The Economist's Tale

The Economist's Tale

A Consultant Encounters Hunger and the World Bank

★

Peter Griffiths

ZED BOOKS
London & New York

The Economist's Tale: A Consultant Encounters Hunger and the World Bank
was first published in 2003 by
Zed Books Ltd, 7 Cynthia Street, London N1 9JF, UK,
and Room 400, 175 Fifth Avenue, New York, NY 10010, USA

www.zedbooks.demon.co.uk

Everything in this book happened. However, to protect the guilty it has
been necessary to change the names, nationalities and organizational
affiliations of the people involved.

Designed and typeset in Monotype Joanna by Illuminati, Grosmont
Cover designed by Andrew Corbett
Printed and bound in the EU by Biddles Ltd, www.biddles.co.uk

Distributed in the USA exclusively by Palgrave, a division of
St Martin's Press, LLC, 175 Fifth Avenue, New York, NY 10010

A catalogue record for this book is available from the British Library
Library of Congress Cataloging-in-Publication Data available

ISBN 1 84277 184 1 (Hb)
ISBN 1 84277 185 X (Pb)

Contents

FOREWORD

Is the Story True?

Everything in this book happened: the facts, the figures, the dates, the interventions by the World Bank, the interviews with civil servants and potential importers are true. Even the Cabinet Paper is quoted verbatim.

The economics is correct, but has been simplified to keep the storyline clear. A full analysis of the food and agriculture sector, with its dozens of interlinked industries, would be many times longer than this book, and would be opaque to anyone but a handful of specialists.

The biggest constraint in writing the book was the law of libel. Some of the people I met were incompetent, some were corrupt, some were evil. Most of the others had peccadilloes that they would not like to be made public. The only way round this was to ascribe real actions to invented characters. For example, while the World Bank did intervene as I describe, there was no Resident Representative in Sierra Leone at the time, and no World Bank office there. I have changed nationalities and institutional affiliations, and many characters, such as Brendan, are invented. In one or two instances, people may appear identifiable, as there was only one Minister of Agriculture, and only one General Manager, but in each of these cases I have invented characters and actions.

Steve Lombard did exist: he did stop a famine in Tanzania and he did get fired. Mr Kamara did take me to the hospital in Bo during the rioting. The Nordic doctor did repair refrigerators for the polio campaign. Chief Margai did wear a ring.

Why did I write this particular book?

I wrote this book because this was the only food crisis where I have been near the centre of events at the key times. I knew the facts; I saw the decisions being made; I saw why they were being made; I influenced them.

In other food crises, I have not known the full stories. When Steve Lombard was stopping the famine in Tanzania, I heard what was happening second-hand. Elsewhere, I have worked on a crisis brought about by IMF/World Bank interventions, but the interventions had been made by people I never met, four or five years before I arrived in the country, for reasons I could not fathom.

The duty of the individual

This book shows that it is individuals who cause poverty, under-development and famine, by their actions, by their failure to act, and by their failure to speak up.

Some individuals choose to be incompetent, dishonest or down-right evil. Some are pressed to be by their employers, their family or their society. Others tolerate incompetence, dishonesty or evil because they are afraid. They may be afraid that they will lose their jobs and starve. They may be afraid that they will be beaten up or killed. Or they may be afraid that they will be seen to be making a fuss.

Workers in the aid industry have to bow to pressures from clients, consultancy firms, donor organizations and the whole aid system if they are to continue to work in aid. Like most of my colleagues, I try to do my best within the limits of what can be achieved. I suspect, though, that often I have acted within the limits of what is good for my career.

Unless the aid industry tackles this problem, it will achieve as little in the future as it has in the past.

Dear Jane,

Ever since you were a little girl, you have been embarrassed by my job. What could be more boring, more uncool than to be an economist?

Yet economists kill – or save – many times more people than generals, especially if you consider that most wars are fought as an instrument of economic policy.

This is the story of one battle between economists. It was only a small battle: the number of lives that could have been lost was rather less than the number lost by the combined armed forces of the British Empire during the Second World War, though a lot more than the USA lost in two world wars and Vietnam put together.

The story is drawn from my diary of four months working as an economic consultant in Sierra Leone. The diary shows how an economist works and thinks in the real world, which is not how economists in the universities work or think, but is a lot more exciting. At least, I think trying to avert an impending famine is exciting.

The events, the economics, the crisis happened. Fiction it is not.

Read it and you will know more about me.

Your loving father,

Peter

The Task Ahead

The White Man's Graveyard, they call it; the poorest place on God's earth. It looked like a tropical paradise this morning, as I ate a breakfast of pawpaw and mango on the terrace of a four-star hotel, and looked out over two miles of deserted beach. True, when the plane landed last night, we had gone through the most decrepit international airport I have ever seen, but it was too dark to see the city or the countryside on the way to the hotel, so I had not seen any of the signs of a country on its knees.

All I knew at breakfast time this morning was that my job here was to look at Sierra Leone's food situation. I had to do an economic analysis of the food policy, find out if there were any problems and come up with solutions. All by myself. All in four months. Today I was going to have to try to find out what my job really was. Of course, my tasks were set out in the written Terms of Reference in my contract, but these TOR are always a polite fiction. In fact, anybody who has anything to do with drawing them up has their own hidden agenda, whether it is increasing their personal power, firing the Managing Director, getting a large aid budget for the country, or diverting some of the aid into their personal bank accounts. Unless I can find out what these people really want, I will not be able to develop a solution that they will accept and implement.

As I was musing about my programme for the day, a wiry black man of about 35, dressed in a grey safari suit, came up to my table.

'Good morning, Sah,' he said cheerfully. 'I am Mohammed

Kasama; I am the World Bank driver for you. I have come to take you to the office.'

We shook hands and I introduced myself. He said that he was going to be my driver for my whole four months here. I was delighted to hear it for several reasons. He is cheerful and speaks excellent English. More important, perhaps, he is a Muslim, and probably does not drink, which extends my life expectancy considerably. In Zambia, there was an appalling death rate because drivers drank heavily, then drove at high speed on excellent roads. A government Land-Rover had a life expectancy of 2,500 miles, and a police motorcycle of 600 miles – and their drivers about the same.

We drove two miles down the coast from the hotel, with the empty beach on one side and a golf course on the other. Then the road swung inland through rice paddies, and uphill into leafy suburbs. The car pulled up outside a 15-foot-high whitewashed wall, with the blue flag of the World Bank fluttering above it. Mohammed hooted, and a uniformed guard opened the high steel gates. We drove in and parked in the compound. I got out and went into the office building, where I asked if I could see the Resident Representative.

While I waited, I wondered what to expect. I was curious about the man who had set up this consultancy project and arranged the finance for it. The World Bank Resident Representative, its ambassador, is the most powerful foreigner in any poor country. A country like Sierra Leone would be getting perhaps three-quarters of its foreign exchange earnings from foreign aid, and three-quarters of its government budget too. The World Bank is the biggest aid donor, so it can exert a lot of power by increasing or reducing the amount of aid, or by switching it from one sector to another. It is not just its own aid: it orchestrates the aid programmes of most donor countries. The Bank uses this power to make the Government adopt right-minded policies. The Bank's local Res Rep has a big say in how the power is exercised.

He did not rise to his feet when I entered his office, but motioned for me to sit on one of the chairs in front of his desk. He seemed to be in his mid-forties, and was obviously French by his accent. When he introduced himself, I heard him to say 'Murat', like Napoleon's marshal, and he seemed to be modelling himself on the *beau sabreur* himself, with his dapper figure, his moustache, his swagger and his imperious manner. When I looked at his card, I saw it was the more prosaic 'Mauratte' but I had difficulty in seeing him as anything but an aspiring cavalry commander.

He began his briefing, 'You are here to get the Government to change its food policy and its food marketing. The present system is a disaster, and it is seriously damaging the economy.'

I tried not to look surprised, but my Terms of Reference had not suggested that the present system was a disaster, or that I would be doing more than a routine economic study. This was my first glimpse of the hidden agenda.

'The major problem is that there is a government monopoly on exports of the main crops, coffee and cocoa, and on the imports of the main food crop, rice. All of these have to be marketed through the Agricultural Marketing Board, which is a Government-owned company.'

I nodded to keep him talking, though he did not seem to need any encouragement.

'When the British Empire ran this country,' he continued, 'they established monopoly marketing boards to protect the farmers against traders who cheat them and give them low prices. They did it in England first, then in Africa and in places like Australia and New Zealand. We French did the same, especially in West Africa. Perhaps it was a good idea then, in the 1930s depression. Perhaps, but I do not think so. Today there is no question: they are a disaster, you understand. It is World Bank policy to get rid of them.'

I did understand. It was all familiar ground, as I had spent the last few years trying to reform, control or close down state marketing boards. All those that I have seen are corrupt or inefficient, with the result that farmers get almost nothing for their crops.

'The Agricultural Marketing Board originally dealt with export crops only,' he explained. 'It became powerful because it controlled much of the economy. I think the Colonial Government was happy with this because they did not trust the multinational trading companies or the Lebanese traders.'

'Lebanese?' I asked myself, startled. Then it clicked: I had wondered why there were so many Arabs at the airport last night – this is hardly the country to invest your petrodollars – but they must be the Lebanese who had settled in West Africa before the First World War. I had heard that they controlled trade here in the same way that Indians do in East Africa and Jews in South Africa.

But he was reaching his peroration. He rose from his chair and stood silhouetted against the window. He paused dramatically, then raised his hand to his moustache, twisting the end with a flourish. He declaimed, not addressing me at all, but speaking over my head to the wall behind me. Evidently it was a set speech, perhaps one he was rehearsing before giving it to a committee in Washington.

'The Agricultural Marketing Board is corrupt and inefficient. It is supposed to be a non-profit-making company exporting coffee and cocoa for the farmers. In effect, though, a percentage of everything they export goes to a private account in a bank in Switzerland.' He looked at me, and explained in a normal tone, 'The French and British brokers are helpful in arranging this, you know.'

'Yes,' I said, 'I do know.' Then I caught myself. I was believing his story because of what I had seen elsewhere in Africa, not because I had any evidence that it was happening here in Sierra Leone. I must be careful: certainly I must listen to everybody's opinions, but I must withhold judgement until I had checked the evidence.

He looked over my head again, and continued to declaim, 'Up to two years ago, there was another marketing board, the Rice Corporation. Its job was to make sure that the people in Freetown and those in the diamond fields got enough to eat. They used to buy the rice from the farmers, store it, mill it, and sell it to the people in the towns. For many years it worked well, you understand: farmers got a good price, and the people got enough food.

'Then about five years ago the farmers stopped producing enough rice to feed the country. They produced less and less, and now the country imports half its rice. The reason was, I think, that the Rice Corporation was corrupt and inefficient, so their costs were high, and they paid the farmers a price too low.'

I nodded. It was a common enough story in Africa.

'But,' he continued, 'the people still had to eat. So the Rice Corporation imported rice, and the Government subsidized the price. Again, it worked for some years. Then the economy got very bad, and the Central Bank could not supply the foreign exchange that the Rice Corporation needed to buy rice. There were some shortages, and food riots. The Government knew that the state-owned Agricultural Marketing Board had plenty of foreign exchange in London banks from their exports of coffee and cocoa. So it closed the Rice Corporation, and told the Agricultural Marketing Board to take over rice imports.'

'Right,' I said, just to keep him talking. It was an odd story: some bits like high operating costs and subsidies hung together, but other bits sounded strange. I would have liked to ask him some serious questions, but these would have stopped him in mid-flow, and I would not have found out what he thought was going on. I usually save my serious questions until the speaker has finished putting forward his view of the situation. Or I use a question to change the subject if he gets off track. In a perfect interview, I would control the direction by body language and a few 'Uh huh's, with no questions or other interjections at all.

'This worked,' said Murat. 'The Agricultural Marketing Board does today import enough rice. Prices for farmers here are still too low, because there is the subsidy on imports, you understand. So farmers do not grow much rice. Already I have said that the Agricultural Marketing Board is corrupt and inefficient, so it does not pay farmers to grow coffee or cocoa for export either.'

'This means that Sierra Leone imports much rice, and exports little coffee and cocoa, so the economy is bad today, and will be very bad tomorrow. That is evident.'

The story sounded only too familiar. The collapse of agriculture in one African country after another was for the same reasons. Still, I must not let myself believe him until I had checked his facts.

Then he stood up again, so he could look down at me, declaiming from on high. 'What you are here for is to close down the Agricultural Marketing Board. You are to persuade Government that it is the fundamental of their problem. They are to privatize and deregulate the market. They will then have a FREE MARKET [he said it in capitals] and the economy will start to work again. We, the World Bank, will support you absolutely.' He puffed out his chest, as though waiting for applause.

He looked at me again, and spoke in a normal voice, 'There used to be some other factors to do with the exchange rate, but they are not important now. I have the expert on that from our headquarters visiting Freetown now. I have arranged for him to see you at two o'clock tomorrow. His name is Jed Welensky.'

He paused while I wrote this down.

As soon as I had finished writing, he brought the interview to a close and showed me out of his office. I had not been given the time to ask my questions, so I would have to visit him again, or get the information from someone else.

It had been an odd meeting, partly because of his personality and partly for what he had said. There seemed to be a lot of common sense in his diagnosis of the problem, but I had got worried towards the end. It had looked more and more as though Murat thought that I was an employee of the Bank whom they had brought in to push World Bank policy. I am not. I am employed by the Sierra Leone Government, and specifically by the Ministry of Agriculture, so I owe my duty to them, not to the Bank. All the Bank did was to lend Sierra Leone the dollars to pay me, so they are not even a party to my contract. As for the suggestion that it is my job to push World Bank policy, it is an insult: even if I were employed directly by the Bank, I would produce honest, independent analysis and advice. I am certainly not going to fake my analysis when lives are at stake, as they are when I am working on food policy.

Careerwise, though, I cannot afford to upset the World Bank, as I get two-thirds of my income from doing consultancy from them. I will have to tread carefully.

Meeting the Minister

As I stepped out of the air-conditioned World Bank offices, I was struck in the face by hot, humid, air. It was now 9.30, and the day had started to warm up. It must already have been 80 degrees Fahrenheit, with 100 per cent humidity. More or less what I should have expected of a country bang on the equator at sea level, but it still came as a surprise.

Mohammed was dozing in the front seat of the car. He looked up and greeted me cheerfully, then jumped out of the car, and ran round to open the passenger door for me. Too late: I was already getting in.

He drove me to my next appointment at the Ministry of Agriculture. We left the new suburbs, and drove into the old residential district. The houses are wooden, with balconies. They were all painted lovingly once, but the paint is starting to come off, leaving bare wood, dark grey and weathered. Much of the paint that remains is covered with mould – the blue-black mould that grows everywhere with this heat and humidity. Surprisingly, these houses are attractive in a run-down way. There was no pretence at drains or a pavement, just wide ditches on each side of the potholed tarmac, and grassy verges.

We drove at a slow crawl through the traffic jams of the city. The traffic moves at a snail's pace because the streets are narrow, almost medievally narrow. How can this be in Africa? The cities of Central Africa were laid out on a grand scale by visionaries who could imagine that a piece of empty veld was going to be a great city someday. Their roads were laid out wide enough for an ox wagon pulled by sixteen oxen to do a U-turn – twice as wide as Regent Street. Here in Sierra Leone, the Colonial Office seems to have planned a village and to have been taken by surprise when it turned into a city.

Mohammed said that the congestion was because the city is built on the narrow plain between the mountain and the sea. Well, maybe, but that does not explain the narrow streets – not just narrow, but blocked. The buildings on each side of the street in the business area are mostly shops, with the owner's flat upstairs. There are hard earth or concrete pavements here. The shopkeepers seemed to have rented space on the pavement outside their shops to street traders, who set out their wares on packing cases, or on the ground. This means that nobody can walk along the pavement. Instead, they have to walk on the street, blocking the traffic. To make things worse, some of the more adventurous traders have extended their stalls into the street, making it narrower still. In fact it looks as though quite a few of the brick buildings have been added on to, so they extend into the street. The best way to deal with this encroachment is the Pakistani way: every year or two the army drives a tank where the road ought to be. This leaves quite a few buildings lacking a room or two.

At the city centre, I saw an ornate colonial High Court building and a few dozen newish buildings of four to six storeys. Evidently this is the business centre. Here the tarmac runs the full width of the road and there are concrete pavements – no bare earth here. Between the pavements and the road are open drains 18 inches wide and 4 feet deep. They must have very heavy rain.

Mohammed passed the time in the traffic jams by giving me my first lesson in Creole, the local lingua franca.

'Paddy, Kusheh O' (Hi friend – Paddy being Scouse for mate.)

'How de body?' (How are you?)

'I well, ow youself?' (I am fine. How are you?)

'O we go see back.' (See you later.)

Once I clicked to the accent, it made sense. It is largely English words with a local grammar. Something to learn and practice. Not that I will ever learn enough to hold a real conversation in my four months here, but I will have to interview a lot of people using an interpreter. If I can get through the first two or three minutes of formal greetings, I can establish myself as a real person, and they will speak to me rather than to my interpreter.

Of course, as in nearly all Commonwealth countries, the official language is English, and education is in English. It is the uneducated urban poor that speak Creole, while the rural tribespeople speak their own languages as first language.

We arrived at a large, four-storey, concrete-and-glass building in a wide, fenced compound. I recognized it immediately: the Friendship Building. A lot of countries in Africa have one, built by Chinese aid and called 'Friendship' in the local language. This was where the main government offices were: Whitehall if you like.

I went into the building without being stopped by the guards, and without seeing any – and you can't do that in Whitehall. The lack of guards does suggest a relaxed political system.

The first impression was of darkness, as I stepped out of the bright sunshine. Even when my eyes adjusted, I could not see much, as the corridors were lit only by a small window at each end. The walls were painted Public Works Department grey, but there were heavy black stains all along, where sweaty people had brushed against the wall – and in this hot, humid atmosphere, everybody is sweaty all the time. The floors had grey and white plastic tiles, but these had come off in the most-used parts, leaving the rough concrete as a floor.

I was here to visit the Minister of Agriculture, who is officially my client, the person I submit my report to. I found his secretary's office, a small room mostly filled by her plain wooden desk, with just enough space for four wooden chairs for visitors. I was ten minutes early for my 10.30 appointment, but she told me that the Minister was running about an hour late. I sat down, exchanged pleasantries with her, and then read my notes of the meeting with Murat, the World Bank man.

At 11.30, two white men in suits burst into her office.

'Good morning,' said the leader shortly, in a plummy English accent. 'We are the Economic Reform Mission from the World Bank in Washington. We have a meeting with the Minister at eleven thirty. Shall we go in?' He put his hand on the door handle.

'I am afraid that the Minister is with someone,' said the secretary firmly. 'Please sit down and I will get you some coffee. I will tell him you are here.'

'No. Our appointment is for 11.30. We are in a hurry. We will go straight in.' He opened the door and they walked in.

I looked at the secretary appalled. She shrugged and said, 'These Washington people are always like that. They think that they are giving away their own money, and they want us to be grateful to them. They think that because they are giving money away, they come before anyone else.'

I like to think that I never behave like this, but there is some truth in what she said: my attitude does change when my job is to give money away. When I am analysing the situation and giving advice, as I am this time, I have to behave like a normal person. Sometimes, though, when my job is to approve a donation or loan of several million dollars, the reception I get from the locals is quite different. Everybody is helpful and goes out of their way to get me the information I need. They wine me and dine me. Yes, this reception does have an effect on me. Yes, I do feel the power of having money to give away. And, yes, I do start thinking that it is my money.

The office door opened and the Minister appeared, saying goodbye to his previous visitor and taking a long time over it. He then greeted me effusively, and sat me in front of his desk next to the men from the World Bank, asking me about my health, my trip, my hotel and how I was liking Freetown. He started asking me about my business. He may have been asserting the importance of courtesy, or he may have been deliberately insulting them. Either way, they were going apoplectic.

I explained what I was there for, and he gave me five minutes of generalizations about policy, then said that he must deal with his next visitors – with the clear suggestion that they would have been booted out of the building there and then if there had not been a lot of money involved.

This meant that my courtesy visit was completely wasted. Normally I would expect to impress my name and mission on the Minister, to find out the policy constraints and to get the Minister to tell his underlings to help me. Because of the behaviour of the Washington people, I achieved none of these objectives. This is quite serious, as I cannot arrange to see him again for another courtesy visit. I will have to wait until I have something substantial to say, and, even then, I may have to wait four months before the wrap-up meeting when I submit my report. His influence will be important if my recommendations are to be put into action, but I am not even sure if I would recognize him again. Shortish, fine-boned, yes. His face had the high cheekbones and hooked nose that suggest Arab blood: presumably he was from one of the northern tribes that had intermarried with the Arabs of the Sahara. Smartly dressed, dapper even. And very charming.

Interesting, that jargon use of the word 'mission'. Short-term consultants always come on a mission; a delegation from Washington comes on a mission. I do not know if it comes from the bomber missions of the US air force, of if there is meant to be something of the missionary venturing into the great unknown heart of Africa. I tend to think, rather, of the television programme *Mission Impossible*.

★

I went downstairs from the Minister's office to the Planning Department (How is it that in all Commonwealth countries the department is part of a big ministry, while in Britain the ministries are part of the departments?) The Director of Planning is the man whom I am going to have to work with for the next four months, so I have to see him before I talk to any civil servants. His secretary told me that he was away at an international conference, and would not be back until tomorrow.

I was annoyed. I had had only one real meeting on my first day, and I could see no chance of getting another. What a waste of time.

The Expats

As I walked from the Planning Department towards the main entrance, I saw the blue and white logo of the World Food Programme on the door of an office. It was an organization I would certainly want to contact quite soon, so I knocked on the door and walked into the office. A small, round, white man in his fifties seated behind the desk said 'Come in! Oh, I see you have. Well sit yourself down.' He was an Irishman, from Cork I would guess.

I introduced myself. 'Good morning. I am Peter Griffiths. I have just started a consultancy for the Ministry of Agriculture. It is a study of food supply and food policy. I was wondering if you could give me any help.'

'Brendan Bandon's the name,' he replied, then went into his standard introduction. 'I'm head of the World Food Programme here.

I have been working in Sierra Leone for eight years now, I have. The job is distributing food aid. Sure, it is not famine relief or anything like that. Just seeing that any food aid given by the different donor countries ends up in the right people's mouths. A lot of it is food for work, to finance rural roads, swamp drainage and so on.'

We started the game of establishing our credentials, swapping details of where we had worked and who we have worked for. Most of my interviews with expats start like this. I do it partly so they will take me sufficiently seriously to give me the information I want, and partly so they will take me sufficiently seriously to read my report when I submit it in four months' time. The people I talk with are trying to establish that their views are worthy of respect and should be incorporated in my report.

This time I lost hands down. I have only worked in the Third World for the last six years or so, in eight or ten countries, while Brendan has been in Africa for thirty-five years, starting as a palm oil buyer for Unilever in Nigeria in 1950. However, we have worked in quite a few of the same countries, so we established a common bond. It is surprising how sometimes you can click completely with someone in a couple of minutes.

Once the preliminaries were over, I started to ask him questions, but Brendan stood up.

'Time for lunch,' he announced. 'Now, will you come down to the Casablanca with me. It's the consultants' watering hole, so it is. You will meet all the expat consultants and aid workers there, and get all the gossip.'

He drove me through the city to the sea shore, with Mohammed following in the other car. We parked opposite where the fish were landed on the beach. There was a crowded fish market, half on the shore, half in an old building with a rusty corrugated iron roof. Canoes and small fishing boats were unloading their catch. Lined up next to them were a dozen passenger boats for the river trade, each about 30 feet long, with an open cabin below and a flat deck above for cargo. They were beautifully, brightly, decorated, painted as lovingly as any barge, and they flew enormous flags, red or green or blue. Another splurge of colour came from the clothes of the people in the market, bright primary colours standing out against the grey

of unpainted wooden houses and the pewter of the sea. I suddenly
felt chilly, as the sea breeze blew away my dripping sweat.

The Casablanca was a comedown after this. We went down a side
street near the fish market, and walked to a three-storey building.
The ground floor was taken up by bazaar-like shops, open to the
street. Above were two storeys built as a house for the trader, with
a wide balcony projecting from the top floor. The whole building
had been painted white once, but now the ubiquitous blue-black
mould had covered most of the surface. A small door at the side had
a peeling sign above it: 'Casablanca Restaurant'. Brendan and I went
in and up the stairs into a bare, white-painted room about 30 feet
by 20. It was not impressive: tables with whitish plastic tablecloths
for the diners, and a small bar in one corner.

At the bar stood half a dozen Europeans drinking beer or spirits.
They were dressed in safari suits, or, more informally, in white or
blue shirt and grey or dun slacks. This seemed to be the normal
business dress: informal perhaps, but colourless compared to the
clothes of the people in the market across the road.

More of them sat at the tables around the room. At first I thought
that they were all Europeans of some sort or another, but there were
three Indians and another Asian, Filipino perhaps. Probably there
was the odd American among them. It looks promising: a mix like
this makes for good conversation.

I noticed that there were no Sierra Leoneans here, no black ones
anyway. Perhaps they cannot afford it. I suspected, though, that this
restaurant was being preserved as somewhere that expats can talk
freely, and that it would be bad form to bring your local colleagues
here.

We sat down and ordered. Brendan recommended garlic prawns,
hummus and pitta bread. It was wonderful, the combination of
Lebanese cooking and fresh seafood from the market fifty yards
away.

A couple of expats joined us at the table.

'I am quite furious!' said one, a blond-bearded Swede called
Thor. 'I arrived here three months ago for a two-year contract, but
I cannot get anywhere to stay. Every time I find a house or a flat I
want, the administrators at the World Bank tell me that I cannot take

it, because the owner wants the rent in dollars. They say that it is illegal and I must pay in leones, but the owners will not take leones.'

'True enough,' said Brendan, 'That's the law, so it is. The UN used to take the same line. Then someone came in with a written offer to rent a house for dollars, and the letter was signed by the Attorney General himself. They realized that it was a lost cause. Would you not go to the UN Res Rep and ask him for a copy. It should convince the World Bank office wallahs.'

'But they also say that $5,000 a year is too much to pay,' said Thor, indignantly. 'I cannot get even a small flat for that. The World Bank keep telling me that they know that an expat has just got an excellent flat for $2,500.'

Everyone laughed, and looked at Brendan, who blushed.

'Well, true enough, I did get a flat for $2,500,' he admitted, 'but that was three years ago, on a three-year lease. The lease ended last week and, about a month before it ended your woman from the estate agents came to my house with the contract for the renewal. And amn't I after paying her one year's rent, $2,500, in cash. Well, she took the money and has not been seen since. The estate agents fired her three months ago, so they tell me.

'Now the estate agents want me to pay up. It seems that rentals have shot up in the last three years, so they now want $5,000 a year. I have to pay it because it would take me forever to find a flat as good as the one I have.'

I lent across to Brendan and asked him discreetly about changing my dollars into leones.

'Simple,' he said, and led me across to the bar. He introduced me to the barman, a Lebanese, fat, unshaven and looking like Peter Ustinov playing the Middle Eastern villain in a wartime British thriller. 'This is "Boss" Seaga. He owns this place. Just give him an English cheque, and he will give you the leones. He always gives a good rate.'

Boss turned out to be affable and I agreed to bring in my cheque-book next day. Apparently, every month or so one of the regulars posts Boss's accumulated cheques to his London bank account, using the diplomatic bag. Brendan told me that Boss had been changing money for years, when a black market existed, because of exchange control and a shortage of foreign currency. He told me, though, that for the last six months foreign currency had been freely available at the banks, so the black market had vanished, but, for some reason he could not understand, Boss was still able to give a better rate than the banks.

I used to have a conscience about using the black market. Then one day in East Africa, I went into a bank to change my money, virtuously avoiding the black marketeer on the pavement outside. The cashier looked surprised, but changed my money at the official rate. He then rushed out of the bank to the black marketer, changed my money at the black market rate, and pocketed the profit. I started to notice how many hotel cashiers asked me if I wanted to change money at the official rate, with the implied offer that if I did not fill in the official exchange control forms, I could get the black market rate.

This means that I do not worry any more about exchanging money on the black market. I do worry, though, that I do not worry.

As I finished my meal, I told Brendan that I was exhausted after yesterday's flight, and I was going back to my hotel. I could not visit any Sierra Leonean officials until I had met the Director.

'Nonsense,' he said, 'There's no reason to do that at all.' And he insisted on taking me on a guided tour of Freetown. We sent Mohammed back to the office and got into Brendan's car.

First Brendan took me up the mountain that towers over the city, the original Sierra Leone or lion mountain. He drove uphill through town, then turned onto a steeply climbing road, a series of alpine hairpin bends. I kept getting flashes of fantastic scenery, which vanished as he swung into another bend.

The view from the top was dramatic – a thousand-foot drop to the city on its narrow plain between the mountain and the sea. Beyond that was the Atlantic Ocean, with the thunderheads of the monsoon blowing towards us.

To the right of us was an enormous bay, miles wide – five miles at least, perhaps ten: how do you tell? On the other side of the bay, I could see the airport where I had landed last night. I had wondered why it was across the bay, but now it was obvious: there was no flat land this side.

'It's the biggest natural harbour in the world, so it is,' said Brendan, with a proprietorial pride. 'During the Second World War it often had 150 ships here waiting for a convoy. The mountain is 1,000 feet high here and rises to 3,000 feet a couple of miles inland, so it gives a wonderful protection against the weather.

'It is enormously important strategically of course: this is where the Atlantic is at its narrowest, between South America and Africa, so it commands all the shipping lanes. In colonial days, it was the headquarters of the British South Atlantic Fleet.

'You see the concrete emplacement here. This was for the big guns. They had an enormous range, being so high up.'

'And now?' I asked, 'Who uses it now? If it isn't a British base, whose is it?'

'Nobody's, nobody at all's' replied Brendan. 'It's just an ordinary harbour for Sierra Leone, though far bigger than they need. It's also used for cargoes that go to inland Guinea, to the north of here. They take them by road from here to the northern border.

'Just occasionally it is still used as a naval base, though. The British used it for the final stage of the Falklands invasion, which shows how important it is still. They had to pay Sierra Leone £3 million for the privilege, but they couldn't have done it without the base, I'd say.

'Of course the Russians would give their eye teeth to have it as a base but the Americans are terrified at the thought, so they are. The old president, Siaka Stevens, was quite pro-Russian at one time, and hinted that he might let them use it. The Americans pumped in money to stop him doing it. I think he also charged the Russians for not letting the Americans use it. He was an operator.'

I filed away the information. Could there be some sort of international strategic dimension to my job, instead of straightforward food policy?

We got into the car and drove to the foot of the steep mountain road, to where the road levelled at the top of a gentler slope, perhaps 300 feet above sea level. Brendan parked in front of an old two-storey stone building, with wide wooden verandas, the weathered wood showing beneath the peeling grey paint. It was not a big building, big enough for fifteen or twenty offices, and it had a sign outside it: 'Ministry of Agriculture, Computer Section'. It was a building of character, completely different to the concrete and glass of the Friendship Building where the Ministry had its headquarters. It looked a good hundred years older than anything else I had seen in Freetown.

'These are the Tower Hill offices,' announced Brendan. 'They don't look very grand at all, do they? But they were the headquarters of the British South Atlantic Fleet during the war. The admirals used to sit on the veranda sipping their pink gins, and looking out to see if Jerry was coming.'

I looked around, and indeed we were sufficiently high to be able to see a wide arc, three-quarters of a circle, covering the Atlantic and the bay.

After this, I did insist on going to my hotel. I was exhausted from yesterday's journey. I was also hot and sweaty. I went back to the hotel and had a shower, then slept like the dead.

As I sat in the bar of the hotel before dinner, I saw that the bar girls were buying their drinks with tickets, not money. I asked one of them what was happening. She told me that the manager gives each of them a book of tickets when they arrive in the morning to look for customers. This means that they can spend hours sitting comfortably at the bar or by the pool, sipping their drinks and waiting to catch somebody's eye.

I noticed that one girl had decided to blow all her tickets on dinner in the dining room. A high-risk strategy, but it worked. While she was waiting for her food, she was making eyes at a young tourist. Within five minutes, he had joined her at her table, and they were deep in conversation, with him apparently unaware of her profession.

I have not seen this ticket system before. It may be relevant that it is a French-owned hotel with a French manager. Or perhaps it is just that I never usually work in areas where tourists go, so I do not know how tourist hotels operate.

An Englishman sat next to me at the bar. He introduced himself: a retired colonel, no less. He was in charge of security for a diamond mine up-country. 'They like us ex-servicemen because they can trust us. You see, we get the Queen's pension, and we lose our pensions if we are caught stealing.' He looked appraisingly at me, then said 'I can see you are an experienced traveller: I don't have to warn you about having sex with the local women.' Obviously, he had come over when he saw me talking to the girl, to warn me, as though I was a junior officer joining his regiment.

Meeting the Officials

TUESDAY, 5 SEPTEMBER

'Paddy, Kusheh O! How de body?' I greeted Mohammed this morning. We continued my lesson as he drove me into town. I know that I was attempting to pronounce English words with a heavy Sierra Leonean accent, rather than saying the Creole word, but I hoped it showed willing. Perhaps it did, or perhaps he thought 'Patronizing neo-colonial, thinking that all he has to do is speak English slowly and loudly.'

'How do?'
'Morning O!'
'Gud Evening O!'
'Na Who Dat?' (Who is there?)
'I de go.' (I am going.)
'You de write.' (You are writing.)

'Den pikin de play.' (The children are playing.)

If I concentrate on the words that are like the English ones, I will build up a vocabulary quickly, though I may miss some of the commonest words. A lot of the words are straight English: lift, petrol, fitter (mechanic), spanner, motor car, spectacle(s), parlour, yonder, trousers, junction.

Today I met Foday Bombwe, the Director of Planning in the Ministry of Agriculture. He is my contact man, and I report to him, so in one sense he, personally, is my client, rather than the Minister or the Ministry or the Government. One of the big problems of this sort of consultancy is that I have so many people who can be thought of as clients: the Minister, the Ministry of Agriculture, the Government, the nation, the Director. Somehow, I have to keep all of them in mind when I work, and I hope I can keep all of them happy with my report.

Foday's office was quite big, but smaller and starker than the office of a director in Whitehall. The bright sunlight on the trees outside the window made the inside look dark and gloomy in contrast, and there was no sparkle in the pale grey of the walls and the grey painted steel desk.

Foday himself was tall and had a middle-aged spread, though he seemed to be in his early forties. I introduced myself to him, and expected that we would talk about my mission here. Instead, he started complaining.

'I've just got back from a conference in Zimbabwe,' he said aggressively. 'Harare is a wonderful city where everything works, just like a European city. In fact, better than a European city. It shows what the white men did when they thought that they were going to stay in a country. Here the white men came much earlier, two hundred years ago, and they did nothing. Nothing at all. Just look around you. They came to get big salaries for twenty years, then they retired on full salary. They did not have to live with the results of their mistakes and their idleness.'

He glared at me accusingly. Then he relaxed a bit, 'Sorry: jet lag. Still, I was amazed to see it.'

I was really alarmed. This is my contact man in the Government, the man I report to. If we do not get along, this job is going to be very difficult indeed. His hostile greeting was not a good omen.

We then restarted the conversation as it should have gone. He opened with the usual 'How do you like the country?' and I parried with the usual 'Beautiful country, nice people.' Then we switched to the years he spent in England getting a Ph.D. Slowly the tension vanished, and the atmosphere became more relaxed.

He started to talk about my mission here. He made it quite clear that I had been foisted on him by the World Bank with the help of the FAO (the Food and Agriculture Organization of the UN) and the UN itself. He, himself, was a highly trained planning specialist, and believed that what was wanted was not my advice on food policy, but someone to write project proposals to extract cash from donors. In other words, he was opposed to my mission from the start. Another bad omen.

He said that he could not understand why I was working with the Ministry of Agriculture, if I was interested in food policy. He went on to explain that most food marketing, storage and processing was the responsibility of the Ministry of Commerce. He was surprised that I was not working for them, or at least reporting to an inter-ministerial committee. He revealed, intentionally or not, that there was strong rivalry, or even hostility, between the Ministry of Agriculture and the Ministry of Commerce, so I may have a lot of trouble in getting any cooperation from them. It looks more and more as though I am stepping into a minefield.

We started to negotiate on resources. He said that from tomorrow he would give me a young Sierra Leonean economist, Thomas Clarke, as an assistant. The assistant's job is to find out who I should see, to arrange my appointments, to dig up statistics, and to act as interpreter if necessary. However, his most important task, one that nobody ever mentions explicitly, is to tell me about the politics and micro-politics of the situation.

In some countries, it is a popular job for several reasons. It gives young professionals the best possible training, working with someone who is competent and experienced, and learning how to get results fast. I know that I wasted years of my life finding this out for myself, when I could have learned it in a couple of months by working with someone who knew. Second, it gives them a chance to make friends with international consultants who may be able to help them get a well-paid job in one of the international organizations like the World Bank or FAO. Third, they get the chance to travel with the consultant and see their own country, at a time when their own government cannot afford to let them do even essential travel. Another benefit is left unstated. The young economists who are about to go to Europe to do a master's degree are particularly keen to work as an assistant, as a consultant's report can usually be cut-and-pasted, and presented as a dissertation. (I know that at least of three of my reports have been used in this way.)

In spite of this, the job is not popular in some of the middle-income countries, where there is plenty of money for travel, where the civil servants are busy with other work, or where they have too many consultants visiting them anyway.

I asked Foday about other backup. He said that he was going to give me an office of my own in his department. This is wonderful, as I thought I would have to work from my hotel room. He also said that he was allocating a secretary/typist to work with me full time. This is also a luxury, though I cannot see myself having enough typing to keep her busy for more than a few days of my four months here.

He took me through to the typists' room and introduced me to the seven women who work there, their small wooden desks crammed together. Amanda Parker is the one who will work with me. We shook hands and made the usual small talk. I assumed from the name that she was Creole (descended from freed slaves) and Christian, rather than tribal and Muslim or with traditional beliefs, though I could not tell by looking at her – the Creoles do not seem to have any white blood. She is young and pretty, with hair that has been plaited into an amazing pattern.

Then Amanda said 'Please give me all the typing you can. I want to keep up my typing skills, so I need a lot of practice. I have also got shorthand qualifications, so I would be very pleased if you dictated everything. You see, there is no paper in the Ministry, so we do not get a chance to practice. Just bring in some paper and we will all type for you.'

I looked round the office, and indeed there was no sign of paper. Nothing was being typed: the in-trays and out-trays were empty, and there was nothing on the desks except a few old and worn Mills & Boon paperbacks.

I noticed, too, that there were no electric typewriters: all were manuals, the sort that were used in my father's office when I was a boy. In fact, when I thought of it, I remembered that even the Minister's secretary had a manual typewriter, not the electric IBM golfball which is the current status symbol. Nor had I seen any computers or wordprocessors in the whole building. I asked Foday why.

'No electricity,' was his terse explanation. Then he relaxed a little and expanded on it. 'We used to get power cuts for a couple of hours one or two days a week, which was a nuisance, but we could manage. For the last six months, though, we have only had power once, and that was for three hours one Friday afternoon. We have had to put away all the electric typewriters and buy any old manuals we could obtain.

'We keep our ministry computer at our office in Tower Hill, because they have electricity all the time. They have to have electricity there all the time, because they are next to the army's magazine. The ammunition and the explosives have to be kept air-conditioned. There is only one other part of the city where there is usually electricity, and that is on the eastern side of the city, near the President's Palace.'

I remembered the Tower Hill offices, the Georgian stone building, and thought how strange it was that it should be the only ministry building with electricity.

'But what is the problem with electricity?' I asked.

'We are short of foreign exchange to buy the oil,' he said briefly, and changed the subject.

I asked him to give me a letter of introduction 'to whom it may concern'. He dictated a letter to Amanda, and told her to collect a sheet of headed paper from him in his office. The letter of introduction is not just routine: in some countries, people will not talk to you without the formal introduction. If I am working in a police state, it is particularly important, as people are reluctant to talk to strangers, and informers may accuse you of being a spy if they see you asking farmers about their crops. I am not sure yet whether or not Sierra Leone is a police state, but I am being careful.

★

It was a relief to be able to get down to real work after this, having cleared my lines of communication. I was able to make courtesy visits to the other key officials in the Ministry, to the Permanent Secretary, to the Director of Agriculture, to the Director of Research and to the Director of Veterinary Services.

Mainly I was trying to establish that I was a nice chap, and not a threat, and at the same time that I was sufficiently competent that my report would be worth reading when it came out. I also asked them who I should visit in this ministry and in others, and why I should see them. All the time I was listening for clues about the constraints and micropolitics I would have to allow for.

Then I was able to make a start on some of the junior officials, who are heads of units. These are professionals — economists and agriculturists — so they could give me some solid information. I still had to do the sales pitch and listen for tensions, rivalries and vested interests though.

The offices are nothing like as swish as a British mandarin's. The Friendship Building is a large concrete-and-glass building with grey painted interior walls and grey and blue-grey plastic floor tiles. Everything about it is utilitarian. There are utilitarian grey steel desks for director and above, and utilitarian wooden desks of a standard pattern for all administrative and professional officers, with small wooden desks for typists and clerks. There are no carpets, so size of carpet is not a status symbol. The Minister has a big office, with his secretary's office opening off it. The directors and heads of unit each have a big office to themselves, while the junior professionals are two or three to a room. It strikes me as egalitarian compared to most organizations. Perhaps it is a hangover from the Colonial Office ethic that we are a tiny group of similar chaps, and we cannot really afford to put on airs if we are to get on with each other. Status is important, of course, but we do not have to keep asserting our status, because our salaries and positions are published each year.

At the end of the day, I had a collection of old consultancy reports and statistics to read. Most will turn out to be irrelevant, of course, but I am hoping that some of them will be useful. It is depressing that the directors are so little interested in them that they hand out their last copies to a passing consultant, when everybody knows that consultants never return the reports they borrow. (I do, but I am eccentric.) Of course, with no electricity in the Ministry, they cannot give me a photocopy, though Mohammed tells me that he can easily get photocopies from one of the Lebanese shops which has a generator. Mohammed is turning out to be one of those useful people who always knows the one shop in town which has stocks of a scarce commodity, and who always knows where to buy black market goods.

The Casablanca

WEDNESDAY, 6 SEPTEMBER

I went to the Casablanca for lunch, both because it is convenient to the Ministry, and because I wanted to cash a cheque.

As I went in, I slipped Mohammed a dollar and told him to get himself something to eat. He is supposed to pay for his own food and he is far better paid than the government drivers, so it is not really necessary. However, I learnt long ago how important it is to keep the driver happy. For example, we hired a car and driver in the Sudan, and the hire company said they would pay the driver's salary, subsistence and overtime. He was wrecking the project, turning up a couple of hours late for work and generally wasting a lot of valuable consultant time. Then I realized what had happened. The car owner was skimping on the driver's subsistence and not paying him any overtime at all. I paid him the very small amount involved and we had no more problems at all. In a country like Sierra Leone the wage rates and subsistence allowances were set years ago, before inflation, and are quite inadequate today. I top them up. Apart from anything else, I do not want to trust my life to a hungry driver.

The rule at the Casablanca seems to be that someone sits at a table, and anyone coming in just sits next to them. I sat next to Thor the bearded Swede, who was complaining that the United Nations had just funded a project to send twenty Sierra Leoneans to America to train as helicopter pilots.

'It is ridiculous. There is only one private helicopter in the country, and three army ones. It is as though they think that a helicopter comes by magic, as soon as you train a pilot.'

'Yes,' agreed Brendan. 'They did the same ten years ago, and there were no helicopters at all then, so didn't all the pilots become taxi drivers.

'It wouldn't have worked even if Sierra Leone had had the helicopters,' he continued. 'Nobody would employ a pilot without five or six years' experience. You need special skills to be a bush pilot, whether you are flying a helicopter or a light plane. There is no radio or radar at the bush airstrips. Even in Freetown International Airport, they switch off all systems and the landing lights until an airliner is expected, to save electricity. Then, before it lands, they shoo away the cows grazing by the runway. The bush pilots have not got proper maps, just the small-scale map of the whole country. And then there is the weather. Six months of the year, they are flying through solid rain and then, in January, visibility is half a mile because of the dust from the Sahara. We have lost quite a few experienced bush pilots in the eight years I have been here.'

Then a typical Hooray Henry came and sat at our table – an Englishman with a penetrating public school voice and a loud braying laugh. Minor public school then a lot of rugger, I guess: he is tall with the thick neck and chunky torso of a lock forward, and has a mop of blond hair. Everything about him should have been guaranteed to set my teeth on edge, but it didn't. I liked him. His sardonic sense of humour appealed to me.

Henry (his name really is Henry) has been working in Freetown for the last ten years, and he seems to know everything that is going on. He is with one of the big five accounting firms here.

The conversation at the table got quite lively as we discussed a financial scandal involving one of the nationalized industries. Thor turned to Henry and asked him 'You audit them, don't you? Is it true or isn't it?'

Henry stiffened, and a mask dropped over his face. 'I never comment on these rumours. My firm audits most of the big firms here. I could use my privileged information to deny some of the ridiculous rumours that I hear. If I did, though, what would you think when I did not deny a story? You would believe it of course. That is why I never make a statement, even to deny a story that is clearly nonsense.' It came out pat, a well-rehearsed statement. I had got a look at the hard businessman behind the façade.

How does anyone with the training of an English accountant and the ethics code of one of the big five accounting firms operate here? He is auditing the accounts of corrupt, state-owned companies and aid projects riddled with corruption, yet he clearly never blows the whistle. If he did, everybody would immediately switch to one of the other accounting firms.

Does he discuss his findings with the Managing Director or the Project Director, and agree what to cover up? Or does he just produce clean audit reports? If he just turns a blind eye, corruption will blossom. The only time I have managed to get any action on corruption was when I found out that the junior accountants were on a fiddle. Perhaps the auditors had found it already, but had not told the Managing Director because they thought he was in on the racket. I did tell him, as it was threatening the survival of the firm. It turned out that he did not know about it, so seven accountants ended up in jail.

Mind you, I do not know what the ethical standards of the big five are anywhere else in the world. Nearly every time there is a major scandal in Britain, with a business collapsing because someone has been pinching hundreds of millions of pounds, it turns out that the firm has been audited by one of the big five.

In the silence after Henry's statement, while everyone was trying to think of a safe topic of conversation, I ordered my food. I do like the Lebanese food. I started with hummus, and then went on to fried fish, fresh landed an hour or two ago on the beach across the road. Simple but delicious. Henry, I noticed, was ordering his second double gin since he had sat down.

I asked the group at the table about Freetown's electricity supply, as Foday had not been willing to explain it. Henry took my arm, and led me across to the window.

'Stick your head out and listen,' he ordered.

I did. I heard a little traffic but not much, as we are in a side street. I was not sure what I was supposed to be listening for. Then I got it. There was the deep rhythmical thudding of a large, slow diesel engine. Then I realized there was another engine in a different direction, then another. I looked at Henry enquiringly.

'That is the sound of the new Africa,' he said dramatically. 'What you can hear is the private diesel generators producing electricity. All the larger firms have one. Your hotel has one. The Casablanca has one. I have one at home. So do most businessmen and expatriates. The little shop at the corner that does photocopying has a small petrol generator. They have to, because of the power cuts.

'But these small generators are expensive to run. They are 25 per cent efficient, compared to 75 per cent efficient for the generators in a power station. This means that they use three times as much fuel to produce one unit of electricity. Personally, I believe that if they stopped all private generators and used the same fuel in the power station, there would be plenty of electricity for everyone. It's also the cost: these small generators cost money. With the same money we spent buying them, we could have built a couple of new power stations. It is individual capitalism gone mad.'

He shook his head, looked down at the table, then took a large mouthful of gin and tonic.

'This all started when the World Bank made the Government privatize the oil refinery,' he went on. 'When the Government started to have foreign exchange problems, the refinery would not supply the power station with oil, so there were power cuts. Those of us who could get hold of dollars on the black market just went down to the refinery and bought the diesel with dollars. We used it for our cars and for our new generators. The projects did it too: all their aid is in foreign exchange, so they did not even have to use the black market. The refinery was delighted to get our dollars so they could stay in business. Then it spiralled out of control.

'Now the rest of the country, those without dollars, only get electricity when someone gives Sierra Leone oil. In practice, that means Libya. Something about this country being nearly half Muslim. I don't ask.'

I looked at him and wondered. He was telling me a good story, not waxing indignant about incompetence. He seemed to be an interested observer, not a participant and certainly not a victim. Perhaps, though, he enjoys telling a good story like this because he cannot tell the really juicy ones about his clients.

His story reminded me that I desperately wanted to drink pints of water. I was dehydrated because I had been sweating all morning. At least now I know that the reason the fans in the government offices had not been working was lack of electricity: I had been wondering if the locals were used to the heat and did not need fans.

Exchange Rates

Mohammed drove me from the Casablanca to the World Bank offices where the Res Rep had arranged for me to meet his visiting economist.

A tall blond man stood up as I entered the office, gripped my hand firmly and said, 'Hi, I'm Jed Welensky' in an accent that was clearly American.

He seemed to be a really nice guy. He said that he works on the Sierra Leone desk in the World Bank in Washington and comes here now and again to try and persuade the Government to get their economy in order. He had been here for a week, and was set to leave on tonight's plane, but he would be back for another week in a month or two.

Then he started to explain the key problems as he saw them.

'What was really hammering the economy was the exchange rate. Up till six months ago, the Central Bank fixed the exchange rate between the dollar and the leone. They had set it at $1 = 7 leones, but this was artificial. It should have been about twice this, $1 = 14 leones, for most of the last five years.'

I nodded, to show I understood, and to keep him talking. I had seen something similar in most Third World countries I worked in.

'Of course,' he continued, 'when the Agricultural Marketing Board exports its coffee and cocoa, it gets paid in dollars on the world market, and it gets the same number of dollars whatever the exchange rate is. However, when they changed their dollars at the Central Bank, they were getting only half as many leones as they should, seven leones per dollar instead of fourteen. In effect, the Central Bank kept half of all export earnings as a hidden export tax. This was in addition to the ordinary 30 per cent export tax which they are quite open about. Take the two together, and make allowance for the inefficiency of the Agricultural Marketing Board and you have the farmer getting perhaps one-fifth of the full export value of the crop. This very low price explains why coffee and cocoa exports have fallen so sharply in the last few years.'

I was surprised to hear this analysis from a Washington man. It was only five years ago that we economists in the field were trying to explain the effect of an overvalued currency to them. But, yes, I had seen it all before. When I was in Tanzania in the early 1980s I had made myself unpopular by showing that 95 per cent of the farmers' cash income was being taken away from them by an overvalued currency, plus marketing board corruption and incompetence. It is difficult to say just how serious an overvalued currency is, but everyone now knows that even a short period of an overvalued currency can have a dramatic effect: only a couple of years ago Thatcher bankrupted a third of British manufacturing industry in three years in the same way – an overvalued currency effectively taxed exports, making them unprofitable, and at the same time it subsidized imports, so they undercut local production.

'The other side of the coin,' Jed continued, 'is that the overvalued currency was subsidizing imports: they cost half as many leones as they should have. The subsidy came from the hidden tax on exports – that is to say from the farmers and the miners.

'Obviously, this meant that anyone who got hold of subsidized dollars for imports could make huge profits, either by importing, or by selling the dollars on the black market. A lot of important people got rich.'

What he was saying was that, in a kleptocracy, the ruling politicians keep an overvalued currency as the easiest way to steal money. They can easily steal a quarter of a country's export earnings in this way. Corruption is the main reason that the Third World stays poor, and this form of corruption is the worst.

'You want to know about food, don't you?' He asked. 'Well the overvalued currency was disastrous. It meant that imported rice cost half as many leones as it should have done. Then there was an explicit subsidy as well. This meant that Sierra Leone consumers were paying less than half the world price for rice. Of course, the local farmers could not compete at this price. It was not worth their while to grow rice for sale any more, so they just stopped producing. Over two or three years, production fell until the farmers were producing enough for themselves, but no more. So now all the rice for the towns is imported.'

'I understand,' I said, encouraging him to keep talking.

'This solution was fine for the consumers in the short run,' continued Jed. 'The overvalued currency meant that half the miners' and farmers' export earnings were used to subsidize imports, which was great if you were not a farmer or miner. For them prices were so low that either they reduced production, or they smuggled their output abroad. It is easy to smuggle diamonds, of course, but it is surprisingly easy with coffee and cocoa too – you just bribe the customs officer.

'Suddenly there was no money coming into the Central Bank from the normal exports, so the Rice Corporation couldn't get the dollars to import. There was not enough rice imported, and there were food riots. The Government had to act fast. They closed down the Rice Corporation and handed over rice importing to the only organization with dollars, the Agricultural Marketing Board. They have dollars from exporting coffee and cocoa, and use it for importing rice. Obviously this could only work in the very short run. With exports declining, the money would soon run out. Something had to be done to push up prices to the farmers, and fast. It was a real emergency.' He looked to me for confirmation, and I nodded.

'We had to lean on Government, and hard. The World Bank, the International Monetary Fund and the United Nations. Between us, we control most of their aid, and all their financial support.'

'Well!' I thought to myself, 'A nice guy perhaps, but a ruthless enforcer underneath.'

He continued, 'Six months ago they agreed to float the currency. There is no longer an overvalued leone, with the rate fixed by the Central Bank. Instead, there is a Free Market. Anyone who wants foreign exchange can buy it. The exchange rate is set by supply and demand. The rate is pretty realistic now, which means much higher prices for farmers and miners. This should mean a big jump in production in the future.

'The Free Market is the only way to do it. In the past Sierra Leone has tried to devalue by changing the official exchange rate, but it never works. Within two or three years, the currency is overvalued again. We had to take all control away from the Central Bank.'

I thanked him profusely and left. His explanation had filled in a lot of the gaps in Murat's explanation of why the economy was collapsing: in fact the two accounts were complementary, rather than conflicting. His explanations had rung true: they seemed to tally with what I had seen elsewhere in Africa.

However, I was worried about his conclusion. Yes, it seemed obvious that devaluation had been needed, but it did not seem at all obvious that floating the currency was the right way to go about it. The 'Free Market' (with capitals) is a political dogma, not an economic one. I am not an expert in international exchange rates, but I cannot help noticing that all the rich, developed countries have had fixed exchange rates for most of this century. Their first attempts at floating the exchange rates in the late 1970s showed that it was a high-risk strategy. The Bank of England and the Federal Reserve Bank had to be ready to spend their gold and currency reserves to stabilize the exchange rates, rather than leave them to the free market. But Sierra Leone does not have any gold or currency reserves, so there cannot be market intervention to support the currency.

I had seen the International Monetary Fund produce the bright idea of a freely exchangeable currency before. If a university-based economist makes enough unrealistic assumptions, and assumes away enough real-life constraints, he can prove that this is marginally more efficient economically than a fixed exchange rate. When they introduced foreign exchange auctions to Zambia four years ago, the rate fell from 2 kwacha = \$1 down to 7 kwacha = \$1 in just three weeks. The rich countries of the world do not let themselves be used as guinea pigs for some half-baked academic theory: why should the poor?

I was even more alarmed to hear that the International Monetary Fund was involved. They are a group of Washington-based economists who make whistle-stop tours around the world telling countries to change the way they run their economies. If the country does what it is told, it gets access to international loans and to loans from the International Monetary Fund itself. If it does not do what it is told, it is cut off from the international financial system. They have left a trail of disaster through Africa.

The United Nations

When I came out, I asked Mohammed to take me to the offices of the Food and Agriculture Organization of the United Nations. They were a mile or so away, up the hill. The FAO Resident Representative negotiates with Government, signs contracts for aid projects, arranges visas, and provides backup for people on aid projects.

I must have come at a slack time, because the secretary showed me straight into the Res Rep's office. He was a German, called Abensberg. Like the World Bank man, Murat, he had a large air-conditioned office with a big desk and a picture window with a view of the South Atlantic. Unlike Murat, he was friendly, especially when I told him that I had worked for a couple of years for the FAO and so was 'one of us'.

'You English always called this coast "the White Man's Grave-yard"', he said. 'Yes, it was. Two hundred years ago, most white men who came here died within two months, from malaria mainly.

The British colonial civil servants who ran the country could retire on full salary at age 40. That was the theory. However, nobody lived that long until the beginning of this century. It was Ross, the malaria expert, who made the difference. He introduced anti-malarial measures that made it quite safe. By 1934 it was so safe that, for the first time, the British were allowed to bring their wives here.'

He looked down at his desk and pondered. His fingers reached out and fiddled with the blue FAO flag on its little flagpole on the desk, the ambassadorial flag that flies from his car when he drives from the office.

'But do not forget that today it is still the black man's graveyard. Black people are a bit resistant to tropical diseases, but not much, especially when they do not have enough to eat. Today the life expectancy here is about 50, compared with 75 in Europe. It is the lowest in the world, even worse than Ethiopia, in spite of all their famines. Half the babies born here die before they reach the age of 5.'

I was appalled. The death rate in the rest of sub-Saharan Africa is pretty awful, with every country, including South Africa, expecting one in three children to die before they are 5 (compared with one in fifty in Britain). This is far worse.

He went on. 'I am sure you know that in most poor countries the low life expectancy is mainly because of lack of food. Disease is important mainly because they are too badly fed to resist infection. In Sierra Leone, too, there is not enough food. You will soon see this for yourself. There are no fat people. Many children have thin arms and legs, with their joints showing clearly. They are pot-bellied because they do not have enough protein and their stomach muscles waste away. Their hair is reddish instead of black, their skin is floury instead of shiny chocolate. As you know, I am sure, this is serious malnutrition. The children will not live.'

He looked down at his desk, twiddled the blue flag and was silent. Then he looked up at me.

'Malaria is the real killer though. The dry parts of this country get over 2,500 cm of rain, and the wet areas around 8,000 cm.'

He saw me trying to do mental arithmetic and laughed. 'You English! That is about 100 inches and 300 inches: 8,000 cm is about ten times the average rain in your country or mine.'

Only two things irritate me about the Germans. One is that they speak our language more grammatically than we do. The other is that they can switch from metric to imperial measures as easily as this.

He continued, 'The wet time is now, from April to October. From now it gets drier, and in January there is no rain at all, as the harmattan blows dry, dusty, wind from the Sahara.

'In the wet season, it rains heavily all the time. The rivers flood and turn into swamps: one-third of the country is covered by swamp. Everywhere there are mosquitoes. This means that it will never be possible to control malaria in the country areas. In Freetown, though, it should be quite easy to control the mosquitoes and prevent malaria. You need drains to remove the water they breed in. You spray stagnant water with paraffin to kill the larvae. You spray insecticide on the walls. You put wire mosquito netting on the windows. You get people to sleep under mosquito nets. All cheap, simple and low-tech. In the 1930s, 1940s and 1950s there was no malaria in Freetown. The bigger the city, the easier it is, so it should be much easier now than it was then. Modern drugs should make it easier still. However, the Government has 'other priorities', and does not enforce these simple measures, so malaria is rife.'

'Yes,' I agreed. 'The same thing had happened in Zambia and Tanzania when I was there.'

After this depressing start, he went on to tell me who I should see in the various ministries. He also told me which FAO projects and other projects I should visit and which would be a waste of time. This is really why I came to him: seeing the right people can make or break a mission. I always make a point of visiting the FAO Res Rep in any country I go to, even if I am working for someone else entirely, as in this mission.

The projects he mentioned covered the whole range. Some were small projects, with an expat supervising spending money for aid, like Brendan's food-for-work project. Some were providing technical assistance, like experienced research workers for a research station. Some were nationwide, providing animal health medicines to all regions. Some were the latest fashion, Area Development Projects, which take one district and try to improve everything at the same time: agriculture, roads, bridges, clinics, small workshops, local government, and so forth.

Abensberg gave me a list of some twenty projects scattered round the country, together with contact names and telephone numbers, as well as useful people to contact in Government.

'You can't telephone up-country,' he said. 'The telephones do not work any more. You have to radio to make an appointment. The Ministry of the Interior has a radio network, and it will pass the message to the project. In fact, even in Freetown it is not easy to telephone.'

I looked at the list. A lot of Area Development Projects, a few farm mechanization projects, fertilizer distribution projects, etc., but nothing at all closely related to my work. I had expected the odd project on agricultural marketing or storage or price policy which would have done some work I could use, and which would have the statistics, but there was nothing. I would have to do everything from scratch. I was going to have to do five years' work in four months.

I will just have to see as many people as I can, and hope that someone can help. Abensberg has pointed me towards people who have some idea of what is really happening, even if they are not economists, or food policy experts. Everybody always claims that they know what is really happening, but it is difficult to find out who really does. In most countries, people think that they would lose face if they said 'I don't know,' or 'I have no power over that.' Instead, they talk as though they do know and are able to change things. This can send me chasing a lot of red herrings.

I will have to talk to all these people, get isolated scraps of relevant information and try to build it into a jigsaw. It is detective work, made all the more difficult by the fact that I do not know which information is relevant, or which information is correct.

There was one good bit of news though. Abensberg told me that an FAO food supply expert from Rome was in Sierra Leone this week. He led me down the corridor, introduced me to the expert, Batangas, a Filipino, and left us to get on with it.

I introduced myself, and said why I was here. We then went through the usual sparring, saying where we had worked and who we worked for. He turned out to be a permanent employee of the FAO, based in Rome, and he had worked with them for twelve years.

Batangas' job is to visit each West African country in turn for two weeks a year and prepare their Food Balance Sheets. The idea is simple: you get figures for total food production and divide by the number of people to get food consumption per head. Of course, you have to allow for imports, exports and level of stocks, but the calculations are simple. The practice is more difficult in a country where statistics are unreliable, and where even the census of population could be wrong by a third to a half. It would be hard enough to get the right statistics, both meaningful and accurate, in Britain.

Batangas told me that he just ignores import and export statistics. I asked him how he could do this, when the figures show that the country imports half the rice it eats. He explained his logic. He believes that most of the rice that is imported is not eaten here at all; it is smuggled out to Liberia up the coast, or to Guinea inland. The smuggling is profitable, because rice is artificially cheap here. The price is kept down by a consumer subsidy as well as by the fact that the leone is overvalued. (I was about to question this – Welensky had said that it is not overvalued any more – then I realized that he was working out a Balance Sheet for last year.)

He told me that the traders just buy the cheap rice from the Agricultural Marketing Board depot, drive it across the border and sell it for US dollars in Liberia or for CFA francs in Guinea. (This is the currency used by the ex-French colonies in Africa.) Either way they get the world price in a convertible currency, and they make a fat profit.

'This is important for food policy,' he told me earnestly. 'It means that if you stop all food imports you will not change the amount eaten in the country. You will just stop the smuggling. This policy will save the country a lot of money, foreign exchange particularly.' He looked at me proudly, confident that he had solved a major problem.

Well, he had told me all he thought he knew about the subject, so now was the time to ask questions, to probe.

'That is very interesting indeed,' I said sweetly. 'How do you know about the smuggling?'

'Well, everybody knows that there are queues of rice lorries at the border, waiting to go through the customs.' he said.

'You mean that the smugglers go through the customs with something as obvious as a lorry load of rice?' I asked, trying not to sound incredulous.

'Yes, this is a corrupt country. All they need is a small bribe for the Sierra Leone customs officers, and another one for the customs at the other side.'

'Have you seen the lorries queuing yourself?' I asked, a little too abruptly.

'Well, I saw lorries heading for a customs post in the north once. However, I had to go away after a short time. If the smugglers had noticed me, they would have attacked me. Or they would have told the Special Branch to arrest me and deport me. You know how it is?' He looked at me for confirmation.

I nodded agreement. Expats are carefully watched.

'It is not just what I saw myself,' Batangas continued. 'In my job I visit FAO projects all round the country, and also experts in other projects. They live in the country and know what is going on.'

I wondered how much travelling round the country he really did, in a two-week visit spent mainly on collecting statistics. I started asking questions, to see if there was any way of checking his theory.

'How do you know the amount that is smuggled?'

'How do you know how many trucks go across the border in a year? Is it hundreds or thousands?'

'Do they go every day of the year, or did you happen to pick the one day when they were going?'

'How do you know that it was not a perfectly legal shipment to Guinea? After all, Freetown is the normal port for inland Guinea.'

'How do you know that the sacks on the lorry were rice, not maize or even fertilizer?'

I did try to ask these questions as softly and disarmingly as possible, but he saw the cumulative effect of a string of questions he could not answer as aggressive. He stiffened and said, formally and coldly, 'It is my job to take a view on the situation. I base it on the statistics, on the information I gather, and on my own experience.'

I do not like to leave a meeting on such unfriendly terms, so I thanked him profusely, switched to idle gossip about the FAO and other countries he had worked in, then left.

★

My worry is that when there is no hard evidence and there is no economist working full time on food policy, both Government and the aid agencies will base their decisions on myths like this.

Of course, this myth could be true. Certainly subsidies and the artificial exchange rate kept local prices below the world price in the past, so smuggling may have been profitable. Equally, though, the story could be complete nonsense. There is no supporting evidence at all. I must keep an open mind and look for evidence one way or the other.

How far can I rely on Batangas' 'taking a view' based on his experience? Not at all, I think. He gives the impression of being one of those people who have been in aid forever, but who have learnt nothing from their experience. FAO has a lot of them, very highly paid permanent staff members whom they cannot get rid of, and who they have to keep busy on simple routine tasks like this. A lot of them are Indians who came in as friends of friends when the FAO Secretary General was an Indian. The Indian Government was so embarrassed by them that it now vets any Indian joining an international organization to see that they are of international standard.

Batangas' story is important, if it is correct: it means that the country is self-sufficient in food, rather than importing half its rice, and this has obvious implications for food policy. How could I check it though? I went straight back to Foday Bombwe, the Director of Planning, and asked him where I could get all the figures that Batangas had used: production of the various food crops, stocks at the beginning and end of the year, consumption statistics, and import and export statistics.

He laughed humourlessly. 'There are no figures at all for stocks, production or consumption. When he asks me for them, I refuse to give him any, because we just do not know. What he does then is employ my junior economists as "consultants" to get the statistics. They need the money, so they invent figures for him. He prepares his Food Balance Sheets; FAO publishes them; we put them in the waste-paper basket; everybody is happy.

'As for the import and export statistics, I do not know how accurate they are. You must ask the Central Statistics Office, though they have not printed any for a long time. In fact, the Central Statistics Office is now running more than six months late for everything. Even the national accounts were six months too late for the budget, so it had to be based on pure guesswork. It is not inefficiency: it is because the European Commission has paid them a lot of money – in foreign exchange – to do a special statistical collection, so they have stopped all their real work until the EC work is finished. Nobody can see any possible use for the statistics the EC wants – they are for some silly international comparison the EC wants to do – but money is money.

'But if you really want to know about our production statistics, you must come to our meeting with the World Bank, here at 8 a.m. on Friday morning.' He smiled meaningfully, and winked.

Why was Foday so open with me, and why did he blow the gaff with such obvious enjoyment, after our guarded initial meeting? I suppose the fact is that his department has no responsibility for statistics. He can enjoy telling scurrilous stories about the FAO and the EC, and it does not matter to him what I think about the Central Statistics Office.

Doing Business in Freetown

THURSDAY, 7 SEPTEMBER

Behind the bar, Boss Seaga was holding forth on the difficulties of doing business with the Government.

'My brother, he sells to the Government. Of course, he wants to do business with no bribes, like in Europe, I think, but here it is not possible. Always he had to pay a bribe to get the contract, but now it is much worse. If he wants to get paid, he spend most of his time going round the Ministry to pay them to sign the papers. Then he must pay the Ministry of Finance to get the cheque. They keep wanting more money, and already the bribes cost more than what he sells them.'

'True enough,' chimed in a man standing next to me at the bar. 'You know I run the cigarette factory and we pay taxes to Government?'

I nodded.

'Well,' he continued, 'I know for a fact that someone, who shall be nameless, imported a whole container load of Marlboro into this country and paid only $5 customs duty – that's right $5, not $500 or $5,000.'

'But didn't you see that story in the paper, Mr John?' Boss asked him. 'There was a fire in a house two streets from here, and the people inside threw packets of money and gold coins out of the window to save them. The people outside stole most of them, of course. But the owner was a customs officer. He said, "Never mind. There is plenty more where that came from."'

That is the reality, I suppose. To an economist it would be much better for a government to tax luxuries coming into the country than to tax export industries. With a totally corrupt customs department, it is a waste of time even attempting import duties, while export taxes on government monopoly exporters are easy.

'You exaggerate,' said Thor the bearded Swede. 'You don't always have to bribe. Only today, I got my telephone connected. I was quite happy to pay a bribe, but nobody asked me.'

'Didn't anyone say that they had lost their pencil?' asked Henry.

'Well, yes, she did,' Thor agreed, 'so I lent her mine.'

There was a roar of laughter from the people at the bar, and Henry explained, 'The correct reply is to give her 50 leones and say, 'Why don't you go and buy yourself one.' She must have thought you were a real nutter.'

The conversation turned to actual theft. One of the expats complained that his camera had been stolen from the bedroom of his house. He knew that one of the servants must have stolen it, but which one of the six? He was going to have to call in the police.

Boss Seaga interrupted, 'Hell no. Those bastard policemen thief everything else in your house. You must get a potman. He is the magic man. He will light a fire and put a clay pot on it. It is full of plants and medicines. When it is hot, he puts it on the stomach of your servants. If the man is not the thief, nothing happens. If it is the thief, it sticks to his stomach. Then he gives back what he has stolen. It always works.'

There was a chorus of agreement.

'Using a potman can only work if the person feels guilty,' said an American priest standing next to us. 'The way they work it in Government, nobody feels guilty.

'For example, our project is located in the Ministry of Health, and we have our offices there. Last month we had a robbery, and all our paper was stolen.'

'Paper?' I asked, surprised.

'Yes, paper,' he replied. 'Haven't you noticed that you can't buy plain typing paper in town? You have to pay a fortune for poor quality. So we paid dollars and imported ours direct from the World Health Organization headquarters in Geneva.

'Anyway, as a priest, I have my own way of finding out what happened. The actual theft was ordered at director level. Everybody in the building got a cut, from the Minister to the office messenger, though the messenger only got two leones.

'I think it is a way to make everybody part of the system, so that everybody shares the guilt, and nobody feels very guilty at all. This means that your potman would not find the person who stole my paper.'

'Myself, I don't use potmen,' said Brendan, 'because I can always tell when my supervisors are stealing. Their job is to take rice and distribute it to people working on a 'food for work' programme. It is a great temptation for them to sell it to traders instead.

'Once they do that, though, they start eating well and drinking well. Then they get fat. Sure, nobody gets fat on the wages we pay, even though we pay three times as much as Government. As soon as I see someone putting on weight, I transfer them to a new district, where they promptly lose weight again.'

Our food came, so there was a break in the conversation. I took the opportunity to ask Henry what had happened to the exchange rates.

'Up to the beginning of this year, Government controlled the exchange rate,' he said. 'It was 7 leones to the dollar. It was overvalued of course – I reckon that 10 leones would have been about right. Then the World Bank and the International Monetary Fund came in. Instead of letting the Government devalue to the right rate, which they had done a couple of years ago, they made them float the exchange rate, so it was set by supply and demand on any day. It became a free market without any controls whatsoever.'

I nodded. I noticed, though, that he thought the currency had been 40 per cent overvalued, while Welensky, the World Bank man, thought it had been 100 per cent overvalued.

He continued 'You see, these Washington bankers think that every country in the world has money markets like New York or the City of London, with thousands of traders handling billions of dollars a day. Here the sums are tiny. A car salesman importing half a dozen Mercs can change the supply and demand for a day, and change the exchange rate. It is a very thin market.

'These Washington bankers also think that businesses want foreign exchange so that they can import. Businesses here don't, not now anyway. They want to get all their assets out of the country. The exchange rate today represents how desperate they are.'

He waved to the waiter and ordered another double gin.

'How it happened was like this. As long as the exchange rate was fixed, the business community thought that the economy was reasonably stable. It did not matter too much to businesses that the leone was overvalued, because everybody used the black market.

'Once it was freed, though, nobody knew what was going to happen next. In the first week of trading, it dropped from 7 leones to the dollar down to 15 leones. As I say, it should have been 10. Because it was falling so fast, some people panicked and started to shift their capital out of the country. This pushed the leone down to 20 to the dollar, so more people panicked. It is still falling.

'It is like a bank going bust because everybody wants to take their money out at the same time.'

He was clearly upset. He took a pull at his gin, and put the glass down hard on the table.

'It is easy to say "I told you so", but I did tell them. So did the commercial banks and businessmen. At least, we told the Government, but we could not meet the International Monetary Fund people to tell them. They never talk to people like us. They despise people in poor countries. They despise businessmen.'

True, but they also despise me, a micro-economist working on practical problems in developing countries. The only people they do not despise are people with Ph.D.s in macro-economics, and, even then, they must be Ph.D.s from an American university.

This has been a long and exhausting day. I enjoy meeting people and talking to them, but interviewing requires me to think constantly and hard, to get every nuance from each statement.

I am also putting on an act. I have to show that I am in some way different from all the dozens of other consultants who call on them every month, that my report at any rate will be worth reading. They suffer from consultant overload, seeing far more consultants than they can remember, and getting far more reports than they can read, much less act on. In Jamaica, a couple of years ago, the World Bank sent in a consultant just to identify what consultancy reports had been produced over the previous two years. She found 1,300 reports for an island of 3 million population, one for every 2,300 people!

To show that they should read my report, I indicate that I respect their opinions. I am polite. I ask for their advice. I listen. But I do listen with total absorption, and few people can resist having people listen to them with total absorption. I am not pretending: I am absorbed. Even if they are obviously talking rubbish, I want to know what people like them believe, and why they believe it. I also want to know who else believes it.

And, of course, I am trying to get something positive from the meetings, ideally their active support. I am hoping to get guidance on who I should see, and what the political constraints are. And, of course, to get some hard facts.

Finding the Facts

More useful phrases from today's Creole lesson.

'How de body?' (Answer: 'De body fine; de wallet empty.')

'A de work na Agriculture, were y'self?' (I work in the Ministry of Agriculture. Where do you work?)

'A de go in bar for drink Star bia.' (I am going to the bar to drink Star beer.)

'Let we go blow na bar.' (Shall we go and relax at the bar?)

'Do you no wast me tim.' (Please don't waste my time.)

★

My first meeting today was the one Foday had invited me to, on production statistics.

The meeting was to referee between two projects, both funded by the World Bank, which were producing completely different estimates of rice production in a major production area. One was the Agricultural Statistics Project, the other an Area Development Project. They used identical methodology – it is pretty standardized around the world. They selected a village at random; then a random farmer in each village; then a random one of his fields; then a random square metre in that field. They cut the rice in that square metre, and multiplied the amount harvested by 10,000 to give the yield per hectare. Since they both visited several hundred farmers, this should have given a pretty accurate estimate. Two projects using identical methodology in the same area should have produced almost exactly the same results.

Only they didn't. They disagreed by 80 per cent on the total area planted to rice, and by 60 per cent on the yield per hectare. The surveys could have been done on different continents.

This is alarming to me, and should alarm anyone involved in running the country. If we do not have any idea at all of how much rice is produced, how can we know whether people are starving?

Both projects were determined to show that they were right, and had sent their Project Director and all their graduate staff to defend their estimate. The economists in the Ministry of Agriculture had come along to watch the fun.

Both sides said forcefully that they had stuck scrupulously to the standard methodology, so the other side must be wrong.

We heard them out. Nobody was tactless enough to raise the possibility that one or both estimates were pure invention. Often the enumerators decide that walking for hours through the bush in the heat of the day is too much like hard work, and that it is a lot pleasanter to sit in a pub inventing the figures. It is not just idleness: if the enumerators invent a farm, they can pocket the farmer's fee. Sometimes it goes a step further, with the supervisors inventing both enumerator and farmer, so that they can pocket the enumerator's salary as well as the farmer's fee. When we were doing a similar survey in Zambia, our solution was to devise our own IQ test and to give it to anyone who applied for a job as an enumerator. We rejected anyone who seemed to be intelligent enough to fake the results convincingly. Of course the others tried inventing their results, but it was easy to spot this.

Murat, with all the panache of Napoleon's *beau sabreur*, rose to the occasion. He stood up and said 'It is my decision that we will use both these surveys. We will take an average of the two estimates.'

The one decision that is certainly wrong.

I kept my mouth shut. Murat could have had me fired and sent home at any moment.

Conclusion: we know nothing at all about the amount of rice produced in the country. Yesterday I had found out that we did not know anything about how much rice was exported either. The country's food policy is based on total ignorance.

I went into the department and got my letter of introduction from Amanda. It was perfectly typed, with no errors at all. Again, she asked me to give her a chance to practice her typing and shorthand. What a difference from the typists at home!

Evidently she had had her hair done last night, because it was plaited in a new and more complicated pattern. This devotion to personal beautification must be compatible with fundamentalist

Christianity: she had a Bible open by her typewriter, while the others were reading Mills & Boon.

As I walked past Foday's door, he called me in, and introduced me to Thomas Clarke, the man who was chosen to be my assistant on this mission. He looked to be in his late twenties. He was tall, handsome and black, with a deep, booming voice. I am guessing that his English name means that he is Creole.

Clarke is an economist in Foday's Department of Planning, on the bottom professional grade, though he seems to have been in the department for six or seven years. He has worked with a few visiting consultants before, so I think he knows a bit about organizing us. He seems to be bright. He has a local economics degree, which may mean anything. Twenty years ago, in the mid-1960s, Sierra Leone's university was run as a college of London University and gave proper London degrees. Sierra Leone may have kept up this standard – Zimbabwe certainly has – but I read an article by someone who taught in Malawi, saying that their degree was equivalent to O levels. Thomas has also got a master's in a British university, which, again, can mean anything. It could be the same master's degree I got, but it could be the low standard that they reserve for Third World students. Universities are under strong financial pressure to get foreign students, who are paid for in hard cash, and to pass them. For the moment, I will take him at face value and assume that he is well trained and bright.

I spent an hour with him, discussing what I am trying to achieve and how I want to go about it. I want him to be more than just a guide and an interpreter – Mohammed could do that very well.

Thomas took me to the Ministry of Commerce, which is responsible for all marketing of processed food and all imported food. It also covers all the storage, milling and marketing which was done by the now defunct Rice Corporation as well as the coffee and cocoa marketing of the Agricultural Marketing Board. I suppose the reality is that, if the Ministry of Commerce only covered manufacturing industry, it would be so small as to be non-existent, so it has to cover a lot of agriculture as well.

Anyway, this means that the Ministry of Commerce is the parent ministry of the state-owned Agricultural Marketing Board and is technically in charge of it. It may not really be in charge of the Board: often a marketing board is so powerful that it controls the ministry that is supposed to be controlling it – the power comes from control of the cash.

Thomas arranged the high-level courtesy visits, introducing me to the Permanent Secretary and Director. He then took me round to meet all the economists in the building who had been at university with him. He seems to be on good terms with everybody, which could be handy for this job.

The important man to meet turned out to be the Chief Economist, a grave man of about forty, tall and lean. He was not one of Thomas's friends, and was not particularly welcoming. He sat us down and gave us the official Ministry story, which is that the Ministry of Commerce sets the prices of agricultural export crops. The farmers get world prices minus the marketing costs of the Agricultural Marketing Board. I waited for him to expand on this, but he clammed up completely. This is the same story that I got from the World Bank, but without any mention of exchange rates, corruption, export taxes, and so on.

We then switched to rice, and he explained why a country that used to be self-sufficient in rice was now importing half what it eats. The main reason he gave was inflation. Up to a couple of years ago, the Rice Corporation marketed the rice, buying it from farmers, storing it, milling it, then selling it in the cities and the diamond fields. They paid the farmer the full price they received, less their marketing, storage and milling costs. They announced the price that they were going to pay well before the rice was even planted, so that farmers did not face the risk of low prices at harvest time. The system worked for many years. Then there was rapid inflation: the value of the leone fell by a third between the time the rice was planted and the time the Rice Corporation bought it. This meant that farmers got a third less in real terms than they had been promised, and they lost money. They could not afford to buy fertilizer and improved seed, and they stopped producing a surplus for sale.

He spoke formally, distantly. I think he was making it clear that rice marketing was nothing to do with the Ministry of Agriculture.

So far, his line had been blaming inflation, which was clearly not his ministry's fault: it was the fault of the Ministry of Finance.

He continued, explaining another effect of inflation. The Rice Corporation had based all its calculations on the actual costs incurred, ignoring inflation. It paid the farmers the price it had announced before planting, then sold the rice at this price plus actual marketing, milling and storage costs. Certainly it recovered its costs in money terms, but all costs had gone up by a third by the end of the year. This meant that it did not have enough money left to buy the next year's crop at the new price, nor to maintain its mills or stores at the inflated costs. First, the mills stopped working, then the stores fell into disrepair.

He did not present this as a failure by the Ministry to make the Rice Corporation adopt a realistic inflation accounting system. He presented it as the Rice Corporation acting on orders from the President. The President was determined to keep down food prices to reduce inflation and civil unrest, so he ordered the Rice Corporation to sell at a loss.

The result of the President's decision was inevitable. With this fall in production and the collapse of the marketing infrastructure, there was nothing left to do but import rice.

Yes, it was necessary to import, but the Rice Corporation was bankrupt and the Central Bank had run out of foreign exchange. Freetown started to run out of rice, and there were serious riots. As an emergency measure, the President ordered the Agricultural Marketing Board to import rice, paying for it with the foreign exchange that it had got from coffee and cocoa exports. The Rice Corporation was redundant, and its assets were taken over by the Agricultural Marketing Board.

It was a credible and familiar story, but a different one from the two told to me at the World Bank. Murat had said that it was due to corruption and incompetence, and Welensky had said it was all due to an overvalued exchange rate. However, I do not think that the three stories clash: the different forces combined to cut prices to farmers, and to stop them from producing a surplus.

I am sure that the Chief Economist was telling me what he saw to be the truth, but I am equally sure that he knew that he was not giving me the whole story. He gave me a credible story, which put the blame squarely on the Ministry of Finance for allowing inflation, and on the President for ordering the Rice Corporation to sell below cost. The story completely exonerated the Ministry of Commerce and the two marketing organizations it was supposed to be controlling. Never mind: I did not expect a confession.

When I asked for other information, such as statistics, the accounts of the marketing board, or any consultancy reports on agricultural marketing – they would normally be freely available to a consultant – he said that this information did not exist, and anyway he would have to get clearance from the Permanent Secretary before he released it: a clear snub.

The Casablanca

I arrived early at the Casablanca for lunch. It was only my fourth visit, but Boss Seaga greeted me as an old friend. He had the same three days' growth of beard as on each of my previous visits, and he was sweating profusely, in spite of the fan behind the bar. He leaned over and fixed me with his eye.

'I was born in Sierra Leone, Mr Peter,' he said. 'My father, all our fathers, came here from the Lebanon before the First World War, because they did not like being in the Turkish Empire. My father had little money, so he could only get to West Africa. If he had had more money, he would have gone to America, like other Lebanese, and I would be American.'

I tried to imagine him as an American businessman, slim, clean-shaven, wearing gold-framed glasses and a lightweight suit with a Rotary pin in the buttonhole, then I quickly turned off the thought before I started laughing.

'The Lebanese had no money, so they started little businesses,' he continued. 'For example, before we came here the farmers who wanted to sell a few kilos of cocoa and coffee had to go all the way to town and sell it at the buying station of a big company like Unilever. We Lebanese went to the villages and bought one or two kilos from each villager. We sold it to Unilever at bulk prices and made a profit. Then we found that we could get even better prices if we sold it to them at Freetown docks. It was good for the farmers, and it was good for the big companies. After we had been here for twenty years, we had all the trade from the villages to the docks, and the big companies stopped trading inland.'

He had fixed me with his eye, as though he was the Ancient Mariner, determined to tell his tale. I do pride myself on my interviewing skill, my ability to get people to talk, and keep talking, but I was not using it now, rather the opposite: I was trying to break away to get some lunch. In vain: he continued firmly.

'Even today, when the Agricultural Marketing Board does all the export, they have to use Lebanese traders to go to the villages and buy the crops. Half of the firms who are buying agents for them are Lebanese, not black Sierra Leoneans.

'You ask me why Lebanese are such good businessmen, Mr Peter? I will tell you. I like to tell you it is because we are more clever than the other Sierra Leoneans, but it is not true. We are good businessmen in this country because we do not cheat other Lebanese. Of course, I will make a good bargain, but I will not cheat him, and he will not cheat me. So I do not have to watch my back all the time. A black Sierra Leonean, he knows that everybody tries to cheat him, so he try to cheat them first.'

As he talked he leaned against the bar counter, his belly guarding the cash drawer, like any trader in the bazaar. Waiters kept coming up with orders, and he poured the spirits without moving from the cash drawer. Somebody wanted to pay their bill, so he moved his belly away and made change. All this without breaking the flow of his story, or taking his eyes off me.

'You know, Mr Peter, in the old days there were Lebanese, and some were Christian and some were Muslim. It did not matter. There were very few of us and we all knew each other and did business with each other. Then, ten years ago, Israel invaded the Lebanon and the civil war began. Lots and lots of Lebanese came here. They came to get away from the war, and they came to make money. The old Lebanese, who came here when my family came, they put all the money they made into their businesses here, and they build factories and shops. The new Lebanese send their money to the Lebanon to buy guns.

'They have an agreement, though: they do not fight here. Instead, they send the money home to buy guns to kill each other's brothers and cousins.'

He looked down, dejected, then looked me in the eye and said firmly, 'Mr Peter, it is nonsense. I was born in Sierra Leone, and I am Sierra Leonean. My family helped build up the country, and it is my country. I am not from the Lebanon and I do not mind what happens there. These new Lebanese are destroying the country.'

The flow was broken when the door opened and a group of expats entered, led by Brendan and Hooray Henry. They went straight to the table to eat, and I took the opportunity to break away from Boss's life story and join them.

'I've just had a letter from Damien,' Brendan announced to the table at large. 'He says he has recovered from the accident and will be coming back next month.'

He saw the blank look on my face, and someone else asked 'Who's he?'

'He was a consultant here, he was,' Brendan explained. 'He was staying at the same hotel as you, Peter. He was driving to work one morning and went off the road into the ditch by a paddy field. He went through the window, and cut his face to ribbons.

'All the passers-by rushed to the car. They eased him out of the window, and laid him gently beside the road. They stole his wallet, his shoes and his glasses, and they were starting on his clothes when the hotel manager happened to drive past. He recognized Damien as a hotel guest, and drove him to hospital. Sure, they would have left him there to die, stripped bare.'

Henry harrumphed, 'Bloody lucky he didn't kill anyone when he went off the road, or they would have lynched him. They know damn well that the police won't do anything, so they take justice into their own hands.'

'Anyway,' said Brendan, firmly resuming his story, 'the hospital saved him, though they have almost no equipment. I thought they did a grand job on his face, though he was still bruised and puffy when he went home. Damien, of course, didn't think so, though frankly he was no oil painting before.

'And didn't he go on about it?' he said, looking round the table for confirmation. 'He kept saying that his insurance would pay for the best plastic surgeon in England to restore him to his former beauty.'

'In this letter, though, Damien says that the English plastic surgeons were impressed by the face job, and asked him who did it. When he said it was Charles Touray, they said "Well, that explains it!" Apparently, he made quite a reputation for himself when he trained in England.'

There was a break as the waiter came and took our orders. I had some of the small, spicy, Lebanese sausages with pitta bread.

'I've just been doing some calculations,' came Henry's drawling voice. 'That star plastic surgeon of ours, Touray, is being paid $150 a year. Not much, is it, really?

'What!' I exclaimed, '$150 per *year*? Per month you mean.'

'Yes, per year. I've just worked it out. He gets 4,000 leones a year. That is a government surgeon's salary. Remember, it used to be two leones to the pound until England devalued in 1967. The government salaries were set when 4,000 leones was a lot of money.'

I can't work Henry out. Sometimes he seems to be amoral, other times quite concerned. I was going to say that he appears to have a social conscience, but really he is a cynical outside observer of the system.

'Embarrassing though it may seem,' came the calm, authoritative voice of the English bank manager on my left, 'I actually get paid more than all my staff put together. It is not that I get paid so much – only half as much again as I get in England. It is that they get paid almost nothing.'

Thor came and sat at our table. He was beaming. He had taken Brendan's advice: he had gone to the UN Res Rep and had got a copy of the Attorney General's letter asking for rent to be paid in dollars. This had been enough for Murat to cover his back, so he had given Thor clearance.

Thor had a moral problem, though, 'The first time I went to the house, this morning, there were six people waiting outside, all wanting to work for me as servants. No! I do not approve of having servants: I think that it is wrong for one man to work for another like that.'

'Employ them!' boomed Henry. 'It costs you bugger all, and each one you employ keeps a family alive. Damn your socialist conscience.' Everybody at the table agreed loudly.

'If I do that, how much do I pay them?' asked Thor.

'Can't remember,' replied Henry. 'The firm pays them for me.'

'The normal rate is about 80 leones a month, I think,' said Brendan quietly. Then his voice rose. 'I pay them twice that. I wouldn't be wanting to pay them so little that they can't send their kids to school. I also give them a sack of rice a month.'

'But that is so patronizing, so paternalistic!' protested Thor. 'Why do you not give them the money instead of buying rice for them? Let them decide how they want to spend their own money – your employer does not decide what you must spend your money on.'

'No!' came Boss's voice from behind the bar. 'That is a bloody bad thing. They want that you buy them rice. When they buy rice in the market, they buy it one cup at a time, so it is expensive. When you buy it, you buy a full bag, so the price is one-half. They have no car, either. They cannot go into the city centre, buy a bag of rice and take it home in the back of a car like you. And a sack of rice is more than they need. Their wives will sell some in the market and make money to buy other food.'

Brendan returned to his point doggedly, 'But you can't just employ a cook. There is a social obligation on you to employ a house servant and a gardener, especially if you have a garden. You also need to employ at least two security guards, one for the day and one for the night. Why, I am not quite sure: there is always someone around in the daytime, and the night guards are useless. My guard is usually fast asleep, wrapped up in his army greatcoat and balaclava – in this heat! Once or twice, I have driven the car right up to him where he was asleep. He didn't wake up with the sound of the engine, nor with the headlights in his eyes, nor even when I sounded the horn a foot away from his ear.'

Henry interrupted him, 'You've got to be bloody careful. You can't just wake the buggers like that. I shook one of them awake once, and he jumped up, half asleep and absolutely terrified. He picked up his machete and went for me. I was only saved because he realized just in time that a white man was not likely to be a burglar trying to kill him.

'But what really annoys me is the pretence,' he continued. 'I know that they work somewhere else during the day and they are going to sleep half the night. I keep telling them to sleep from 6 p.m. to midnight, so they can stay awake after midnight, and guard me when I am asleep, but will they, hell? They must pretend that they do not have another job, and that they are going to stay awake all night. So they stay awake in the evening and go to sleep when they think I have gone to bed.'

'No problem,' said Boss from behind the bar. 'The guards all come from one village near Yoruba Town. It is not the guard that protects you; it is the whole village. If someone thief from one of the houses that they guard, the whole village finds out who did it. Then they chop him with their machetes, perhaps kill him.' The thought evidently gave him great satisfaction.

'Someone certainly woke my guards last night,' came the Welsh voice of Owen Veterinary. 'I was sitting on the veranda at about 8.30 last night when there was a blare of music from next door. A disco at full blast, and I really mean full blast. It was actually shaking the glass in the windows. We could not talk and even the guards could not sleep. All this in spite of the fact that we are a good fifty yards from the house next door, and there is a big wall in between.

'I sent out one of the guards to see what was happening. He reported back that everybody living within half a mile had also sent their guards to complain. They were banging on the gate and telling the guards inside the compound to tell their bosses to turn down the music. Only it was a party given by some Lebanese teenagers while their parents were away. Here they are the super rich, and like the super rich anywhere, they couldn't give a damn about anyone else. So they told their guards to tell our guards to go away, and our guards told us.

'This went on for a good two hours, with the music blasting out painfully. They must have hired a proper disco sound system, and they were using it to its full capacity. Then suddenly it stopped completely, utterly. There was no sound at all. My guard came back laughing. He had noticed that the gilded youth had parked their cars outside the compound. The message was conveyed to them that if they did not shut up immediately, their cars would be wrecked.'

I was wrong about there being no black Sierra Leoneans in the Casablanca. There are some black women. I am not too sure about their status. Some of them seem to be girlfriends come to join their expat companions for lunch. Some seem to be more freelance, which is not to say they are bar girls who sit at the bar to try and pick up custom: that would be socially unacceptable in what is in effect an expatriate's club. No, they come in, usually two of them, and sit at a table with someone they know as a friend. They are always cheerful, and improve the level of conversation at the table no end.

The Weekend

SATURDAY, 9 SEPTEMBER

What have I achieved at the end of my first week here? I have done most of my courtesy visits, and started on the information-collecting visits. I have a pile of old consultancy reports to read, though there does not seem to be a lot that is relevant.

I have heard a lot of people's opinions. Most will probably turn out to be wrong when I start investigating them, though. The World Bank team gave me the most complete picture, but that does not mean that they were right. The Ministry of Commerce gave me excuses and self-justification, but this does not mean that they were wrong. A lot of other people gave me stories and scraps of theories, which do not fit into what I now see as the big picture. The fact that they do not fit may mean that they are wrong, but it may equally mean that I am not working with the right big picture.

I am going to have to spend the rest of my time here checking all the stories I have heard and trying to fit the facts together. It is detective work – fascinating, but difficult. Usually I cannot check the facts directly: it would be impossible to sit at the customs post counting smugglers' lorries for instance. I have to work out a way of checking the stories indirectly. This is not going to be at all easy, because one of the things that I have found out is that all the statistics are wrong: we have no idea how much rice is produced, how much is consumed, how much is smuggled out of the country, or what the prices are in the local markets. And this is for a controlled good, where Government is the monopoly importer. If we do not have these figures for rice, we most certainly do not have them for other foods – maize, cassava, palm oil and alcohol.

All this means that I have not yet got enough information to spend this weekend doing economics or starting to rough out my report. It is frustrating, but it always happens in the first week. Still, it means that I can relax with an easy conscience.

So I sat under a palm tree and read the guidebook. It seems that Sierra Leone became a colony two hundred years ago, a couple of years earlier than Australia. In fact, they were going to send the convicts here, instead of to Australia, until they noticed the death rate. Instead, they used it as a place to dump released slaves, on the assumption that blacks were immune to African diseases. The first lot were the slaves who happened to be in Britain in 1770 when the courts held that King Alfred had abolished slavery in England nine hundred years before, and that it had been illegal ever since. Any slaves in Britain were shipped off immediately. This ruling, of course, terrified the slave-owning American colonies, and triggered the American War of Independence. British forces released a lot of slaves in this war, most of whom ended up here. One of Washington's own slaves was resettled here, where he disgraced himself by becoming a slave trader himself.

From 1806, when Britain abolished the slave trade, there was a British naval squadron stationed here, to capture slave ships and free the slaves at Freetown. They continued to operate until the USA and Brazil abolished slavery in the 1860s.

The released slaves formed a little colony of their own, in Freetown. They came from some two hundred African tribes, including Ghanaians, Nigerians, Congolese and even East Africans. As they had no common language, they created a pidgin, Creole, which is basically English words with a West African grammar. I gather that the Creole spelling of Creole is Krio, with the 'le' hardly sounded. The Creole people are the descendants of these released slaves and have no European ancestors. They are a minority in the country, but they have always dominated the civil service and business, because they are better educated. They are all Christians because the doctrine of redemption is striking to someone who has just been released from the hell of a slave ship by a Christian warship. And, I suppose, because the missionaries offered free education.

The rest of the population are the local tribes who were here at the time the British arrived. About half are Muslim, and the rest are either Christian or have traditional beliefs. There were few Muslims here before the British arrived, but the British actively encouraged Islam, because they noticed that the Muslims were law abiding and teetotal, while the Christians behaved just like British Christians.

The guidebook does not say anything about religious conflict, of course, so I will keep my eyes open. It sounds like an explosive mixture.

SUNDAY, 10 SEPTEMBER

I was chatting to one of the young waiters at the hotel last night, and I arranged to have a drink with him when he was off duty on Sunday, on neutral ground, at Alex's Beach Bar down the road.

We sat at a table on the beach and had a beer. He talked of his education and his ambition. He was almost in tears as he talked of the tiny ambition he had left, a house of his own, and of the fact that he would not achieve it.

'It is not too much to ask for, is it? Just two rooms and a parlour?'

No, indeed, it should not cost more than $150 at local prices to build a house like this, and his father had managed it.

He had good A levels and he had thought that they would get him into a good job, much better than his illiterate father's. Instead, he had spent three years searching for a job in a collapsing economy, and was very grateful indeed to get a job as a waiter.

He got this job six months ago, and when he got his first salary he took it round to pay it to the personnel officer. The normal thing is to pay the first three months' salary as a bribe for getting the job, then a percentage of each subsequent wage packet as a bribe to keep the job. He was surprised, and grateful, when she refused to accept it on the grounds that the French hotel paid her properly, to do a proper job.

This purchase of jobs runs through the system. They were saying at the Casablanca that one of the directors in the civil service had to pay $4,000 to get his job. This is twenty-six times his present annual salary. How is he going to steal enough to pay for it?

In fact, it is rumoured that some of the international civil servants are doing the same. There has always been this bribery/extortion in the UN headquarters in New York, of course, but this is rather different. A consultant from a poor country comes out to do a job here. Whether or not he is any good, the Sierra Leonean Director hauls him up and tells him that he will report to the international agency that he is incompetent. On the other hand, if he hands over half his fee, the Director will give him a glowing report and recommend that he is employed full time. Consultants from poor countries are vulnerable to this extortion, because they are rich even if they get only half an international salary. It is a much higher salary than they would get at home, it is tax free, and there are perks like a duty-free car. Europeans, Americans, Australians, and so on, are not so vulnerable, as they can get much the same salary at home.

Of course, I personally would never pay a bribe to get a job. The bribe is paid by the company who employs me. Typically, the contract requires my company to employ some local consultants on our team, so the company employs them through a local consultancy firm owned by the Director who awards the contract. He supplies some local academics, who get a tiny proportion of this fee, and are naturally unenthusiastic about working. I know nothing: I do not get involved in the negotiations, and I keep my eyes shut. The only times I have seen anything were once when no bribe was paid and once when the bribe was late. Suddenly, everything started to go horribly wrong, with non-cooperation, hostility, trouble with my inception report, and so on. I told my company what was happening, they paid the bribe, and I carried on.

The system shelters me from having to see the reality of how my jobs are secured, while my waiter friend sees only too clearly how jobs are secured and kept. We passed a pleasant couple of hours before returning to our different lives.

Should I be discussing my sex life in this journal? Is it relevant to my work? I suppose you could argue that it affects my perceptions of the country and the way I tackle problems. If I have no contact with the local women, it is easy to overlook them in the analysis. In Pakistan, for instance, I can go for a month at a time without seeing a woman's face. When I visit a house, I am not allowed to enter until the women have been shooed into a back room away from me. The women in the streets have a hood over their heads, and peer out through an embroidered grille. Of course, when I prepare a project there, or analyse a market, I do try to analyse the 'gender dimension', but this is not the same as taking women into account.

Sierra Leone is completely different from Pakistan, even though it has a large Muslim population. Here I have women secretaries at the Ministry, who are attractive, who speak excellent English, who are articulate, and who do not wear the veil. True, I have not come across any women professionals or senior civil servants. However, I find that whenever I go into a bar, I am surrounded by beautiful women looking at me admiringly. I would like to think that it is because of my irresistible personal attraction, but I know that it is because of the size of my wallet. My daily subsistence allowance, the cost of staying at a moderate tourist hotel for just one day and eating there, is more than a year's salary for a Sierra Leonean graduate. Some people would argue that simply because I could easily buy many local women's services, I will despise all women here, and possibly, by extension, all Sierra Leoneans. In fact, the bar girls I have met here are intelligent and charming women and I enjoy their company. I do not buy their sexual services, for reasons of my own like having a girlfriend at home, a fear of disease, and a distaste for purchased sex. Still, I do have long conversations with them, just because it is the only chance I get to talk to women. I pay them for their time, of course, because, like me, they are professionals selling their time to make a living.

Here the job of a bar girl at one of the top hotels is a prized position only open to intelligent and educated women. A woman should be able to earn enough to keep her whole family alive – husband, children, parents, even uncles and aunts – at a time when survival is a challenge for anyone.

There is a different group of women here, who shack up with the single expats, then disappear discreetly when wives and girl-friends arrive from Europe. Some of them, I think, are bar girls who have moved into a more lucrative and more pleasant work environment. Some are secretaries, or whatever, who have met expats at work and have moved in with them, as a way of feeding their families. Sometimes, no doubt, it is true love. Several of the local people have introduced me to their fanciable sisters and cousins, and were disappointed that I did not take up the offer. They were by no means pimps, just people facing hard times. If I had one of the women move in with me, ten people would have been fed for a year.

The local girlfriends are welcome in hotels, restaurants and even clubs. I have sometimes seen them being introduced to senior civil servants and their wives, all of whom treated the arrangement as normal, and all of whom treated the women courteously.

There are two groups of expats here, the single men and the families. The families have their own tight social circle, and they do not mix with the single men much. They certainly do not meet people like me who are on short-term contracts. This makes con-sulting a desperately lonely business, especially outside the capital city, where there are few consultants.

I do not know what the etiquette is here. Do the 'respectable married women' ever meet the companions? Do they treat them civilly? Or do they move in circles that do not overlap at all?

Some expat men move from one group to another. They are family men when their wives and children are here for the school holidays, then become hell-raking single men when the family goes back. The next holidays they are quiet family men again. Of course, there is total discretion when wives and girlfriends come over from England. I can imagine hundreds of conversations going, 'Well, of course I trust you dear. I can see that you are exactly that rare type who does not have a mistress here when his wife is in England.'

There are very few women consultants, and most of those that do come here are on long jobs, a year or more. They tend to mix with the families rather than with single male consultants. Why so few? I suspect that as short-term consultants, constantly on the move from hotel to hotel, from rest-house to rest-house, they would be constantly harassed, even in danger. I do not think there is that much danger here, but there is grave danger in a sexually uptight country like Pakistan. I think, too, that many of the men drifted into consultancy after their marriages broke up, leaving their wives to raise the family at home. How the women came into the business I do not know, but they are in great demand, particularly for projects aimed at women.

But this does not answer my question about sex. I suppose I can say that, as a consultant, I am always isolated from the community, and I need all the personal contact I can get. Perhaps I should shack up with someone?

I went for a drink at the Aqua Club with Brendan on Sunday. We sat at a bar on a headland overlooking the bay and watched a scarlet sunset reflected on a pewter sea.

This is not the usual expat yacht club. When I was in Dar-es-Salaam a year or two ago, I joined their Yacht Club, which is a member of the Royal Yacht Squadron, along with the Royals at Cowes and the Royal St George in Dublin, clubs that would certainly black-ball me if I applied. Members are allowed to fly the white ensign on their yachts. In practice, Dar-es-Salaam's club was for white expats only and even Indian expats could not become members. While Africans were welcome in theory, there weren't any, because in that socialist dictatorship none of them would admit publicly that they could afford to join. Any pressure to open up membership was vigorously resisted by the ambassadors of Western countries.

The Aqua Club here is not a member of the Royal Yacht Squadron, probably because they never got round to joining in colonial days. They would never get in now. The membership is mixed, with Africans, Lebanese and Europeans drinking and laughing together. Nor do most of them seem to be here for the sailing or big-game fishing, unlike Dar. Swimming and squash are the attractions.

I saw a notice behind the bar 'Beware of Pirates', and I laughed.

'It is not a joke,' Brendan snapped. 'Freetown is one of the pirate capitals of the world, along with Indonesia and the South China Sea. Merchant ships which come here are armed. They have to pay special insurance rates at Lloyds.'

Then he relaxed a little and explained. 'If you go out sailing, don't you ever, under any circumstances, go to help one of the local boats. At best, they will take your watch and your money. At worst, they may sink your boat and leave you to drown.

'Last month, didn't some of them rob four men from the club about ten miles out to sea, and then knock a hole in the bottom of their yacht. Eight hours later one of our members was sailing past and saw their heads bobbing in the water as they clung to the wreckage, and picked them up, just in time.'

Somebody banged on the bar counter behind us, and I looked round to see the manager announcing that a doctor was going to give us a talk about cholera. It seemed to be a special occasion, as they called all the kitchen staff, the waiters and the boatmen to listen. Then some women and children came in, evidently from one of the shantytowns near the club.

A pretty Swedish girl stood up to speak. She looked about 19, far too young to be qualified, but she announced that she was indeed a doctor, and that she had come from Sweden as part of an emergency aid mission to deal with the cholera epidemic.

Then a Lebanese man interrupted. He volunteered to translate into Creole for the benefit of staff. He translated her plain, correct, English into a wonderfully colourful discourse. All English words, of course, but unusual words in a different order, to give a vivid picture.

She told us that the epidemic had started on the western border but is now raging through the country, and there are no signs of it abating. Her guess is that 7,000 people have died already.

The symptoms are simple. You get diarrhoea and you shit water for four days. If you are still alive then, the disease cures itself instantly. If you lose a tenth of the water in your body before that, your brain is dehydrated and you die.

I am still reeling from the shock. I must have had cholera that time in Dar-es-Salaam – there was certainly cholera about. I had thought it was just a bad case of the runs. I sat on the loo shitting water, day after day. Then, after four days, it suddenly cleared up, and I felt quite OK. From what she said, I must have been close to death in those four days, whether it was cholera or something else. It also sounds as though I only survived because I drank lots of water and used my rehydration salts. It turns out from this talk that they are the only cure.

Nowadays, of course, my standard diarrhoea remedy is rehydration salts every couple of hours, so I always carry a good supply in my suitcase. However, the doctor told us that there was a desperate shortage in Freetown, and the free sachets brought in by the World Health Organization were now being sold for a couple of leone each on the black market. So she told us how to make our own emergency salts. She got everyone to chant the recipe, 'One teaspoon salt, five teaspoons sugar in one litre water.' Some people responded, but the expats were too reserved, and the chant petered out after two repetitions. The Lebanese man who had appointed himself interpreter had more charisma, or a more receptive audience, and he soon had the staff and the locals chanting in Creole. The club members joined in, and so did I.

After this, she had more success in getting everybody to chant 'one capful salt, five capfuls sugar to the water in one Coke bottle.'

She emphasized that the water must be boiled or you just spread the infection. She said that Coke was better than nothing, as it has lots of sugar and some phosphate salts.

The disease is spread by shit in water. I am blunt about it because when I grew up there were polio epidemics every year, killing or crippling thousands, largely because everybody was too polite to tell us that it was carried by shit. The fact that cholera is carried by shit means that there is not a lot that can be done about it in Sierra Leone. The continuous torrential rain floods the earth toilets and spreads the germs into the rivers and water supplies. The epidemic will carry on until the rains end completely. Even then, most people do not have access to clean water or hygienic lavatories. It is a poor person's disease.

After she had finished her talk, I asked Brendan about the epidemic. He said that he had only been vaguely aware of a small outbreak, and had not realized that there was anything like this going on. He called over the Lebanese who had acted as interpreter and introduced him to me. He was a doctor himself, Dr Blel, and he told us what had happened.

'Yes, the epidemic is quite as bad as she says, worse probably. There has been a media crackdown on it, though. That is to say, the Government has stopped anything appearing on radio or television about it, and somehow there is not much in the newspapers. The reason is that the Government is afraid that if there is any publicity it will damage the tourist industry.'

'What tourist industry?' I asked, astonished.

The tourist industry turned out to be the three beach hotels, none of them ever more than a quarter full, which are owned by a pal of the President. He hopes that this will develop into a tourist trade like the Gambia's.

'When they had the first two or three cases,' he continued, 'the outbreak was localized in a small border town on the West, Pamilap near Kambia. If the Government Health Service had acted fast, they would have kept it there and stopped the epidemic. They have emergency regulations which work. For example, no brewing is allowed at village level, because of the difficulties of maintaining hygiene, and no dead bodies may be moved out of the area. However, the tribes believe that everyone should be buried in the place where they were born. One of the first men to die had been born at the opposite end of the country. His family took his body to the home village. There the women did the ritual washing of the body. Then they prepared the funeral feast and brewed the funeral beer without washing their hands properly. Everybody who took part in the funeral feast went down with cholera, and thirty people died.'

I did a double take. It must have wiped out half a village. It would have hit the world news if it had happened in Europe or the USA, but because it happened in Sierra Leone it had not hit the headlines even here.

'It is not the first time we have had cholera here of course,' he said. (I noticed it was 'we' when he was talking as a Sierra Leonean, 'they' when he was distancing himself from the Government Health Service.) 'We had an outbreak in the 1920s, so we introduced the necessary emergency regulations. They are still on the statute book. All that is necessary is for the Minister to announce that they are in force.

'That's in theory of course,' he said, suddenly bitter. 'If the regulations are going to be any use at all, Government has to give them maximum publicity. They have to tell everyone that there is an epidemic. They have to show them that regulations like not moving bodies are common sense, or everybody will ignore them.

'Then they have to enforce them. Someone has to stop policemen from taking bribes to let bodies be moved out of the epidemic area – and stopping policemen from taking bribes is no easy matter.'

In the Markets

MONDAY, 11 SEPTEMBER

My girlfriend in England complains that I walk round supermarkets admiring the marketing instead of doing the shopping. Guilty. But that is exactly what I am paid to do here.

Thomas and I visited the market today. At first sight, the main retail market here looks much like any other Third World market. There are the market women squatting on the ground, each with a dozen or so little piles before them, of okra, or peanuts, or beans perhaps. They sit in the deep shade of the market buildings, on the near-black of the dirt-engrained concrete floor, the bright colours of their clothes muted by the contrast with the sun outside. In one corner are the rice traders. Each has half a dozen open sacks, one for each quality of rice. They laugh and chat with their customers as they negotiate a price. Then they scoop a couple of tin cups of rice into the buyer's basket for the customer, and throw in a little extra for luck.

The surprise is not what they sell in this market, but what they do not sell. For example, there are no tools, although nearly every Third World country would have stall after stall selling Chinese-made knives, screwdrivers, chisels, saws, and so on. There are no stalls selling cloth and clothes. There are no piles of colourful plastic buckets, bowls and plates, the basic necessities of modern living. There are no toys, no batteries and certainly no radios. This is the poorest of the poor countries.

We started in the retail market, talking to the women who sell rice and other food, and then talking to their customers. They have the same loud voices and wicked backchat as market women any-where in the world and the same sense of humour. We started with my attempts at Creole greetings, with me insisting on the full five-minute interchange, even when they were willing to accept just 'How de body?' 'Ah well t'ank ee.' This definitely makes them more willing to talk. I cannot possibly know all the nuances of politeness here. I now know that in Pakistan, for instance, you do not pick up food with your left hand, because that is reserved for wiping your bottom (though the women use both hands for cooking the food). The rules are certainly different here, and I cannot hope to learn them in a couple of months. Instead, I am just scrupulously polite in English mode. I am sure that they recognize this, and pardon any faux pas.

Thomas, of course, acted as interpreter. As he is a handsome young man, he had no difficulty with getting them to cooperate. I am never altogether happy working through interpreters though: I think that I am lucky to get half the facts and none of the nuances. Nor do I want to get the opinions of an interpreter who puts his own beliefs into the mouths of the traders. I would much rather that the work is done properly by someone who knows the language. What I am hoping to achieve today is to get Thomas to understand what I am trying to find out, and how I am trying to find it out. I can then let him do his own interviews without me and, of course, with no interpreter coming between the market women and the economist. He will get different answers, of course, working by himself. If I am there, the market women are likely to think, 'It is a mad Whiteman asking stupid questions. The handsome young man with him is paid to keep him amused and out of trouble. Anything I tell him will be used in England, where it cannot hurt me. Perhaps I will tell him some truth.'

When Thomas goes by himself, they will ask him who he is and who he works for. They may think 'He is from Government. Nothing that Government does is meant to help me. I will tell him lies.' In most of the world, the reaction is the same. If a government official asks a question, the only safe thing is to lie. When I was working in research, I had similar problems. For example, I telephoned an English wholesaler to ask the price of Irish tomatoes on his market. '£1.20,' was his instant reply. A minute later, I listened on an extension while an Irish exporter asked the same man the same question in the same words. This time the answer was '£2.40'. Sometimes they try to get a bit of fun at the same time. In Dublin, for instance, the Government sent an official around the fruit and vegetable market to record prices. The wholesalers promptly started a competition to see who could get him to write down the most ridiculous information. The winner got him solemnly to write down a price for 'Apples, origin Hong Kong.'

This means, of course, that I do not know which is right, the answer I get or the answer Thomas gets on his own, or, for that matter, whether either is right.

There is another completely different class of misinformation. Certainly, the market women will tell some lies. They will say that they are selling cheaper than they really are; they will say that they charge a tiny margin; they will say that they are losing money. The polite thing is to accept this at its face value – there are other ways of finding out. You then have no difficulty in getting the more important information on market structure and market channels where they do not feel so threatened. In the same way, when I am talking to the village moneylender, I accept without blinking his statements that he charges 2 per cent interest per year and that half the farmers never pay him back, and that he never lends money anyway. He then feels less threatened, and tells me how the system actually works. Sometimes it comes out as 'Well, I do not know anything about it myself, but other people tell me that...' or as 'What some unscrupulous people do is...'

When I interview I have to listen very carefully indeed, trying to find out what is true and what is not. I have to keep crosschecking, seeing how one market woman's story compares with another's, and how this checks with what I hear from the rice wholesaler.

I spent this afternoon training Thomas. The first part was not so much training him as showing him that he was a partner in the enterprise, rather than just an interviewer. First, we spent an hour or more discussing what we have learnt from the interviews, going over them in fine detail. Fortunately, he is very sharp. It turns out that he does a bit of trading himself on the side – he says that he has to if he is to survive on his salary – so he understands what is going on, and understands the jargon. He is getting an idea of what I am trying to find out and why.

He had not had any training in interviewing skills before, so he was missing a lot. For example, he was asking leading questions and he was interrupting people just as they started to say something relevant to our enquiry. We had a little workshop on it, and he responded excitedly. He had not even realized that there were interviewing skills and techniques he could use. He is a natural for the most important part of interviewing, which is listening with interest. It is possible to fake interest, I imagine, but I am interested, and once he realized what it was all about, he too became interested. This is important in getting people to talk: few people can resist talking to someone who is interested in what they say. He was listening with his whole body, responding to everything that is said, which was good. However, he was also saying 'Yes', 'Yes' and nodding his head as the market women talked, and from their body language I realized that they were taking this to mean that he liked what they were saying, and that they should say more of the same. When I pointed this out, he laughed, recognizing what he was doing.

He was also translating my open question, 'Where do you buy your rice from?' into a closed question 'Do you buy your rice from the traders in Congo Street?' or even 'You don't go into the country areas to buy your rice do you?' The advantage of Creole is that I could get some idea of what he was saying: I would not be able to pick this up from listening to someone talking the local language in most countries. Again, he had no idea what he had been doing. This is not surprising. In Europe I always tape my interviews, because if I do not watch myself I find myself slipping into the same bad habits: leading questions, 'Do you really do...?' and so on. I cannot tape interviews here, because few people have ever seen a tape recorder, and I think that they would react with fear and suspicion.

Then I taught him how to get people to talk. If you ask the trader a question and she answers it very briefly, do not jump in with the next question and do not move on to the next subject. If you do, you will have lost any chance that she will tell you more. Instead, when she stops talking, just look her in the eye and say nothing. Wait five seconds if necessary. She will feel under pressure to talk. If she does not, say 'Uh huh?' (In the tone of 'Go on') and count again. If that does not work, say 'What else?' (Not 'Is there anything else?' which calls for the answer 'No.')

He is delighted with these basic techniques and cannot wait to get back in the market and see if they work. I think he is going to be good.

As I was walking round the market, two little boys, about 10 years old, attached themselves to me, offering, in excellent English, to do my shopping for me. It is a good service for any expat who does not speak Creole, and it is probably profitable for the boys – they get a tip from the expat, then go round later and get a commission from each of the traders he bought from. However, it was not what I was there for, so I said 'No thank you.'

They kept hassling me, and eventually I lost my temper and told them to fuck off.

They walked off disconsolately, muttering to each other, 'He do spik Creole.'

While I was in the market, I took the opportunity to buy a grass basket for a couple of cents – they are used as disposable carrier bags. I am going to use this as my briefcase for the rest of the mission. The big minus with normal briefcases is that they get stolen. It is the height of cool to walk round wearing dark glasses and carrying a briefcase. People will break into a car or a hotel room to get the ultimate status symbol. Of course, they accidentally take the contents too, often all the papers collected on a long mission, and throw them away as being incriminating. You often see plaintive advertisements in the papers in African countries:

REWARD OFFERED
for the papers in a
briefcase stolen from a Land-Rover
outside the UN offices on Friday 13th.
No Questions Asked.

★

I stood out as the only white man in the market, but not as I stand out in the Philippines, where I am a head taller than anyone else. In fact, Freetown is the only place in the world where I feel small, three or four inches shorter than the average. Even in Pakistan, the Pathans, who were described as giants by the British army in the 1890s, turned out to be no taller than me – the British rankers were half-starved in Victorian times, and seldom made 5 foot 3 inches (they had to be enormous, over 5 foot 6, to join the Guards!).

Here, though, most people seem to be over 6 foot, and some are well over. I thought at first that it might be just the Creoles, perhaps because only the toughest were made slaves and the toughest of the toughest survived the slave ships. But toughest is not tallest: perhaps the slavers raided tall tribes? Then I noticed that the people from the local tribes are also big, which Thomas confirmed. This means that it cannot be genetic. The Creoles come from two hundred different tribes from West, East and Central Africa, so they have nothing genetic in common with each other, or with the local tribes. It must be related to diet. If so, everybody over 20 must have been raised on a very good diet indeed.

Thomas tells me that one of the girls in the office caused a sensation when she was sent to Japan for a computer course. She is tall, beautiful and has wonderful posture. She had great fun there, being surrounded by admiring Japanese men who barely came up to her waist.

My work here is proving difficult, because I cannot start by examining the existing food and agriculture price policy – there isn't one. This is extraordinary because price policy is fundamental. If you do not pay farmers the right prices, they will not grow the right crops in the right quantity. Sierra Leone manages to combine no price policy with the maximum of state intervention: it has state marketing companies for most agricultural products, and it has a state monopoly on imports and exports. The state sets minimum prices for annual crops like rice, well before planting date, and they fix the prices for tree crops like coffee and cocoa before harvest. There are also taxes and subsidies.

From what I can see, Sierra Leone has no coherent policy. There is a mishmash of taxes, subsidies, monopolies, state companies, etc., each introduced at a different time in history in response to a different crisis. Some of the policy measures work in different directions and cancel each other out. Some have no effect whatsoever, and some are plain harmful. The net effect is high taxes and low productivity.

Why has Sierra Leone not got a coherent policy or a unit to develop it? My guess is that a lot of important people do not want one. The policy unit would start by checking the costs of the Agricultural Marketing Board, and looking to see if any of its selling price was being diverted into someone's Swiss bank account. It would then ask awkward questions, like 'Should there be an Agricultural Marketing Board at all? Wouldn't it be better to have private firms competing on the export market?'

Of course, just asking these questions may be harmless. Kenya and Tanzania have World Bank-funded units which ask these questions and do work on policy, which keeps the donor countries and the World Bank happy. The Government does not answer the questions: it files the reports and ignores the advice. This solution had not occurred to the Permanent Secretary in Sri Lanka, who told me that he refused to have a policy unit at all, because, if he did, the World Bank would be able to tell him what to do.

Malawi has never had any policy, at least not in the thirty-three years since 1953. They had a few economists who started to do their job properly in the early 1980s, but Government did not want to know. Half were fired or 'disappeared' and those who are left avoid the subject.

What does all this mean to my job here? How will I deal with food policy when there is no food policy? In other jobs, I have had to try and find a workable alternative to a disastrous policy. This meant changing a lot of people's minds and upsetting a lot of vested interests. In one way, this should be a lot easier: if there is no policy, I do not have to get people to abandon a policy that they are wedded to.

Of course, one of the disadvantages of having no explicit policy is that there is no way of knowing when the policy is suddenly going disastrously wrong.

Vanishing Rice

TUESDAY, 12 SEPTEMBER

It's funny where you pick up the important information. I was at Alex's Beach Bar this evening having a barracuda steak when I got into conversation with one of the expat project advisers from up-country. After quite a few drinks, he told me what his local colleagues had told him about rice smuggling.

They said that there was almost no smuggling by lorry across the border. The smuggling works in a completely different way to the one that Batangas of the FAO had described. In fact, the Agricultural Marketing Board does not unload all the rice consigned to Freetown. Instead, it unloads half of what is in the ship and leaves the other half in the hold. The ship then takes this to another country, where it is sold at the full international price in dollars.

It is easy for the Agricultural Marketing Board to balance its books. All it has to do is to change some of the dollars it earns, at black market rates, and deposit the leones in its bank account, as though it had sold the rice at the local, subsidized price. This means that some people can pocket about a third of the value of the shipment, without even leaving their offices.

This is a far more convincing myth than the smuggling one. It is a lot easier and more profitable. The Agricultural Marketing Board gets the full world price, not what inland Liberia and Guinea are willing to pay for smuggled rice. It is a simple paper transaction: there is no need to travel from Freetown docks through the jungle over bad roads to Liberia or Guinea. (I have just worked it out: if Batangas, the FAO man, were right, there would be 32,000 lorry loads making the trip, using the 5 tonne truck that is usual here. Someone might have noticed!)

Also, it does not mean giving a bribe every time a truck passes a police checkpoint, and again when it crosses the border. Most important, it is discreet. No more than a few dozen people need know what is happening, and they can easily be paid off.

This is the sort of story I will never hear in an official visit to a Sierra Leone civil servant. I expect to become sufficiently friendly with my assistant, Thomas, that he will tell me some of these stories before I leave. Otherwise I have to rely on gossip from expats who have heard stories from their own local friends. Why do they tell me? Partly because they are absorbed in their job and in anything that may affect how they do the job. Partly because it is in the expat culture to bitch about the latest corruption or incompetence in the country they are working in. Partly because they like gossiping and I like listening to gossip. Partly because I have good interviewing skills.

The trouble with getting information in this way is that there is no way you can check it. I would very much like to ask this man's informant to tell me all about it, to tell me how he knows, and to tell me where I could find the evidence. If I did go to him, he would of course deny everything.

Instead, I start with three questions: 'Could it work?' 'Is it credible?' 'Would rational people act in this way?' In this case, the answer to all three is 'Yes'. It is far more convincing than the smuggling story. Next, I have to try and get the evidence. This is not going to be at all easy, as the few people who are in on the racket are presumably being paid off. I will have to think of some other way.

If it is true, what does it mean? It is difficult to believe that more than half the official imports are left in the ship – some substantial amount must be seen to be unloaded. It is quite possible, though, that only half the stated amount is imported. This means that Sierra Leone eats one-quarter less rice than the official figures indicate.

I have just thought, though, that it might be even easier to have a whole shipload not arrive. Would anyone notice, outside the small number of people not on the take?

What a basis for a food policy! One estimate of rice consumption is twice the other. I am going to have to do a lot of detective work to see which is right.

Military Coups

WEDNESDAY, 13 SEPTEMBER

Henry sat at the bar sipping his gin, and gave me a potted military history of Sierra Leone.

'They can be bloody good fighters. One of the Chindit columns in Burma was West African. They went behind Japanese lines, expecting that half of them would be dead within two months – the Japanese tortured and killed prisoners – in fact, it was nearer two-thirds killed. They also had the Black Scorpion commando brigade. They were effective: the Japs ranked them just below the Gurkhas.' He spoke with the accountant's envy of a fighting man.

'After the war, the army went back to the colonial system – one under-strength battalion armed with rifles and batons in case of riots. It was a comfortable life for them, no work, good wages, and a pension at 40.'

'Of course they have not had a war for forty years now, not even a threat of war, and that gets boring. So, about ten years ago, the junior officers staged a coup.'

He paused, and sipped his gin.

'They got into power all right, and got their hands on the Ministry of Finance, so they were happy.

'But the buggers were too greedy. Nobody minded that they got their snouts in the trough like the politicians. That was no change. They made one big mistake though: they didn't pass any of the money back to the army. Result: the sergeants staged their own coup, and chucked the officers out.' He smiled appreciatively.

I was fascinated by the accountant's analysis of history, even blunter than a Marxist's on the central role of economics.

He continued, 'They brought in Siaka Stevens as a figurehead president. He was an old trade-union man who had been in politics since well before independence. They had not realized how shrewd he was as a politician, though.

'Again the buggers were greedy. They kept all the good jobs for themselves and got their percentages on all the rackets, but they did not pass any money back to the army either.

'So, of course, the privates staged their own coup.' He grinned and ordered another double gin from Boss.

'This coup was different. You know the old Government House, the big white house with a wall around it, near Tower Hill Barracks at the centre of town? You do? Well the whole army, all 600 of them, surrounded it and fired off their rifles. The buggers stayed there, firing at nothing in particular for eight whole hours. Then they ran out of ammo. They couldn't think what to do, so they marched back to barracks.' Henry brayed with laughter, throwing back his blond hair with his hand.

'Siaka Stevens used this as a way to bring back civilian rule. Everyone was sick and tired of coups now, so he hanged some of the ringleaders to get the message home. Then he introduced the one-party system, with no opposition party, and he ran it well: he turned out to be a genius at playing off one faction against another.

'He also arranged to take a percentage of everything, and became very rich indeed. Most people here reckon he has accumulated $1.5 billion – yes billion – in fourteen years. Himself, he hints that it is more.'

This is an enormous amount. A crooked politician in a country of this size in Europe, Ireland say, is not going to end up with more than a few million. How did Stevens manage to get perhaps five hundred times as much? And from such a poor country?

Henry said reflectively, 'I suppose I am describing the political system as though it is a business. Sorry, but it is.'

'Siaka Stevens was a lot sharper than most African presidents. He did not want to be shot in a coup, and he did not want to spend his declining years desperately trying to hang on to power. He wanted to retire and enjoy his gains. Of course, he could have just gone on holiday and not come back, and spent the rest of his life living off the money in his Swiss bank. For some reason he wanted to stay here, though. Perhaps he wanted his people to continue to admire him, and envy his success. Perhaps he wanted to keep all his political networks. Perhaps he thought he was enormously popular for what he had done for his country – politicians come to believe their own propaganda. I don't know. All I know is that he wanted to retire in Freetown.'

'So how did he manage it?' I asked, 'Or was there a coup. They have a general as president now, don't they?'

'He managed it all right: he negotiated his retirement a year ago. He was the first African leader to retire voluntarily. It was not easy, as a lot of people were gunning for him. He had to get cast-iron guarantees that whoever took over would not arrest him and take all the money. This meant that he had to get the army, the freemasons and the secret societies to guarantee his freedom. They would also negotiate who would take over the single political party. As I say, he was the supreme fixer, and he fixed it.

'They chose General Momoh, who isn't a patch on the old man as a politician. He can't even control the army. Since he took over, there have been plots and rumours of plots, and even the odd attempted coup. Nothing official, but a lot of army officers have been fired. Nor does anybody know which way the police will go in a pinch.'

'What was that about masons?' I interrupted. 'Are there really freemasons here?'

'Oh, yes,' said Henry, authoritatively. 'We are strong here. In fact, I am meeting your Permanent Secretary at the lodge tonight. The British colonial officials were masons, and they started introducing local officials as members two hundred years ago. The oldest lodge here still wears white tie, tails and top hats to the meetings. It was an important part of running the Empire. They did the same in India. Kipling was proud of the fact that when he became a mason in the 1880s he was inducted by a Hindu and a Muslim.'

I looked at him curiously. I tried to remember if he had given me a funny handshake when we met, and whether he had been using any strange codewords. Not that I could remember. I tried to visualise him with one trouserleg rolled up, and wearing an apron. I gave up.

'It is only the Creoles, really,' Henry continued. 'The people from the local tribes join their own secret societies, even if they are Christian or Muslim. You have heard of the Leopard Men, haven't you, the people who used to dress up as leopards, then kill people with their claws? They used to appear in the boys' books when I was young. Well the originals were here, down in the Southern Province.

'That is one way they balance the civil service. They do not let the Creoles or one of the tribes, the Timne or the Mende, bunch together in one ministry. In your ministry, for example, the Permanent Secretary and the Director of Agriculture are masons, but the Minister, the Director of Research and the Director of Planning are tribals, and belong to secret societies. This stops any one faction from getting too strong.'

Behind Henry's stories, there is information that can be useful to me. I am starting to get some idea of the politics inside the Ministry of Agriculture, and the importance of Christian versus Muslim, Creole versus tribal. I have also previously got some information about conflict between the various ministries. Another bit of politics that could be important is conflict between different aid agencies: so far, all I have found is that the Resident Representatives have different personalities.

Planning My Expedition

THURSDAY, 14 SEPTEMBER

I am still at the stage where the more I learn the more ignorant I feel. I am here to sort out food policy, but I am still not clear what needs sorting out. The World Bank's complaint is largely that there is no Free Market. Murat argues that this is why the country is now importing half its food, but the visiting FAO man, Batangas, is firmly convinced that in fact large amounts of food are smuggled out, and the country is self-sufficient. Then someone at the Beach Bar, whose name I do not know, also said that the country was self-sufficient, and argued that half the rice that is officially imported never even leaves the ship. All I am getting from going round the ministries is opinion: there are no hard figures. Nobody knows how much food people eat; nor do they have any idea how much is grown here.

It is time I went up-country. It will give me a different perspective. In fact, since the statistics are so bad, just looking at things on the ground could tell me more than any statistics. For some consultancy assignments, of course, I could get all the information I need in the capital city, but, even then, I prefer to travel. This is because I want to make the point to the people who read my report that I am the sort of consultant who has talked to farmers and consumers there rather than working in the Ministry and hanging round the Casablanca and the Aqua Club. In my first foreign consultancy, my team leader insisted that I spend more than seven weeks out of a ten-week consultancy travelling up-country. I nearly had to come to blows to get a couple of weeks to analyse the statistics and get the economics done. I still think that he was being excessive, but the report was certainly very well received.

Surprisingly, this means that I often know more about what is going on than the local civil servants. Government has no money for them to travel, so they can be amazingly ignorant about their own country. Last year in Zambia, I had one of the Permanent Secretaries contradicting a statement in my report and telling me firmly that all the roads in Zambia are tarred now, and there are no dirt roads left. Fortunately, the Director of the Roads Department stepped in and told him that only the main trunk roads were tarred.

I know that I learn a lot from talking to farmers working in fields beside the road, from wandering around the roadside markets, and from talking to people queuing at the village rice mill. Some researchers get snotty about 'main road bias' and jeer at consultants like me who never make it into the deepest, darkest interior. They say that there is a strong urban influence all along the main roads, and that is what we see. There is something in that, and I would do more travelling if I had unlimited time and money. In some jobs, it can be relevant: maybe the people in the remote areas have very different problems. Mostly, though, I think the people who talk about 'main road bias' are those aid workers and researchers who think that it is more virtuous to work deep in the interior, preferably living in acute discomfort in the villages. Myself, I believe that they are dealing with the symptoms: the causes are to be found in the president's palace or the ministry headquarters.

British aid seems to be particularly concentrated on such virtuous and uncomfortable deep bush projects. Certainly, I have never seen any British aid project doing anything important or anything that would affect the country as a whole. This is strange, as there are an awful lot of experienced Brits doing important work for other aid agencies.

★

I spent half an hour negotiating with Murat about my trip up-country. Surprisingly for a Frenchman, he was most insistent that I take a Land-Rover, the go-anywhere car. 'It is the only vehicle for up-country roads.'

It is funny how emotional people get about four-wheel drives, especially Land-Rovers. Some people have this enormous macho thing about the ultimate bundu-bashing, go-anywhere vehicle. Others think that Land-Rovers are OK for towing a horsebox down the M1.

I tactfully said that I would accept Murat's advice, but really I was accepting Brendan's advice, which had been based on quite different considerations. Brendan and I agreed that the ideal would be a Peugeot 504, which goes anywhere that a Land-Rover does, and which seats six to nine people in comfort. This would mean that I could take a couple of people from the Ministry with me on the trip. However, Brendan said that there was no fuel up-country. I could not just drive into a garage and say 'Fill her up.' Nor could I expect the projects to give me fuel that they are carefully hoarding. What I am going to have to do is go to the refinery and pay dollars for a 44-gallon drum of diesel. I can carry this in the back of the Land-Rover, so I have enough fuel for the whole trip. (Nearly all cars run on diesel here: it is because Sierra Leone usually gets its oil from Libya, where the crude oil comes out of the ground as nearly pure diesel. Countries that use Saudi crude refine it into petrol plus diesel.)

I am not happy about travelling with a drum of fuel in the back, even if it is diesel not petrol. In Tanzania, I was in a Peugeot stacked with jerry cans full of petrol when one of the local economists lit up a cigarette. A close call.

My friend Mehta in Tanzania warned me that it was extraordinarily dangerous to carry cans of fuel in a car, and he flatly refused to do it. He had worked in Shell before joining the FAO, and he knew. I had to do it because I could not travel otherwise, but he had a ploy. He would get a bar of ordinary English soap from me – I had shipped it from England with my other essentials when I went out there. When he arrived in a provincial capital, he made his courtesy call to the local provincial governor. As he left the meeting, he gave him a little gift from the city, my bar of soap. As ordinary soap is unobtainable, and as my 50 cent bar of soap is worth $10 on the black market, this was gratefully received. When Mehta needed petrol to go home at the end of the week, he called on the governor, who supplied him from government stocks.

Mehta has the right touch with a gift. It should be something unusual, but not valuable enough to be considered a bribe. When he last visited the top FAO officials in Rome, he gave them each a pound of cloves, straight from the trees in Zanzibar.

I am preparing for my trip. I am taking a small suitcase with a few clothes, and a great many mosquito repellents, anti-malarials, fungicides, and so on. Of course, I am not forgetting the rehydration salts in case of cholera. I am taking essential supplies in the form of a couple of crates of coke and a couple of crates of beer. I am not being facetious when I say essential supplies. When there is cholera about, it is essential to have something safe to drink. If I was living in a house, I could take my own water. To do this safely I need a house and my own kitchen, because I would have to boil the water furiously for twenty minutes to kill the germs. After this, I would put it through a filter. I do not trust a cook to do it: I want to see it with my own eyes.

I hear rumours that they are soon going to set up a factory outside Freetown to bottle water in plastic bottles, like the spa water in Europe. I strongly disapprove. It uses enormous amounts of foreign exchange – enough, perhaps, to repair the public water supply for Freetown. It also means that the rich have a way of avoiding cholera that the poor do not. If they were both at the same risk, the rich would fix the water supply. As it is, the rich live in the eastern side of the city where the water is good, and the poor in the west where it is terrible, so there is no incentive.

Alarm at the World Bank

The main topic of conversation in the Casablanca today is the news that the new Director General of the World Bank has fired all the permanent staff, and told them that they have to apply for their old jobs. If this works, it will get rid of all the dead wood in a stagnant bureaucracy. If it does not, the dead wood will get rid of everyone else.

All Washington officialdom is in a state of panic, desperately trying to justify themselves. Suddenly officials are actually visiting the countries they are supposed to be helping. Desk officers are trying to disburse large quantities of loans instead of sitting on the applications. Everybody has adopted what they perceive to be the Director General's extreme right-wing Reaganite position, and is trying to be more extreme than him. The Free Market is the new god.

The smarter operators in the Bank had expected some sort of shake-up. They have been trying to collect their Brownie points for the last year or so. A couple of months ago in central Africa, I was sitting in on a meeting between the World Bank mission and the Ministry of Agriculture Planning Director. The meeting had come to an end when the World Bank man said 'By the way, we have lent you $20 million for a credit project.'

One of the expats in the room started asking questions.

'What credit project?'

'Where is the project proposal?'

'Where is the government's application?'

'Why do you think we need another credit project?'

'Why do you think that it will work any better than any other credit project we have had in the past?'

'Why don't you fund the projects we want funded instead?'

Tactless, and not at all good for his career. Obviously, the Bank staff were desperate to get their Brownie points by disbursing large quantities of money as quickly as possible. Obviously, they did not mind how they did it. Lending the money for a credit scheme meant that they could transfer the money immediately. Using the money for a much-needed irrigation scheme was not on, as it would take years to get the scheme designed and built, and they wanted to get rid of the money now.

The mission then went on a rampage of stopping subsidies and privatizing everything, to establish their Reaganite free market credentials. All done without any analysis, without any attempt to determine the impact, and without any planning of how to get from the present situation to the new system.

The Americans had a similar (or opposite?) dilemma in Malawi. For decades, they had been supporting the dictator Dr Banda, because he was openly pro-West and a vocal supporter of capitalism. Then, about a year ago, in 1985, it dawned on them that virtually all businesses in the country, apart from subsistence agriculture, are owned by Banda himself, by the state, or by a single multinational, Lonrho. The economy was more centralized, more tightly controlled, than Stalin's. He had also adopted Stalin's one-party state, secret police and detention camps. Banda is old, and it is quite possible that his successor will admit that he is a Stalinist, and declare for Russia. It will not take a revolution; nobody will lose their jobs, nobody will do anything that they are not doing already.

When this dawned on them, the Americans made the introduction of the Free Market a top priority. Their knee-jerk reaction was to give a lot of money to privatize the state corporations, to sell them on the stock market as Mrs Thatcher had. It had not occurred to them that there could be no stock market in a country where all firms are owned by the President himself, by the state, or by Lonrho. Nor had it occurred to them to ask who could afford to buy shares, in a country where nearly everybody is a subsistence farmer with no cash income, and most of the rest are poorly paid civil servants. Of course, the result was that they spent a lot of money and nothing happened.

Anyway, this news would explain why the World Bank and Murat were so insistent on privatization and Free Enterprise as the basis for all policy, and as a condition for all World Bank finance.

Into the Interior

MONDAY, 18 SEPTEMBER

'Trek up country' is what they say here for my drive into the interior by Land-Rover. A trek does not have any connotations of taking an ox wagon over the veldt into the unknown.

Mohammed picked me up from the hotel at 5 a.m and drove us to the far side of Freetown, where Thomas was waiting for us.

Dawn broke as we left the houses and drove through derelict industrial sites on the outskirts of the city.

We drove out along what was once a 20-foot-wide tarred road but which now has potholes at the side, where the torrential rain has washed the tar away. I was looking out of the window when a car passed us at great speed on the passenger side, its wheels off the tar, on the bare earth. I was alarmed, but I was more alarmed when, a few minutes later, Mohammed did the same: he overtook a truck on its passenger side. I asked him what the hell he was doing.

'Look at the road, Sah,' he said, offended. 'The tar is good in the middle, but at the side the rain has washed it away, and there are big holes. The people are driving on the good part, on the middle of the road, so they do not get off it for anybody. If anyone want pass, they must get off the good part and go on the earth and bumps. Today, we call this the "passing side". The other side is the side they tell you to pass on when you are doing your driving test. We call it "government side".

'When you are not passing a car, but it is coming straight at you, it is more difficult. Every person tries to keep on the good part of the road as long as possible, and he hopes that the other car gets off first. The big lorries are the worst.'

A game of chicken, in fact.

Thomas confirmed this. He thinks that the rot set in when Sierra Leone switched to driving on the wrong side of the road.

'At the time of our independence, 1960, Nkrumah and all the politicians were talking about a United States of West Africa. As a first step, they decided we would all drive on the same side of the road. We agreed on the wrong side because the French Government insisted, even though most of the world drove on our side.

'Of course it caused a big fuss and a lot of confusion when it happened. One of our MPs made a speech in parliament. He said, "It is going to be difficult to make the change. I propose that we amend the law so that buses and taxis make the change two weeks before anyone else, so that they get time to get used to it."'

I laughed and returned to looking out of the window.

Mohammed pointed out a few leafy branches scattered on the

road. 'You see those branches, Sah? When the men are fixing the road, they put those branches on the road, so that the cars will not drive into them while they work, especially when they are working at a corner. They do not put them far from the hole, maybe ten yards, so cars still hit them sometimes. At night-time, there are no lights there like in the old days; there are still these same branches. You cannot see them until you hit them, so lots of cars and lorries drive straight into the holes.'

I suppose the system is better than Tanzania's, where they leave large boulders in front of the roadworks. This does protect the road workers better, but since the boulders are unlit at night, and since they are the same colour as the tar, people often drive into them at night and kill themselves.

'I was a lorry driver, before I worked in the World Bank,' continued Mohammed. 'I drove at night for my job, but I was careful. It is dangerous. It is not just the road repairs. It is because lots of people think that it is cheaper to drive without lights: it saves electricity. No, Sah. I think that it is better that we always drive in daytime.'

I am surprised to see that all the villages we pass through have comfortable-looking houses with corrugated iron roofs. They are houses, not huts, two or three bedrooms and a sitting room I would guess, with a large veranda in front. They have solid, 2-foot-thick walls, whitewashed or left mud-coloured. Elsewhere in Africa, most people live in round huts, made of poles set in a circle, and then plastered with mud. The walls are perhaps three or four inches thick, nothing like the solid walls here. Elsewhere, too, nearly all the huts are thatched, as corrugated iron is expensive. Obviously, though, the roofs here were put on a long time ago. The sheets have long since lost their silvery shine, and are now just a rusty brown, with holes starting to appear. Nobody is replacing them, or putting corrugated iron on new buildings.

Thomas tells me that there was an economic boom from the end of the Second World War to a couple of years after independence. Coffee and cocoa prices were reasonable and sometimes very high.

There was a diamond rush, and there was large-scale extraction of iron ore, bauxite, titanium and gold. Everybody had a lot of money, even the villagers. That was when everybody had waterproof, corrugated-iron roofs.

One of the Cambridge economists, Ford Sturrock, visited Ghana a few years ago, and the local economists pointed out disparagingly the sort of house the poor people in the country live in, thatched, with walls built of poles and mud in between.

'Actually,' said Ford, 'I live in a mud and wood house with a thatched roof.'

They were embarrassed at having insulted their English guest, and quickly said, 'But I am sure that yours is very new.'

'No,' he said, 'it is four hundred years old.'

They were even more embarrassed. I do not know if he even tried to explain that it was not such a bad thing to live in Madingley Manor, and I doubt if they would have believed him.

★

We travelled for a couple of hours along this road to the first town, Mile 91. Most of the time it was sunny, but there were sudden brief downpours – too much rain to be called showers, and not lasting enough to be called rainstorms. Along the road, there were women with brooms and sacks of unmilled rice. They spread the rice thinly on the tarmac, sweeping it up when they saw us coming. When it rained, they swept it in heaps and covered it with plastic sheets. They did not always manage to sweep it up before we passed, but Mohammed made no attempt to avoid driving over it.

'This rice was parboiled last night,' he explained. 'They put it in a big oil drum and light a fire under it. When it boils they let the fire go out, and it cooks slowly overnight. This makes it softer, so it does not break so much when they pound it to take off the hull. Boiling also makes it taste better. Now they are leaving it in the sun to dry, before they pound it.

You would have thought that each village could have clubbed together to build a concrete drying floor.

On both sides of the road, I see fields of cassava, 6- or 8-foot-high thin canes with a sprinkling of leaves on top. It is grown from cuttings and takes three or four years to mature. When its tubers are harvested, it produces very high yields, over ten tonnes per acre. It is reasonably good food, with lots of calories, but its protein and vitamin content vary enormously with variety. Some varieties have high protein and vitamins, and are a complete food, like rice or wheat, so you can live on them alone. Others are just starch, and you have to have other sources of protein to survive. Cassava is not particularly palatable, but it can be processed into a sort of baby cereal, or into foo-foo, a rubbery, translucent ball of what looks like – and tastes like – laundry starch. The one- or two-year-old tubers can be roasted like potatoes. It is an excellent food security crop, drought-resistant and high yielding, but the Africans prefer to grow the more risky maize and rice, which have a much better taste and texture. The Vietnamese villagers have solved this problem by turning cassava into noodles using village-level technology, but nobody has introduced the technology into Africa. You can also eat the cassava leaves in a stew, where they look like spinach but taste a lot better. There are even some varieties they grow just for the leaves – green leaves, unlike the roots, have first-class protein, just like meat.

With this miracle crop growing so well here, there should be no hunger. There certainly should not be a 'hungry season' when one rice crop has been eaten and the next one is not yet harvested.

I asked Thomas to explain why there is a problem. He laughed, 'In this country, if we have not eaten rice today, we say that we have not eaten. The time when there is no rice and we have to eat something else, we call the "hungry season". Then we eat cassava. We also eat mangoes: the British brought them here from India, because they are ripe during the hungry season.

'No, we do not grow cassava as a main crop. Partly we grow it for the hungry season. Partly we grow it as an emergency food supply, in case we have a bad rice crop.

'If there is a bad rice crop, we can easily get a lot more cassava than usual. We harvest the fully mature, four-year-old crop as usual. We can also harvest the three-year-old tubers and get a good yield. If food is very short, we can eat the one-year-old and two-year-old tubers, but they are thin, and do not give very much food. The one-year-old tubers are small and sweet and you can eat them as they are: you do not have to process them to extract the poison. This means that if you are really short of rice, you can get two, maybe two and a half times as much cassava as normal.'*

'But what do you do next year?' I asked.

'Yes. That is the problem,' he replied. 'When you have eaten the young cassava, there is none left to grow into old cassava. There will be no proper crop next year. Perhaps there will be no proper crop for two or three years. We call it "borrowing next year's food".

'Of course, when we have dug it all up one year, everybody works hard to plant more and more rice to catch up, but it is never enough. In fact, because the people have not eaten very much, they cannot do much work, so they find it difficult even to cultivate the same amount as last year. This means that one hungry year is followed by another.'

'How old are the cassava plants we see in the fields today?' I asked.

He looked surprised, 'Can't you see? They are all young. We had a bad season last year and a bad season the year before. There is no four-year-old cassava in the fields, and only a little three-year-old. Most is only one-year old, or maybe two.'

I was silent. If he is right, the country has none of its normal food reserves. Any disruption of the food supply, another poor crop for example, could result in most of the country going very hungry indeed.

We stopped for lunch at the side of the road: I had brought a cold chicken and sandwiches from the hotel, and we shared them out. I drank my beer, then idly crushed the can in my hand.

---

* When cassava is grown primarily for food security it is usually grown in the way described. In countries where cassava, rather than rice or maize, is the main staple food, it is normally grown as an annual crop, and harvested after one year, or perhaps two. Foo-foo may be made mainly from cassava, or entirely from plantain, or from some mix.

'You must not do that,' said Mohammed. 'The people in the villages want to use the cans. They can make a cup to drink out of. Or they can use the metal to fix things that are broken. You leave them at the side of the road, and when you go by an hour later, they will be gone.'

As we ate, I remembered that I had forgotten to use my tyre pressure gauge. I always carry one, because they do not seem to have any in the developing countries. There are not the garages with air pumps that they have in England. I get the impression that the drivers usually find the only compressor in town, pump until the tyre feels hard, and decide that it is OK. Sure enough, one of the rear tyres was at 25 lbs per square inch, and the other went off the gauge, which is very dangerous indeed. I made him drive slowly to the next town, and we got the pressures right, 28 lbs front and 48 lbs rear.

I kept telling Mohammed how dangerous this was, how easily it could make the Land-Rover turn over, but I do not think he believes me. He also thinks I am an eccentric for making him travel below 50 mph. ('But if you travel at more than 50 miles per hour on a corrugated road, you skim on the top of the corrugations, and you can't feel them.') Both he and Thomas laugh at me for wearing a seat belt, but they are too polite to say what they really think — that I am cowardly and effeminate, I imagine.

After lunch, we started the main part of the trip, visiting projects and talking to their staff. I am trying to find as much as I can about how food is produced and marketed, and about what people eat and why. Much of what I find out is not, at first sight, relevant to my task, but it pays to find out everything. Often what seems at first to be irrelevant later turns out to be crucial. It is detective work.

The projects usually have a local Project Director and local project staff. There may be an expatriate Project Adviser and sometimes short-term or long-term expatriate staff, like vets, agronomists and public health experts. Generally, a Western consultancy firm has the contract and employs all the expatriate staff, and sometimes the local staff as well.

There is a lot of room for conflict; the Project Director thinks that the Project Adviser has been employed to keep an eye on finances, and to see that he does not steal too much (which is true enough). The Project Adviser resents the fact that he cannot get on with his job as a professional because he is acting as a policeman, trying to keep the project's assets from disappearing. The locals resent the fact that the consultant is paid twenty times as much as a local who has the same qualifications and far more experience of local conditions.

The trouble is that any aid worker who raises a fuss about corruption or incompetence will get the reputation of having a difficult personality, of not being able to work with the locals. Any aid worker or administrator who gets this reputation will soon be without a job. The danger is particularly strong in organizations like the UN or FAO, which have both the donor governments and the recipient governments on the governing body. If any official makes waves, the country's representative complains at the top level. The representatives of other countries where aid money is being stolen will certainly support him. Since there are a lot more countries receiving money than giving it, they make a powerful voting block.

The impact is easy to see. For example, the FAO had a project in Pakistan a couple of years ago which went wrong. They bought a fully developed, irrigated farm and were going to start production the moment the foreign expert arrived. The local civil service provided a bit of empty desert instead of the agreed farm and pocketed the difference in price. Instead of raising a fuss, the FAO made their man, a world expert in his subject, spend three years and a lot of money levelling the land, drilling for water, and putting in an irrigation system – all things the local farmers were quite capable of doing. Then they provided another million dollars, and the project started three years late.

When I talk to someone on the project staff, I introduce myself as one of us. Like them, I work in the agricultural sector. Like them, I am not quite in the Ministry of Agriculture, and we can both feel superior about that. Like some of them, I work in the development aid business. Like some of them, I am an international consultant. This means that we can start talking in a private space, where we know the language, the culture, the problems. We are alike; we both know the background: 'If only *they* would understand.'

The immediate result is that they will talk freely and openly about things in our common space, about what their project is doing and what problems they are facing. As we talk, they get more confident that I understand their position, and the talk spills over into areas outside our common private space. They make unguarded political statements or remark on the competence of senior civil servants.

Curiously, some things seem to be OK for discussion in any private space at all, but are not mentionable in public space. Others are explosive in some spaces. For example, when the British Government imposed price control during rapid inflation in the 1970s, the senior civil servant responsible was invited to speak at the British Agricultural Economics Society conference. A lot of us were ready to attack him on the distorting effects of the policy. He disarmed us completely by admitting that the only objective of price control was to persuade the workers that prices were being held down, so that they would think that there was no reason for them to strike for more money. The price control was not implemented properly and so it was ineffective, but if it had been effective it would have been positively harmful. This truth worked in one private space, and it could be told in a meeting open to anybody who cared to attend, even though it would have hit the headlines if the newspapers got hold of it. When I mentioned this view of price control in a confidential report for an Asian government, the Asian Development Bank went ballistic: you are not supposed to say it in this particular private space.

I know this analysis makes me sound like a cynical, manipulative bastard. I am not, or at least I did not think I was until I started writing this diary. This is the first time I have examined what I have been doing during a mission. What I thought I was doing before was meeting people, chatting to break the ice, then asking their opinion.

What are the ethics of doing this? I am open about why I am here and what my main objective is. I do not know what I am going to do with the information I get from any discussion. I do try to get more information from somebody than they wanted to give me when I entered the room. I protect my sources though: I do not say who gave me the information. This is not really for ethical reasons, but just because I know people would refuse to talk to me if they thought I was going to tell everyone what they said. Sometimes protecting sources means suppressing important information that could only come from one person, which may be unethical. (Of course I am not a reporter, so I do not have the same responsibilities as a reporter, or the same ethical code.) More often, I can express it as a theoretical possibility, rather than a matter of fact, knowing that some readers will know it is fact. Sometimes the people who talk to me tell me more than they meant to and reveal that they are incompetent or dishonest. More often, they think that if they have faked the accounts, they have covered themselves completely and I will not be able to find out by other means, so they keep talking. (They are in for a rude surprise.) Ethically, there are problems. I ignore incompetence and dishonesty that is not directly related to my terms of reference – unless of course they are far more important than my own mission. I justify this to myself by saying that there is no point in making enemies unnecessarily, and the people I annoy could wreck my mission by launching a concerted attack on my report. I have to reveal the key problems if my mission is to be a success. However, this may mean that even though my report is accepted, the people attacked will try to make sure I am not allowed to work in the country again.

Visiting the Projects

We picked up the local Agricultural Officer, Fomba, from the Area Development Project. His task was to take us to see what he thought would interest me in the area. First, we went to see a 30-hectare Rice Research Centre, a sub-project of the Area Development Project. This does work on plant breeding, cultivation methods, fertilizers and insecticides. It then does extension, getting the results of its research to farmers. It is run by the Chinese. Thomas told me that it has been run for twenty years by either Taiwan or mainland China, whoever is currently in political favour. Right now, it is mainland China.

The Chinese Project Adviser took us round and showed us a perfectly functioning research station getting high yields. He thinks that it is the ideal country for paddy-field rice production, as a third of the country floods each year. He was upset that he could not get the local farmers to adopt the improved systems, and he complained that they were irrational.

As we drove away, Thomas and Mohammed explained why none of the local farmers would adopt the Chinese methods of cultivation. First, nobody likes 'swamp rice' grown in paddy fields, because it has a bland flavour and a poor texture. They much prefer the taste and texture of upland rice, grown on dry land in ordinary fields (and looking like wheat as it grows). Second, the Chinese system requires a lot of manual work: the Chinese are seen to be working in the fields from dawn to dusk. Third, and most important, people think 'that there is a health risk when they work in paddy fields' – that is to say, they do not live long.

The health risk must be serious to frighten people who already have the shortest life span in the world. The objection to working long hours is not idleness. People living on 1,600 calories a day or less in the hungry season cannot work more than a few hours a day even if they are healthy, and most people here are riddled with chronic diseases, such as dysentery, anaemia and bilharzia. If they are that badly fed and that sick to start with, overwork and a few extra doses of malaria will kill them off. Just to put it in perspective, I use up 500 calories in a one-hour game of squash.

The Chinese can do it because they are much healthier to start with, not having been raised in that fermenting pot of disease which is equatorial Africa. Most of them are professionals – the head of the project is an ex-mayor of Shanghai – so they are presumably a lot fitter than the poor Chinese farmers. They take anti-malarials and have access to drugs and doctors, so they will survive a two-year stint here. And they have enough to eat.

★

This afternoon the Agricultural Officer took me to look at farmers' paddy fields. I am an economist, not an agriculturist, but I thought I might learn something. The paddy fields were much like any others, and we walked over the narrow irrigation canals on little bridges made of three poles side by side, then made our way on the 1-foot-wide embankments. I nodded attentively to what he was saying, but all rice looks much the same to me. I did learn something, though, when I looked to see what was growing beside us. At the edge of the paddy fields, which had been created in a swamp, the ground rose ten or fifteen feet. At first glance, it seemed to be covered with jungle, but when I looked more closely I saw that it was a mixture of useful trees, with coffee growing under its shade trees, and the odd oil palm or bread fruit. As I went closer, I saw a few cocoa trees growing in thick shade, their greeny-white pods growing straight out of the thin white mottled trunks.

On the way back we examined a passion fruit plantation that a Dutch businessman had established, as a new export crop. Unfortunately, he had fallen sick, and in the five months he had been away the weeds had grown 9 feet high, smothering everything. What a fertile country!

Outside the Area Development Project headquarters were the signs of an old sub-project, which aimed to teach local people to plough with oxen. All that remained was a truck with flat tyres and 'Work Oxen Project' painted on the side. I was too tactful to ask if the project was successful. When I was a student, I was told that the definitive research on the economics of ox-ploughing was done at Rothampstead in the 1850s. They found that you have to allow 8 acres of grazing for each acre that the oxen can plough. This means that it works fine in Zambia and Zimbabwe where there is plenty of grazing (or there was before the population explosion). However, wherever there is plenty of grazing, the locals have been using ox ploughs for the last sixty years at least. Here there is little grazing, just a little land left fallow and reverting to jungle.

One of the last colonial government projects in Zambia was an Area Development Project in the Northern Province. It included a state-of-the art dairy farm in the bush. They could have bought top-quality, high-yielding Friesland dairy cows from the local white farmers. The Frieslands have been in Africa for decades and have built up an immunity to local diseases. They are also cheap. Instead, the Brits imported 125 pedigree Jersey cows and bulls from Jersey. These had no immunity to local diseases, they gave low yields, and they produced very fatty milk. The cost was fantastic, £700 per head at 1963 prices – say twenty times as much at today's prices. When I visited the project, after independence, the Zambian manager showed us the herd, and then turned to lead us to the farm office.

'But where's the 125 cattle?' I asked. 'I can only see 25 or so.'

The police investigation showed that he had been selling these expensive pedigreed animals to the local butcher at £5 per head.

The Area Development Project headquarters is in a small town, which was nicely built and laid out in the 1960s. The Project buildings are concrete and glass, and there are new bungalows for the Project staff. The main street has forty or fifty shops, small but modern, and the same number of older ones.

The town has ceased to operate. It no longer has electricity, and a modern town cannot survive without electricity. There is no electricity to pump the water, so the water-borne sewerage does not work. In fact, the sewers are now blocked solid, permanently: if the electricity ever comes back, it will be necessary to dig new sewers. Because there is no electricity, there are no fans, no lights, no refrigerators, and no electric typewriters.

It is the water and the sewage that worry me most, because of the cholera epidemic. In an African village, or an old African town, there would be alternative systems, wells for water and pit latrines. These do not exist here, and there is nowhere to put them between the buildings of a modern town.

'Before independence,' explained Thomas, 'each town was a local authority with its own town council. They charged rates and land taxes and spent the money on developing the town. Each town had its water, its sewerage, its electricity, and its roads. The system worked well, because it is something like our tribal system – chiefdoms. Then, about five years ago, Siaka Stevens decided that this was inefficient. He made central government in Freetown responsible for local tax collection. All the rates and taxes would be collected by Freetown, and then they would send the money back to the towns.

'Well, you know the Ministry of Finance. They have to use the money for what is most urgent. They have to pay salaries. It is like a bird in the nest feeding her children. Always she feeds the one who is nearest and who makes most noise.

'Of course none of the rates and the land taxes went back to the town councils, so there is no water, no electricity. I do not know if Government knew what would happen when they changed the law, but a lot of people told them.'

A little shack in the middle of town has a sign announcing that it is a recording studio. They must have a small generator in the back. I can see some quite basic equipment, and their chief business seems to be done with a mike and a cassette tape recorder, so that people have a real cassette of their own voice. I do not know how long the cassette survives in this humidity: I am told that half of your computer disks become unreadable after three months because mould grows on the surface.

I have been looking at the transport system as we travelled today. The chief form of transport here is the 'poda poda', a 1½ tonne truck with a roof, usually a Mazda. Sometimes the poda podas carry people, some inside the truck, some clinging to the sides and some on the roof, with quite a bit of personal luggage inside. I counted twenty-six people on one, going on a very bumpy dirt road that looked as though it was going to shake them off. More often, they have a general cargo, a few bags of rice, a dozen people, some furniture and a couple of goats perhaps.

They all have brightly coloured mottoes painted on the back for the edification of the driver behind:

'GOD DAE'

'Ah! The World nor Level
God Bless Farmers.'

Every ten miles or so along the road there are roadside markets, places where lorries can park beside the road. Mohammed explained.

'Once I was a lorry driver, and I used to come to these places a lot. You can buy food always there. You can buy fruit or cooked food and Coca-Cola or tea.

'The drivers are also looking for customers. The people waiting here will pay to go to towns along the road, and they pay extra if they are carrying a sack of rice or mangoes. Mostly these people travel in poda podas which are for passengers only.

'I was driving a proper lorry, not a poda poda. If I had only a half-load, or if I was coming back empty, I used to take passengers. The driver is supposed to give this money to the man who owns the lorry. Mostly, they keep it themselves,' he said reminiscently.

'Sometimes the driver buys things. Perhaps, if I was delivering to Rokupr, where they grow lots of rice, I used to buy rice cheap. Then I take it to Freetown and sell it for a good price. If I do this, I get some of the profit, and the man who owns the lorry gets some. You see, the man who sends the load to Rokupr pays the cost of the lorry both ways. If we can get a backload, we can keep all the money he paid us to drive home.'

We stopped at one of these markets and walked round to see what they were selling and what prices were like. Thomas and I were trying to find out the going price for rice when we noticed that Mohammed had vanished. We carried on without him for half an hour and when we returned to the Land-Rover we waited ten minutes before he returned.

He had a smirk on his face, like a cat that has been at the cream. 'I met an old girlfriend, Sah. From when I was a lorry driver.'

We teased him, asking what his wife would think, but he just smiled sweetly.

The Resthouse

The project we visited yesterday put us up for the night at their own resthouse. They make no charge for rooms, so Mohammed and Thomas are staying in the resthouse too. If we have to stay in a town I will stay at a hotel, but they will stay with friends in the town. The government subsistence allowance is far too small, so this is the only way they can get accommodation. I pay for their food and drink out of my allowance as otherwise they would go hungry. I keep telling them that the World Bank is paying, not me (which is largely true), and this is sufficiently face-saving. It does not work in Pakistan, where it goes against all the Muslim traditions of hospitality. I kept telling the Pakistanis that the World Bank or FAO is paying, but they insisted on treating me, or the World Bank, as a guest. (I discovered later that the correct procedure is then to send them an expensive present from Europe.)

Mohammed, Thomas and the resthouse cook removed the drum of diesel from the back of the Land-Rover, put an empty 44-gallon drum in the back, and disappeared to get water from the river. This means that the cook can wash up, and we can wash – I am sweaty and smelly after a long, hot day, and if I do not wash, I get prickly heat.

In the meantime, I sat on the veranda having a couple of beers with the Sierra Leonean Agricultural Officers and economists. This is where they feel they can say things that they cannot say when the Project Director or the expats are around. They cannot normally afford beer, so it loosens their tongues wonderfully. They were drinking the Star lager I had brought with me from Freetown, a very good light lager, perfect for a hot climate. The brewery also produces Guinness, which is thick and heavy, which I could not drink in this heat. However, the brewers have persuaded the locals that it gives them virility. They use the same overtly sexual advertising as in Jamaica: 'Get on top with a Guinness.' This is misleading: ask any Dubliner what eight pints does to your performance.

They also helped me experiment with the local palm wine. I had noticed this morning that every mile or so along the road a few 2- or 4-gallon plastic containers were left at the side of the road. I asked Mohammed to explain.

'Palm wine,' he said. 'They cut the top of the tree and collect the juice in a "plastic". Then it turns to wine. Do you want some?' He pulled up and negotiated for a couple of gallons, which we put in the back of the Land-Rover. It cost a couple of leone – about 20 US cents.

In the evening I tried drinking this palm wine. It was not pleasant. It had so much yeast that it was white, and it was rather sweet. I persevered, though it seemed to be non-alcoholic. The alcohol suddenly hit me at about 10 o'clock and I was drunk.

'It is not alcohol when you drink it,' was the explanation. 'It ferments in your stomach and turns into alcohol there.' They then told me of another drink made of malted millet grains. They put the grains into a big pot and pour boiling water over them, then they put a hollow bamboo pipe into it, and everyone takes turns at sucking up a mouthful or two. Again, it is non-alcoholic when you start drinking and turns into alcohol in your stomach.

It sounds like the perfect way to spread cholera. Come to think of it, it was bloody stupid of me to drink palm wine made in some plastic container that cannot have been properly washed.

In the morning, I found that the outside lavatory was next to the well, because there was nowhere else to put it. Neither had been necessary when there was electricity, but now they were squeezed into a small yard. This is dangerous, as the lavatory is a pit latrine, a whistle-and-thud. It is actually a well that is used as a latrine, rather than for extracting water. This means that the sewage can percolate sideways through a few feet of soil into the well. The pit latrines are not hygienic anyway: the theory is that they should be 25 feet deep so that flies cannot fly up to the top, but the water table here is only 10 feet deep.

Perhaps the reality of the water problem was shown by the following exhortation on the resthouse notice board:

```
From:    Deputy Project Manager,
         Integrated Agricultural Development Project
To:      All Heads of Department and Senior Officers
         Residing in the Main Site Quarters

SHORTAGE OF WATER - MAIN SITE Resthouse

It has been brought to my notice that some people are in
the habit of using water supplied to the above resthouse,
causing water shortage to visitors staying there.
    As this resthouse is used by important visitors both
from here and abroad, I am advising that this habit be
stopped forthwith. Anybody caught collecting water from
this quarter will be seriously dealt with.
    Please inform your families accordingly.

Umaru Bombwe
  Deputy Project Manager

Copy:          Project Manager
Addressed to:  Senior Civil Engineer
               Agricultural Officer, Chila
               Marketing Accountant
               Ag. Chief of Input Credit & Marketing
               Ag. Monitoring and Evaluation Officer
               Administrative Officer
               Ag. Chief Mechanic
               Chief of Input Credit and Marketing
               Confidential Secretary
               Wells Coordinator
               Credit Accountant
               Chief Accountant
               Agricultural Officer, Mile 91
```

More Projects

WEDNESDAY, 20 SEPTEMBER

I visited two projects today. Both had credit programmes. There are no banks here, so farmers cannot just go to the bank and borrow the money for fertilizer and seed at the beginning of the season. Nor can they borrow money to make long-term investments, like planting coffee trees, or buying machinery. The projects fill the gap by acting as banks and lending money to the farmers.

The credit is heavily subsidized by the donors. Personally, I think subsidized credit is a waste of time and money. In most countries, the credit officers do lend to the farmers as they are supposed to, but they lend at the same extortionate rate of interest as the village moneylenders, instead of at the subsidized rate, and they pocket the difference. There is another scam going on here. A lot of the credit officers lend to imaginary farmers, and then claim that the farmer has run away or refuses to repay the debt. Only about 10 per cent is repaid on time.

In fact, I think even unsubsidized credit schemes are misconceived. Generally, as long as you pay farmers a fair price, they have no difficulty in borrowing money locally. What has happened here, and in other African countries I have worked in, is that the farmers are paid a low price, with most of the money being taken by corruption, by export taxes and by an overvalued currency. The farmers cannot cover their costs and repay the money, so they just build up their debt. Every few years Government realizes that this huge accumulated debt will never be repaid, and it is written off. What this means is that the credit is not real credit at all; it is some of the farmers' price, arriving a few years late.

Two men stood at the side of the road this morning, waving what looked like dead rats, 2 feet long excluding the tail.

'It is Cutting Grass,' said Mohammed as he pulled up to let me examine them. 'If it get into a rice field, it cut all the rice, so it look like grass is cut. All the rice fields have a fence around, made with sticks, to keep the Cutting Grass out. They are good to eat. Do you want I buy it?'

One advantage about living in a hotel is that you can refuse to buy a cane rat at the side of the road on the grounds that you have no kitchen, so you do not hurt anyone's feelings.

A few miles further along we saw somebody waving a dead monkey, which they were also selling for the meat. We did not stop: I am squeamish.

★

I see Victorian railway stations in some of the towns, grey-painted wood, with gingerbread trim overhanging the platforms. Occasionally there are signs warning of a railway crossing. However, there is no sign of a railway.

'There used to be a railway here in the old days,' said Thomas. 'The engines burnt wood, and they were not efficient, and lorries were cheaper. So the World Bank made the Government privatize it. Some of our businessmen bought it, friends of Siaka Stevens. They just pulled up all the railway lines and sold them to Britain as scrap metal. That was just before the oil crisis when lorries became too expensive. For some years, we really missed that railway.'

I had been told before that everything of value in the country that was not nailed down had been removed, sold and the proceeds deposited in a Swiss Bank. Clearly, it was not only things that were not nailed down.

I have visited six retail markets today. Three of them were the roadside markets where lorries pull off beside the main road for a break. Two were in tiny townships at the end of the main road, on the border-line between the rural economy and the cash economy, and one was in Makeni, a biggish town, a regional capital. I took a close look at the Makeni rice market. I went to the retail market and also walked round the business centre to talk to the rice wholesalers. I did not have a list of questions to ask, as I was not sure yet what I should be asking questions about – I was trying to find what concerned them. I did ask what happened to the imported rice, though.

The big surprise was that a good three-quarters of the rice on sale is imported. I was completely thrown by this. You do not expect to see imported rice in production areas. Still less do you expect to see such large amounts of imported rice on sale if most is not unloaded from the ship, or is smuggled to other countries as I have been told.

Most is Thai rice, and some is aid rice from Japan. It would be less surprising to see this imported rice in Freetown, as it is cheapest there, next to the docks. It is surprising to see it transported, expensively over bad roads, to the production areas.

It is a real surprise to find that even in the remote townships, right next to the producing areas, most of the rice on sale is imported. It means that most farmers are no longer producing enough to feed themselves. They buy rice with the money they earn working for other farmers, or working in the diamond fields. In other parts of the country, they use the money they get from selling coffee and cocoa for buying rice, but here coffee and cocoa are unimportant – rice has always been the big crop.

Of course, Thomas and I checked and double checked. It was obvious enough that the rice on display was imported, but the retailers confirmed it independently. I don't think Thomas was as surprised as me, but he has not seen what happens in other countries, and he does not get much chance to travel up-country.

Quality and price seemed to have something to do with it. The Japanese rice is excellent, with perhaps 3 per cent broken grains. The Thai rice is poor, about half broken. (The Agricultural Marketing Board claim that they import the much more expensive Thai A1 Superior with 5 per cent brokens. Presumably, the difference in price ends up in someone's Swiss bank account.)

However, Thomas told me I was missing the point.

'You are looking at the number of broken grains, but that is not important here. Look at this rice: it is the most expensive rice on the market, but it has lots of broken grains, nearly half. That is because it is upland rice and it is hand pounded, with a pole in a big mortar. This other rice is cheaper: it has very few broken grains, because it has been through a rubber-roller mill. But it has no flavour, so the price is low.

'We are not interested in the number of broken grains. We are interested in the flavour and in how hard it is when we have cooked it. We all eat rice for two meals a day, every day, so it is important to us how good it is to eat.

'The Thai rice and some of the Sierra Leone rice is grown in paddy fields. We call it "swamp rice". It is not good to eat. In fact, if you serve it to a visitor, it is an insult.'

One possibility, then, is that the best and most expensive upland rice is shipped to Freetown, while the cheaper imported rice is shipped here. I could understand this if transport was free, but it is not. Transport on dirt roads costs ten times as much as transport on good roads, because the dirt roads shake the lorries to pieces. Transport from the village to the mill, and from the mill to the road is even more expensive, because the rice is carried as headloads. Each male porter carries a 50 kg bag on his head, along a narrow bush path for five or ten miles. Women, though, carry most of the headloads and they usually carry only half a bag, and make twice as many journeys.

A farmer will only sell the expensive upland rice and buy cheap imported rice in exchange if the difference in price covers the transport both ways, and covers the dealer's margin. This high transport cost seems to rule out the double journey.

Just to check what I had been told, I asked the traders for the going market prices. At first, they thought I was trying to bargain, and quoted high 'first prices', but they then gave me more credible, though probably incorrect, prices.

The highest price is for hand-pounded, parboiled upland rice, which still has some red skin on it. Machine-milled rice is cheaper, because the red skin has been polished off. Old mills are less efficient than the modern, rubber roller mills, and they leave more red on, so their rice gets a higher price. (The old mills are also less efficient, producing 10 per cent less rice from a ton of unmilled paddy, so I suppose they would not be used at all if the price of the rice was the same. Or at least, that would be so if there was plenty of money to import new mills.) Imported swamp rice is the cheapest. There were at least fifteen different qualities of rice on sale. This means that taste and texture are too important to be ignored in an economic analysis.

In the main street was a small shop with a big sign:

BAKA TRADING CO.
Manufacturers Representatives
Buying Agents for Agricultural Marketing Board
Investment Consultants

The company's real business was buying coffee and cocoa from farmers and shipping them to the Agricultural Marketing Board depot at Freetown harbour. It also buys a range of other crops that used to be important, like palm kernels (which are sent to the mill for oil extraction) and ginger. There are also a lot of battered 44-gallon drums in the street outside, indicating that it does a lot of trade in palm oil.

Further down the road is what was a large supermarket when it was built in the 1970s. It is now a church. This must be the only country where Mammon is being so comprehensively defeated.

As we drove towards the next town, I saw a line of schoolchildren, aged about 8 to 10, walking along the side of the road, on the red earth, to school. They were all carrying stones on their heads — flattish stones about two or three inches thick and a foot in diameter.

'They are taking them to sit on,' explained Mohammed. 'They do not have benches left in the schools. If a boy or a girl finds a stone that is good to sit on, they take it to school. They do not leave it there, or someone will thief it. So they take it home with them.'

We stopped to look at the school. It was built of mud bricks and had an old and rusty roof. There were no doors or windows, and never had been: you need all the ventilation you can get in this heat. There was a blackboard inside, but no sign of paper, books, pens, and so forth.

I checked with both Mohammed and Thomas that it was OK for me to take a photograph. I am acutely aware that last time I photographed a school I was arrested by the army, who threatened to shoot me. I was in Zambia, in a team which included educationalists, and I saw villagers building their own school instead of waiting for Government or an aid agency to do it for them. Very laudable, so I took a picture. Next day, going home, we went past the village again, and were stopped by an army patrol at the bridge. My driver was interrogated and so was I. They seemed to think I was a spy going to send in some white Rhodesian saboteurs to blow up the school, even though this was after Zimbabwe had become independent. They kept saying that if they had seen me taking the photo, they would have shot me. I believed them. They could perhaps be excused for their spy fever, because next to the bridge was the wreck of another bridge which the Rhodesians had blown up a few years before. Eventually, they sent us to a police station thirty miles away, with soldiers sitting in the back of the car, pointing their Bren guns at the back of our heads. The policeman took our details and a statement, then released us, muttering to me under his breath that the soldiers were bush-happy after six months guarding the bridge.

Looking at these children walking to school, I wonder if their education will do them any good at all. It is claimed that someone who has completed primary education will be functionally illiterate within three years, unless they get a job which demands reading and writing. There are not many of these jobs, and even if they did exist in theory our Ministry cannot afford to buy paper, so there is no writing. They cannot even stay literate by reading a lot. In poor countries, and Sierra Leone is very poor indeed, there is nothing available to read in the form of books, magazines or newspapers. There are a few small newspapers in the capital city, and the typists always seem to be reading tenth-hand Mills & Boon, but that is it.

Nobody here can become literate in the way I did – from voracious reading of comics, children's books, then thrillers, detective stories, science fiction and so on, rather than from what I learnt at school. Even university graduates here have read little that was not on their syllabus, because the books are not available. I would like to see Britain sending all second-hand books, remaindered books, even unsold magazines, to the Third World. They should not be educational books, just something people can enjoy reading.

Amazingly, the young professionals we meet are all cheerful and dedicated to their jobs. They believe that they can make a difference, even though they do not have much in the way of resources to do their jobs.

One young man was not so happy. He had been raised in Freetown and went to university there. He did brilliantly. Then he did his Ph.D. in Cambridge, and he thought the sky was the limit. Now he has been dumped in the bush as a project worker with virtually no salary. He has to do a job which does not use any of his hard-learned skills, and he does not get any respect or recognition for his education. He cannot even get enough resources to do this routine job properly. He got quite excited telling me about this, and I think he is headed for a breakdown. What a waste!

Sometimes I worry that I am just wandering around as a tourist. I am getting important information though: there is population pressure and they are running short of land; there is no mature cassava as a food reserve; there is a lot of imported rice being shipped to the rice production areas as well as to the coffee and cocoa areas. This is a sign of a farming system in collapse: the farmers are not producing enough to feed the neighbouring towns, let alone the city: the coffee and cocoa farmers are actually buying their rice in the markets. The big question is where the money comes from for the country people to buy imported rice. I still have to find out, but one possibility is that they sell coffee and cocoa and buy rice with the proceeds. Another is that they work on the diamond fields and bring their wages home.

The smuggling story and the story of rice not being unloaded are looking a bit weaker.

The University

THURSDAY, 21 SEPTEMBER

I have spent the afternoon here at the Agricultural University, and I am staying the night. It is sensibly sited at Njala, a hundred miles from Freetown, in the middle of the production area.

I spoke to the professor and the lecturers in economics. All are bright people with postgraduate degrees from Britain, and it was easy to establish private space – that we academics are different from everyone else – because they had read some of my academic papers (not that I am an academic by profession, but I have to develop theory to solve the problems I encounter in my work, and

I publish it). Thomas had studied under the professor, and was a classmate of two of the lecturers, so there was another private space established.

We discussed the food market and the food situation with great animation, though it is not their area of study. They are not working on policy or marketing and are shaky on the theory. They are production economists and their research is agricultural cost-of-production surveys, which they are doing in collaboration with an English university. They did not want to discuss this work with me, and said that I should talk to the Englishman who is running the surveys. They led me over to his office, introduced us, and left us to it.

Piers Livermore is his name. I know it is wrong to be prejudiced against eager young men with straggly beards, who wear shorts and short socks with sandals. Or perhaps not.

He is a development economics graduate one year into his Ph.D. He has a British government research grant for his study of farm production costs, and is collaborating with the local academics who are doing the field work.

I asked him why he was doing it.

'Mainly because I am really committed to helping the Third World. I think we should know what it means to be a villager in one of the least developed countries. I think that development policy should be based on hard facts about what goes on in the bush, not on the macro-economics of the city.' That is to say, he did not want to examine the policy that caused the disaster, but to measure the disaster as it is today.

I asked him what theory he was using, just a routine question to get him to talk.

'Right now, sampling theory and survey methodology, especially Third World methodology.' He went on to describe how he would analyse the information. It turned out that there was no theoretical basis, just routine techniques.

I asked him what his publication schedule was, a slightly more edged question.

'Well, I finish collecting this year's data at the end of the season, then there is another whole year's data to collect. Then I have to put it all on the computer and analyse it. Finally, I write up my thesis. I hope to submit in about three years' time. Then, of course, I can get down to writing some papers.' That is to say, Sierra Leone will have to wait five years to get any results from this, by which time the results will be obsolete.

'What are the policy implications of your research?' I asked. 'What changes in government's policy, or anyone else's, could it influence?'

He was stumped. He obviously had not thought of this question, even though it was the first question he should have asked himself, before starting the research. I changed the subject and asked him how he enjoyed working here. Immensely, it seemed.

When we had finished our interviews, we went to the university guesthouse where the university was putting us up. It is a well-maintained 1970s building with comfortable beds and furniture, and with the wire mosquito mesh still intact. There was no electricity, of course, but they provided us with paraffin lamps. Thomas and Mohammed have rooms here, as they do not have to pay. Whether Mohammed used his room I do not know: he disappeared into the village to find an old flame. I asked Thomas to go and ask the local academics to join us for a drink, but not to ask Piers, as I wanted the academics to be free to talk.

They relaxed to a couple of bottles of beer and a sympathetic ear. As far as they were concerned, it was not collaborative research at all. It is the Englishman's idea, and they only go along with it because they need the money. They are senior academics, but their university has no money, and so they must work for an English student, collecting his data for him. Worse, the student's project is not fully self-financing, so what little resources the university has are being diverted to support him.

Piers is a nice enough guy, they said, but he is learning his trade from them, although they are not paid to teach him. He had learned a few survey techniques in England, and wanted to use them in any country where he could get cheap local academics to do the work. They were not flattering about his work. He had spent a year in England preparing his survey before he came here. When he came here his survey turned out to be quite unsuitable for local conditions. He had been working on the assumptions that Sierra Leonean farms were like English farms, all having rectangular fields with one crop per field. He had not realized that most fields were odd shapes cut out of the jungle, and could have a dozen different crops all mixed up, sesame, beans, yams, cassava, cocoyams, ginger, and so on. This meant that the figures he was trying to collect, on yield per acre and cost of production of the different crops, were meaningless.

Yes, if you ask a stupid question you get a stupid answer. I was working with an expat statistician in East Africa, who wanted to know how many cattle a single farmer might own, and did not believe people who thought the maximum was about 50. We were driving through the country when he saw a youth herding about 150 cattle. We screeched to a halt, and my colleague asked him, 'Do you own all these cattle yourself?'

'Yes' said the youth. We got back in the car and roared off. I imagine you would get the same answer if you put on a foreign accent and asked an English engine driver if he owned the train, or a pilot if he owned the airliner he was flying.

But the lecturers' criticisms went much further than this. Most agricultural cost-of-production studies in Britain, say, concentrate on the cost of the machinery used and on the cost of inputs, like fertilizers, insecticides, sprays and seed. The cost of labour is a small part of the total, and it is hard to measure. Costing it is difficult, too, when some farmers operate mainly with employed labour while others operate only with family labour, people who are not paid a wage. Should digging a hole in the ground have the same cost if it is dug by an employed farm worker, or by the owner who has a degree in agriculture and a postgraduate degree in management, or by her son of 15? In Britain, this problem is fudged, and they get away with it because labour, other than the farmer's own labour, is a small part of total costs.

Using this methodology in West Africa has always been dodgy, because farmers here use much less fertilizer and other inputs, and labour has always been the biggest part of the production cost. Nowadays, people in Sierra Leone use almost no fertilizer and sprays because they cannot afford them, so virtually all the cost of production is labour. Since there is no local labour market, there is no going wage rate, and there is no way you can put a cost on this labour. A lot of the labour market in the subsistence sector is alcohol based. The farmers' wife brews three or four 44-gallon drums of millet beer (it is a woman's job). Then the farmer invites all his friends and neighbours to help him clear the land and to have a drink. The day is spent with her trying to give out as little drink as possible until the work is completed, and the neighbours trying to get drunk before doing any work. On another day, the neighbours may have their own work party, so it has an element of taking in each other's washing.

'There are more fundamental problems with the research,' said Professor Komba. 'Even when I was a student here, I was told by the lecturers that survey work here was useless because the people are over-surveyed. They have had foreign academics doing surveys here since the 1920s – anthropology, farming systems surveys, consumption surveys, economic surveys, whatever.

'Of course, the academics always select a sample area that is convenient to the university, and that means within ten miles or so of Njala. This means that the same villages, the same farmers, are selected every time. Any time I visit a "randomly selected farmer", and go to talk to him, I find I have spoken to him before, on another survey. I do not think you would find a farm or village here that has not been in a dozen surveys over the years. Some of them are in two or three surveys right now.

'Of course, they are tired of surveys, and they do not want to take part in yet another one. When somebody else comes along and tries to get them to take part in yet another, they may refuse. This high non-cooperation rate means that the sample is not random, and that the results are not statistically valid. Because so many refuse, it means that the few who do cooperate are selected for every survey.'

This is probably true anywhere. When I was doing farm management surveys for Cambridge University, any of the big farms we visited were already taking part in six or eight other surveys. The ones that cooperated, cooperated every time, and the ones that refused, refused every time. There was no randomness.

'Often, though, the ones who do cooperate are not doing it to help, but because it is too much trouble to argue with our enumerators. They do not really cooperate, but they play the game of seeing what silly story they can get the enumerators to write down. This is even better if it is a white man writing down their stories.

'The foreign academics do not understand this: they think that because they have never seen the people of Njala before, the people of Njala have never seen foreign academics before. If we had the money to do our own research, we would do it in a completely different area. It is not just money though: last year the country had no fuel at all for six whole months – it was a major job for the university to get any supplies from Freetown, even food, and no passengers could travel.'

I asked them about the publication of the results. They laughed bitterly. Foreign researchers never publish their results. The facts from the survey are the only results that could be of any practical value to Sierra Leone, but these are never published. There is no academic status in a routine report giving the facts from surveys, especially if it is published by Sierra Leone Agricultural University. On the other hand, there is academic status in publishing theoretical papers that happen to use Sierra Leone data, but these have no practical relevance to Sierra Leone. They expect that after Piers has finished his thesis and got a job as a lecturer he may publish theoretical articles in academic journals, but Sierra Leone cannot afford to buy international academic journals, so they will never see them. Anyway, by then the articles will be obsolete.

Before I came to Sierra Leone, I looked up everything that has been published in academic journals about the country in the last fifteen years. One that seemed particularly relevant to my work was a study of price policy by a German. Yes, they had seen it, a copy of his thesis in German, but nothing in English. Then I asked them about another bit of research I had come across, a household consumption survey published by an American. He has got a lot of mileage out of it, publishing a dozen articles in high-status journals like the *Journal of Political Economy* (the latest one published this year). They remembered him but they had not heard from him since. They had never heard of his papers, and he had not sent copies to them. If this work had been of any potential value to Sierra Leone (it was not) it was wasted, because nobody here has seen it. Still, they were not worried: what conceivable interest could there be in a household budget survey done twelve years ago? In the meantime, coffee and cocoa prices had nearly trebled, then plummeted again. The economy had collapsed and there had been rapid inflation.

I noticed that they did not ask the first questions that would have sprung to the lips of a British or American academic if I had mentioned papers written on work they had collaborated in, 'Was I called a co-author, since I contributed to the survey design? Was I cited? Was I even thanked?' They must have known the answer.

Trekking On

FRIDAY, 22 SEPTEMBER

As we drove away from the university this morning, I realized that I have not seen a single bicycle in Freetown or in the country. And this in a continent where the bicycle is the main form of transport.

'There used to be a lot of them when I was young,' Thomas explained. 'Everybody had one. If a man went to work in the diamond fields for a couple of months, he brought back a bicycle as well as money. The coffee and cocoa buyers used to sell them.

'Then the economy went wrong, and you could not get spare parts. After a bit, tyres wore out or tubes got punctures, and you could not get spares. Everybody put their bicycles away to wait for good times.

'When I went to Oxford to do my M.Sc., I bought myself a bicycle. It was great. I could go anywhere without walking and without taking a taxi. I brought it home with me. In Freetown it meant I was free to go where I wanted, unlike all my friends. It was like having a car. Then the tyre blew. So it is stored in the roof of my house. I oil it sometimes, and hope it will still work when the country has enough foreign exchange.'

His deep voice was quiet, unemotional. He did not seem to be bitter, just fatalistic about something outside his control, something happening to his country, but he did not seem to blame anyone. There is no indignation.

I note that three-quarters of the cars on the road are Mercedes. There are a few of other makes, mainly owned by the projects, and no bicycles at all. This accurately reflects the distribution of wealth in the population.

Our first puncture. We changed the tyre and drove on to the next town. The puncture was not repairable, and none of the shops had a Land-Rover tyre, so we were left without a spare. I thought we would have to cancel the trip, as I was not willing to risk getting another puncture somewhere in the bush, and wait there for a week until we could send to Freetown for a spare. However, Mohammed disappeared and appeared an hour later with a grin on his face, carrying a very old tyre. It was completely bald but would do in a real emergency. We could at least crawl to the next town if we got another puncture. The seller knew he had us at his mercy, and I had to pay the full price of a new tyre in Freetown. Thank God, Mohammed has the gumption to find the only spare tyre in a town like this. No doubt he got a commission though. Smart lad, Mohammed.

Mohammed complained that the VW Passat that he normally drives for the World Bank does not have a proper spare tyre, just a thin little emergency tyre designed not to take up too much space in the boot. The instruction book claims that you can drive 50 miles on it, at speeds of up to 45 miles an hour.

'They are no good Sah. Maybe they OK in Freetown, but on bush roads, they last four, five miles. On bush roads, I get a puncture every week maybe. We bought a proper spare tyre, but it does not fit properly in the boot. Why do they have no proper tyre like the old car?'

I do not think he believed my explanation that it was OK in Germany where you expect one puncture every 50,000 miles and all the roads are tarred.

★

As we drove further inland, I gazed out of the window looking at the scenery. Mostly it looked like unbroken jungle on each side of the car, though I got enough glimpses of trees I recognized, like oil palm trees and bread fruit, to realize that it was not jungle at all, but a mixed plantation of coffee, cocoa, oil palm, and any other trees that might provide food or a bit of money. Occasionally there were small fields at the side of the road, again with a mixture of crops – yams, beans, sesame, a few maize plants and a plot of cassava. This mixed planting gives higher total yields than a field full of one crop, and it reduces insect damage, but it does take more work per acre. Behind these small fields was another belt of trees. Occasionally we crossed a valley and saw a swamp, either untouched, or reclaimed as a paddy field.

What we did not see was a view. This is an incredibly flat country, and we are still not much above sea level. I suppose there must be a lot of small hills, but if there is a hill, we generally do not get any view from it, as there are trees next to the road. Once today and once yesterday we came to the top of a rise and I was able to see beyond the strip of trees by the roadside. Surprisingly I did not see a mass of jungle beyond. Instead, it looked rather scrappy, patches of trees and patches of open ground. It is heavily populated, and there is no spare ground for new fields to feed the increasing population. I suppose this explains why people are turning swamps into paddy fields in spite of the 'health risk'.

I saw a lot of pits in the red soil, 15 to 30 feet in diameter and 10 feet deep. There was water at the bottom of the pits and men were working in them.

'They are diamond diggers,' explained Thomas. We stopped and went over to a pit. There were half a dozen men in it, wearing shorts. Some were standing waist deep in the water, scraping up gravel. Two were washing the gravel to get rid of the soil and loose particles. One was going through the gravel carefully, looking for diamonds.

'We have diamonds everywhere,' said Thomas. 'It is not like South Africa or other countries, where there are one or two diamond pipes. The diamond pipes are the plugs of old volcanoes where the diamonds were formed by the heat and the pressure. It was like that here many millions of years ago, but the pipes were washed away and the diamonds were left in river beds and swamps. In fact, many of the diamonds were washed down from the Sahara when it used to rain there.'

He had switched to his earnest explanation mode. He was speaking slowly in his deep voice, with a slight wrinkling between the eyebrows as he concentrated.

'This is what we call a diamond swamp,' he continued. 'You can see of course that it is not a swamp now, but it was millions of years ago when enormous rivers came here from the Sahara. The fast water washed the diamonds out of a pipe and downstream. Then the river hit a flat area and became a swamp. The water ran slowly, and the diamonds fell down. Then the swamp filled with mud, and the river moved somewhere else. If you can find where there used to be a swamp, there are lots of diamonds.'

'Can anyone dig here?' I asked. 'Do they have to stake a claim, or what?'

'You need a licence,' he explained seriously, 'But any Sierra Leonean can get one. The man with the licence must be born in the chiefdom where he lives. The other workers must be from Sierra Leone. The big problem is capital, cash flow. You see, the man with the licence has to pay the workers all the time, even if they do not find any diamonds. You can see here that they have to throw away the top 10 feet of soil before they come close to where the diamonds are, so he has to pay a lot of wages before he starts to make any money at all. Then he has to buy a water pump and diesel oil, because these areas are low and they soon fill with water.'

He started to tell me everything he knew about the diamond industry in enormous detail. My girlfriend complains that men never talk about their emotions: they exchange facts. Thomas was having a very male conversation. But then, I am male too, so I encouraged him.

'But how many diamonds do they find? How much money do they make?' I asked.

'They expect to find about one diamond for every worker for every month. Mostly they are small diamonds, worth maybe $15. Sometimes they are big, but hardly ever.'

'How do they sell them?' I asked, thinking of all the books I read in my youth, in which the illicit diamond buyers were the villains. In fact, one of the James Bond books starts with him zapping illicit diamond buyers in Sierra Leone. However, I recently read an article which claimed that the demonizing of illicit diamond buying was a ploy to support the de Beers diamond monopoly.

But Thomas dispelled this line of thought: 'In any of these towns we go to, you see licensed diamond buyers. Mostly they are Lebanese, or the shops are owned by Lebanese, but the man behind the counter is a Sierra Leonean. The buyers have to sell the diamonds to the State Diamond Monopoly. The Monopoly pays a 30 per cent export tax and sells on the world market. It is exactly the same as coffee or cocoa.'

He paused and pondered. If he was going to impart information, he was going to impart accurate information. 'No, it is not exactly the same. It is much easier to smuggle diamonds than coffee or cocoa. We think that nearly all diamonds are smuggled abroad to avoid export tax, and to get black market dollars. Of course, the buyers have to sell *some* diamonds to the State Diamond Monopoly, or they lose their trading licence.'

I remembered the English colonel who was in charge of security for the diamond companies, the one who warned me to stay clear of the local girls, and I asked Thomas who he would have been working for.

'Oh, yes. There are the big international mining companies too. For example, there is the Sierra Leone Selection Trust. Once they were the only people allowed to mine diamonds here. The colonial geological survey discovered diamonds here, then the colonial government said that only the Sierra Leone Selection Trust was allowed to mine them. Just like South Africa I think.

'But this was not like South Africa, which was settled by whites who took everything: it was a protectorate for the native people. The people asked why they should let a foreign company take all the diamonds out of the country. So, just before independence we were allowed to mine too. The country had to pay the Sierra Leone Selection Trust a lot of money in compensation.

'There were two reasons the Colonial Government wanted to

work with the Sierra Leone Selection Trust, not the people. First, there would be no smuggling. Second, they use industrial mining methods, which are more efficient: when they mine a swamp, they get every last diamond. These pits you see here, they miss a lot.' He waved his hand dismissively.

'So what is the position with the big companies nowadays?' I asked.

'I do not know. Nobody will talk much. Perhaps they continue to mine efficiently, perhaps they do not do any smuggling themselves, perhaps they pay all their export taxes, perhaps they do not pay any bribes.' He shrugged his shoulders.

Mohammed broke in, 'You see the men who dig here. They all try to thief a diamond. Sometimes, they thief two, three in one dry season. The men who work at the Selection Trust, they also steal. So every family in Sierra Leone has three, four diamonds, and they hide them in a tin under the floor of the house.'

This morning's project HQ is on a high river bank, looking over a river which might be from *Saunders of the River* or *Heart of Darkness*. It is a wide, wide river, green and greasy in a way the Limpopo never was, with unbroken jungle on each side.

I introduced myself to the Project Director, then went to talk with the technical officers. We did not go into their offices, but went and sat outside on a headland overlooking the river and enjoyed the breeze. We sat in wicker chairs under an umbrella and had an ice-cold beer, courtesy of the project. We talked about food and marketing and credit and the progress of the project. I got lots of information which I am trying to fit in with what I have learnt already. Sometimes I get new theories, surprising facts, flashes of insight, but more often it is just like today, more anecdotes, more facts and different perspectives, which slowly build up into an understanding of what is going on.

Dugout canoes kept arriving on the river bank beside the compound. The women paddled the canoes to the bank, waded ashore until they were ankle deep, shook loose the sarong-like cloth that they had tucked about their waists, then put on bras, dazzlingly white against their sun-blackened skin, so they were not entirely topless when they went into the town. They picked up their baskets of vegetables and went into market.

Bare-breastedness is common here. It is hot and humid ten months of the year, and hot and dry the other two, when the harmattan comes down from the Sahara. Clothes are uncomfortable in this climate. Most of the women in the villages wear a sarong and are bare from the waist up. In town, they usually wear a blouse or a T-shirt. When it is hot, they roll the T-shirt up under their armpits, so their breasts can cool in the breeze. The fact that more than a third of the population are Muslim and another third are Christian does not seem to have any impact on this. I have not seen a single Muslim chador or veil. Nor have I seen a woman cover her face or hair – quite unlike Pakistan, where I have spent a month at a time without seeing a woman's face. Everybody seems to accept that you need ventilation in a hot, humid climate, and it is only in hot, dry deserts that you need to cover yourself completely to keep the hot wind out.

I also get the impression that religion and sex are completely separate, as is slowly becoming the case in Europe. Our churches ruled for centuries by the strategy of finding a strong, fundamental, instinct, and making us feel guilty about it. Irish Catholicism is still doing it, as are some versions of Islam. The local version of Islam seems to be completely relaxed about sex. It is not just Mohammed's girlfriends that make me think that. People are quite uninhibited in the bars at night. What is more, one of the most devout Muslim women I have met here, someone who is quite fervent, had a child when she was not married, indeed when her boyfriend was in England for a year. It does not seem to have upset anyone.

The Agricultural Officer from the project took us on a short tour, to see key activities of the project. As we were leaving the town, he pointed to a large low shed, with new cream paint on the walls and a new corrugated iron roof.

'That's the FAO Fertilizer Project. That's Phillips's car there: he must have come from Freetown today. He runs the project. Do you want to see him?' he asked.

'Yes, let's see what he is doing,' I said enthusiastically. It is much more informative to see what someone is doing in the field than to listen to him in his office in Freetown.

We drove up to the shed, parked and went into the little office at the end. Phillips was a tall, gangly Englishman with red hair.

'Hello,' he said welcomingly. 'You were lucky to catch me here. I have just arrived from Project HQ in Freetown. I am on a whistle-stop tour to make spot checks on all the fertilizer depots. I am just squatting in the supervisor's office for a couple of hours.' I looked around. The supervisor's office: that explained the basic wooden desk, the six wooden office chairs and the two new filing cabinets. A low-status office for a senior clerk.

'The justification for this project is simple,' he explained. 'There is no distribution system in Sierra Leone for agricultural inputs like fertilizers and insecticides. There are no shops supplying them to the farmer. There is no banking system. This project is filling the gap. We distribute fertilizers and insecticides to outlying areas and sell direct to the farmers. We arrange credit so that they can buy it. Frankly, if it wasn't for us, all the fertilizer that was imported would lie rotting in Freetown docks.' He leant back in his wooden chair, confidently proud of a job well done.

I asked him which farmers bought the fertilizer and what they used it for.

'Well, that's a problem,' he said, a bit deflated. 'We couldn't keep up with the demand a couple of years ago when coffee and cocoa prices were high. The growers here bought sprays for their trees, of course, and they would spend some of their earnings on fertilizers, so that they would be sure of having plenty of food in their villages. In the rice areas, the farmers bought a lot of fertilizer, because there was a good price for rice, and it was profitable to use the fertilizer.'

He paused, looked me in the eye, and said, levelly but passion-ately, 'I tell you, I really thought that this project was doing some-thing great for this country.

'But then it all collapsed in the last two years. The country is using one-fifth as much fertilizer as it was.'

I was amazed. This is an enormous fall. I have never heard of anything like it happening anywhere else in the world.

'Why, you may ask?' he continued. 'Well, first the coffee and cocoa prices fell to almost nothing. The growers didn't have enough money to buy fertilizer. In fact, quite a few of them just abandoned their trees: didn't weed, didn't prune. They could not afford to buy any sprays either, so black pod disease has caused enormous damage to the cocoa crop – and this is another reason why cocoa production is not economic any more. No, today they are just working flat out trying to grow enough food to live on, without the benefit of fertilizers.

'Something similar happened in the main rice area. The price of rice has halved, so it doesn't pay to use fertilizers any more. They just grow enough to feed themselves, and have no surplus to sell.'

What he was describing was an enormous collapse, an agricultural revolution in reverse. In a couple of years they have gone from a prosperous peasant agriculture to subsistence, living on what they can produce, and not having any surplus to sell. What he was saying also put a new light on the population pressure on land. I had seen that there was not a lot of spare land, virgin jungle. If you use lots of fertilizer, you can feed the population from a small area, but once you stop using fertilizer, you have to cultivate more land to get the same amount of crop. If there is not the extra land, you go hungry.

'It's getting worse,' he said, his voice rising and starting to tremble. 'If the farmers couldn't afford to buy the fertilizers last year, they certainly can't afford them this year. Since the leone was floated, import prices have quadrupled. There is no chance that we could sell any.'

'I tried to persuade the Government to subsidize it, to keep it at last year's prices. They agreed. Then the World Bank stepped in. They are opposed to any form of subsidy, and threatened to cut off Sierra Leone's aid. I was furious. I raised all hell with them. I pointed out that one bag of fertilizer produces two more bags of rice. This means that you get the same result importing 100,000 tonnes of fertilizer or 200,000 tonnes of rice. Since a bag of fertilizer and a bag of rice cost much the same, this would halve import costs. Seems bloody obvious to me, but I am not an economist.

'I don't know if they got the message. They kept disagreeing with me and using long economic words, but eventually we were allowed to keep some subsidy, not enough.'

I could imagine the scene. He may be an agriculturist by training, but he has a sharp economic mind: in the final analysis economics is not about money or inflation or balance of payments, it is about goods and services. His concentration on rice and fertilizer got down to the nub of the problem. It sounds as though he was arguing with highly trained economists who knew all the academic theory, but had not related it to goods and services.

'However, the subsidy is not relevant,' he continued. 'The Government has not got the foreign exchange to import fertilizers and other inputs, so there is no question of subsidizing them. All we have is a little fertilizer given by the Canadians. It is a gift, so we can charge what we want for it and tell the World Bank to bugger off.'

The Canadians are considered eccentric by the other donors. Before, during and after they give a country something, they go round all the local officials and ask 'Is this gift going to help or hinder you? Will it upset local markets? How will it affect local farmers? How will it affect local manufacturers.' When they came to me in East Africa, I was able to say that we had no fertilizer factories, and would be delighted to have any fertilizer they could give us. If they had offered us wheat instead, I would have had to do a lot of thinking before accepting: as they are aware, dumping a large quantity of grain on the local market can depress prices and put local farmers out of business.

'I was proud that I ever got this project off the ground at all,' continued Phillips. 'The Government had promised us everything including staff and lorries. They promised us brand-new lorries. In fact, they gave us some ten-year-old lorries left over from another project. Normally you can only expect to get two or three years' work out of a lorry before it shakes to bits on these roads, so you can imagine what condition these were in.

'Well, I started using them, and they worked. Then I found out that the drivers were misusing the lorries. They should have been driving out with a load of fertilizers, then driving back with an empty lorry. Instead, they were buying firewood in the bush, bringing it back and selling it in Freetown. It was strictly against regulations, and my first impulse was to sack the lot of them. I waited, though, and thought it over for a couple of weeks.

'Then it occurred to me that you have two main problems in this kind of project. First, the drivers do not look after the vehicles, and this would put my lorries out of action in a month or two. Second, the drivers will go to their home villages and have a week's holiday. When they come back to work, they tell you that they had a puncture, or a mechanical breakdown. Either of these problems could bring the project transport to a halt.

'However, if the drivers were making money from selling wood, they would give loving attention to maintenance, and they would be working all the hours God made. And wood is a light load: it does not damage the lorries.

'That is what happened. The lorries are still running three years later. We even had the odd driver buying black market tyres out of his own pocket to keep the lorry on the road.'

'Sierra Leone Revolutionary Youth Farm Centre' read the notice.

'Ignore it,' said Thomas. 'They did start a Revolutionary Youth Movement when Siaka Stevens was friendly with the Russians, but nobody liked it, and this is the only camp now. It is not important.'

How different from other countries I have been in. Zambia, Malawi and Tanzania all have big, strong youth movements based on the Hitler Youth — based on it, not just having some superficial similarities. Massive indoctrination, combined with military training and a bit of vocational training. Most important, they are a powerful and instantly mobilized force for crushing political dissent.

This raises the question, 'How do the politicians here in Sierra Leone keep control in without this muscle?'

Finding the Facts

One reason I travel up-country is that I am afraid that I will be blinded by statistics if I only talk to civil servants in the capital. There is always the danger that if there are no statistics on something, I will think that it does not exist. When I am working on food policy, it is a great temptation to work only on maize and rice because there are voluminous (though inaccurate) statistics on them. In fact most policy documents and academic studies of food and famine concentrate entirely on them, and ignore the foods that provide most of the calories: vegetables, meat, fats and alcohol, for instance.

I have discovered that palm oil is an important part of the diet here, though there are no statistics on its consumption. Some reports tell me that it accounts for as much as 40 per cent of the calories consumed. This is possible, I suppose, as some Brits get 40 per cent of their calories from oil and fat, living on a diet of chips, burgers and fry-ups. Other reports tell me that palm oil provides only 20 per cent of the calories. Nobody knows who is right.

This morning's visit was to a state-owned oil palm factory. It was not working. The manager told us that he had not been given the foreign exchange for essential spares; nor could he get a loan to buy palm fruit from the growers.

But I cannot see how the enterprise could ever have broken even, with the amount of government interference it had. Government decided that all the oil produced there must be sold at the state-controlled price, which is a good one-third below the free-market price, and well below the break-even price. Obviously, the traders or politicians who bought it from the State Oil Palm Factory at this price promptly resold it at the going market price. Obviously the factory made a loss. This is probably the main reason the company could not afford spares. They had never produced enough to export, which was just as well, because the world price for top quality oil – calculated at official exchange rates with a 30 per cent export tax removed – would leave virtually nothing.

As we left the State Oil Palm Factory, we saw traditional processing of palm oil. The oil palm tree is a rather stumpy palm, with a trunk that is very rough from where previous fronds have been cut away. The farmer ties an 8-foot rope in a loop around the tree and his waist, and climbs up to the fruit, which he hacks off. I watched somebody doing it, climbing the rough tree, silhouetted against the sunlight behind. Very picturesque.

Mohammed interrupted my admiration of this bucolic scene. 'It is dangerous Sah. Sometime the rope breaks. Sometime he cut himself with the machete. In the rainy season, also, it is too wet for the snakes on the ground, so they climb the trees. We get two crop of palm fruit, but in the rainy season many people leave the fruit on the tree, because of the snakes.'

'Yes,' Thomas agreed. 'This means that in practice we get less than half the yield from palm trees that the Malaysians do, even though oil palms come from West Africa originally. It is just not economic to export from here.'

We stood sweating in the sun and watched the traditional oil extraction process. The fruit bunches were 2 feet in diameter, a clump of individual fruits, red and black and the size of golf balls. These were boiled, then thrown into a cement-lined pit about 5 feet deep. Barefooted men trod the steaming fruit into an orange pulp while it was still hot. It looked painful. The palm oil gradually seeped out and separated from the orange pulp.

The oil from plantations is clear and white (and turns to solid white cooking fat in a colder climate) but this oil was deep orange. They told me that farm-produced oil had a lot more flavour, and that it would fetch twice the price on the retail market. The producers deserve it, because it is hard and painful work, and because a smaller quantity of oil is produced than with powerful extracting machinery.

The only road signs I see look as though they have been vandalized. Someone has taken them down, knocked lots of holes in the metal, and then put the signs back again. Mohammed tells me that the Roads Department do it themselves. It means that nobody will steal the metal signs to fix holes in their roofs.

As we were going down a dirt road through a village, there was a fluttering of feathers and a bump. Mohammed stopped, and picked up a dead duck. He was upset, which surprised me, as he seems to aim at any chickens he sees.

'Very unlucky to kill duck, Sah! They say that if you kill duck you will kill a person.'

In Makeni retail market, I noticed eight market women sitting in a row on the ground, their produce spread on a mat in front of them. They were in the best position in the market, where everybody had to walk past them, and this means, of course, that they could charge more than the people in the less accessible places. Everybody in the market charges the same price for a pile of beans, or a cup of rice, but the quantity in that pile or that cup varies: the traders in the best position, right by the door where everyone walks past, have smaller piles; the traders in the back have to have larger piles to attract people. I was wondering why it was that women seemed to be so dominant in trade, and so invisible in government.

Mohammed broke my reverie, 'You see those eight women Sah? They are all the wife of the man who owns the shop over there. They all do sell for him.'

'How do you know?' I asked: I had not seen him talking to them.

He grinned. 'Oh Sah! I used to be a lorry driver. I drove everywhere in the country. I know about people everywhere. I had a girlfriend here. She tells me.'

Of course, women and children are a productive asset. A boy of ten is considered old enough to be sent out into the bush on his own to guard a herd of cattle. In Zambia, when I was working on cotton, which is a labour-intensive crop, I was introduced to the two most successful peasant farmers in the country. One had thirty wives — he got a couple more with each year's profits — and the other had two wives, each with thirty children, which must be some kind of record.

Officially, Sierra Leone has gone metric, but I could see little sign of this in the market, and some of the old measures were still being used. One was the round cigarette tin which once held fifty Players. Some of the original tins were still being used, old and battered, with most of the paint worn off, but mostly the traders were using small enamel mugs. For some sales, they were using the enamelled tin plate, which used to cost a penny, and which is still called the penny pan, and the larger version which is the thrippenny pan. For larger sales, they were using the debbie, or four-gallon paraffin tin. As far as I can see

2 cigarette tins	=	1 penny pan
2 penny pans	=	1 thrippenny pan
20 thrippenny pans	=	1 debbie
2½ debbies	=	1 gunny bag
2½ gunny bags	=	1 woolpack

There are a large number of other containers I have not been able to identify.

My interest is not just idle curiosity. The weights and measures used can have a big effect on the validity of the prices quoted. For example, in Tanzania I was intrigued to see that wholesalers were buying potatoes at the same price per debbie as they were selling them. What they had done was beat out the sides of the debbie they used as a buying measure, so it held more than 4 gallons, and beat in the sides of the debbie they used when selling, so that it held less. I bought samples, one a full debbie as they were buying it, one a full debbie as they were selling it. When I weighed the potatoes, I found that they were charging a 30 per cent mark-up, which was reasonable.

★

Tonight I am not staying in a resthouse, but in a hotel in town. Thomas has arranged to stay with one of the local economists who had been at university with him, and so he has saved paying for the hotel. If he stays with a friend, and if I pay for his meals when we are together, he just about breaks even. It works both ways: the friend stays with him when he visits Freetown. Mohammed had another solution. He spruced himself up and headed for town, to look up yet another old girlfriend.

The hotel is definitely a comedown from the project resthouse and the university resthouse. It is made of mud bricks and mud plaster. It was painted once – strident blue and red – but the paint has weathered and peeled to reveal the mud underneath, and the colours are now quite mellow. It looks as though there has been no new wall paint in town in the twenty years since the diamond boom, though perhaps it was only seven years ago during the cocoa boom, and the heavy rains have a more devastating effect than I think. The roof is the rather attractive brown rust of old corrugated iron. I have seen no indication that anyone in this country ever had any roof paint. If they had put a coat of 'red barn paint' on every seven years or so, the corrugated iron would last fifty years.

The street outside is tarred up to the hotel, and turns into red earth as it continues down the hill. The tarred road is actually a lot worse to drive on, as it has enormous potholes, some going from one side of the street to the other, and the sides fall six inches vertically. The potholes in the earth are rounded, so there is not the same sharp drop down, and vertical climb up. Tanzania eventually bulldozed the tarmac off its main trunk road because of this, to turn it from an appalling tarred road to a bad dirt road. Their political dogma is that the colonial government never put any infrastructure into the country, and if there is no infrastructure, obviously you cannot maintain it: hence the potholes.

There are steps up from the street to the hotel's veranda, and I arranged to meet the Project marketing officers and a couple of their friends there this evening.

First, though, I made my room safe to sleep in. Fortunately, I have a little bottle of DDT powder given to me by the FAO in Rome a few years ago. I sprinkled some of this on the mattress to keep the bed bugs at bay. Apparently, the powder is quite safe: it is only when it is dissolved in oil to make a spray that it is absorbed through the skin. Then I gave a quick spray of mosquito killer inside the mosquito net, under the bed, then around the room, so that the room would be safe to sleep in when I went to bed a couple of hours later. (I sometimes use mosquito coils, slow burning pyrethrum, which keeps killing the mosquitoes all night, but I always wake up with a filthy headache after using one, so I suppose they are poisonous to me as well as the mosquitoes.) Then I put on a long-sleeved shirt to protect my arms. Finally, mosquito repellent on ankles, wrists, neck and head, and I was ready to go out.

No, I am not obsessive. I know that bedbug bites are itchy but not dangerous. With mosquitoes, though, it takes just one bite to give you malaria, and this can kill you. The malaria here seems to be treatable, but there is a new strain in Zambia which kills you in nine hours; the fever boils your brain.

All preparations ready, I went onto the veranda to meet the project staff. It was dark, of course, and the hotel brought out a paraffin lamp for us, which soon attracted moths. There were three comfortable chairs, and some people sat on the veranda wall. After quite a few drinks, one of the Sierra Leoneans, the Project Engineer, I think, started talking about diamonds, and filled in some of the gaps in Thomas's explanation.

'Twenty years ago, two-thirds of this country's exports were diamonds. Today the statistics say that it is less than 10 per cent, which is nonsense. Look around you: everywhere people are digging for diamonds. There is more diamond mining than there ever has been. The law is that they must all be sold to the State Diamond Monopoly, and they must pay an export tax. It is just the same as the coffee and cocoa exported through the Agricultural Marketing Board.'

His voice was rising to a higher pitch, as he started to rant.

'So what is happening to the diamonds? Obviously, it is all smuggled abroad. Who is responsible? It is not the diggers. Oh no! It is the top politicians. It is the diamond traders. Especially it is the Lebanese diamond traders. The Lebanese are everywhere and they own everything. New ones come here from the Lebanon every day. They come with nothing, and within two years they are millionaires – dollar millionaires in fact. How do they do it? There is only one way possible. They buy diamonds at the official price and they smuggle them abroad. They do not have to pay the export tax, and they get a good exchange rate. Anything they buy they make at least double as profit. The money all goes to buy guns for the Lebanon. You have heard that?'

I nodded, encouraging him to continue. Yes, it was racist rant, but it was exactly the story I had heard from one of the local

Lebanese, Boss Seaga of the Casablanca.

'As for the Diamond Monopoly! You think that the Agricultural Marketing Board is dishonest, but the Diamond Monopoly is far worse. Who is on the board? Politicians and Lebanese.

'You heard the news, didn't you? You heard that a board member of the Diamond Monopoly was flying out of the country in his private plane last month, but the customs stopped it and examined it. They found it was full of diamonds being smuggled out. His own. Even if they were the Diamond Monopoly's, they did not pay export tax. Of course, he is too important to prosecute: he is paying everyone.'

I had not heard this, but I had read in a book on the Sierra Leone diamonds that this sort of thing used to happen regularly thirty years ago, before independence.

'Then there are the big international diamond mining companies. They have enormous mines and find millions of diamonds. They also have their own airstrips. Are you going to tell me that they sell everything they produce to the Diamond Monopoly at a low price?'

'Everyone know the foreigners thief our diamonds. That is why all the workers try to thief diamonds from them. We have a proverb in Creole, "When t'eef t'eef t'eef, God laf."'

His voice was high and wobbling, as he reached his peroration. Then he stopped, gulped, and in a soft, fierce voice concluded: 'I tell you, it can't last forever. Already Libyan-trained guerrillas are fighting a civil war in Liberia. It will soon spread here: it is only a matter of time. The people will support them. The people want to get the money from their own diamonds; they do not want to see crooked politicians and foreigners getting it.'

The Southern Province

We spent a couple of hours talking to the local chief, who also seems to be something of a politician. I was intrigued, as I had heard how important chiefs are in West Africa. In areas of white settlement, they had been treated as parish councillors, which was more or less their traditional role. However, the Colonial Office, which ran those countries with no white settlers, operated the policy of indirect rule, ruling through the traditional chiefs, as the cheapest, easiest (and least democratic) way of running a country. This meant giving them a lot of power and wealth that they had not had in traditional society. The first thing countries like Zambia and Tanzania did after independence was to abolish the power of the chiefs.

Chief Margai did not fit my image of a chief at all. His farm was much bigger than the average, but still cannot have been more than 5 or 10 acres. His house was not a mansion; it was a four- or five-roomed whitewashed bungalow built of mud bricks. The floors were cement, smoothed and red polished. The furnishings were plain and local. Certainly not a mud hut, but not the squire's manor either. It reminded me more than anything of the small houses that the unsuccessful white farmers in Zambia and Zimbabwe live in.

He was dressed in a plain, locally made safari suit, comfortable and suited to the climate, more or less what a shopkeeper or civil servant would wear. The only flash of colour was a reddish copper ring on his right ring finger, half an inch wide, hand beaten by a local craftsman. It had a big lump of glass set in it, looking as though it came from the bottom of a Coke bottle. Rather tacky, I thought.

When he spoke, he was anything but tacky. He had his finger on the pulse of what was going on. He talked about the economic pressures on different groups of people. He talked of the effect of local, national and international politics. He mentioned in passing that he had been on the board of the State Gold Monopoly. I looked at the ring on his finger. Yes, it was yellower than copper, and it was shiny: could it be 24-carat red gold?

We had tea accompanied by the cheap biscuits which seem to be sold in all the small general stores in Africa. He talked on, and mentioned that he had also been on the board of the State Diamond Monopoly. I sneaked another look at the ring on his finger. Certainly, it could have been a lump of glass off the bottom of a Coke bottle, but it could equally well have been an enormous uncut diamond. How do you tell?

Evidently a man of simple tastes, a man whose authority in the district and indeed in the country did not require ostentation. But then, the diamond ring was making the point discretely but powerfully that he could have been ostentatious if he had wanted.

As we drove away, Thomas said, 'You know his two brothers were the first two prime ministers after independence? Albert Margai and Milton Margai. They are both dead now.'

There seem to be two kinds of small town, one in the diamond areas and one in the agricultural areas. In both of them, there is a small permanent population of civil servants, including teachers, police and agricultural advisers. In the bigger towns, especially the provincial capitals, there are also project staff, including a handful of expats. There are also some traders and some small businesses. Generally, traders bring all the rice that the town needs from Freetown. Locally based people sometimes get a bit of rice cheaply, or for nothing, from their relatives on the farm, possibly as some recognition of land rights, for if they were to go back to the village they would have to be given some of the village land to cultivate.

It is far too wet to dig diamonds in the rainy season and the seasonal labourers go back to their farms, so then the two types of town have the same type of population. When the rains stop, large numbers of agricultural workers leave their farms and head for the diamond fields. A few of them work for one of the big diamond companies which use industrial mining techniques. Most work as labourers for someone who can afford to take out a mining licence, and can pay the workers until they find the diamonds.

There should be good money to be made from this, I gather. Mohammed, who seems to know everybody and to have worked everywhere, told me that the diggers did not always get what they should. 'Sometimes you hear that they have found a big diamond, worth millions of leones. Then you find out that the man who found it, the man with the licence, only got a few hundred leones.'

To me the economics is the same as the coffee and cocoa market. The dollars earned on the international market are converted at the official exchange rate. Since this rate was overvalued until a few months ago, the Diamond Monopoly used to get far fewer leones per dollar than they should have. Then there was an export tax on what was left. The producers were getting less than half the world price for the diamonds. Result: there is a big incentive to smuggle. However, if there is enough money to be made from smuggling, little will be going through the official channels, and the diggers will actually get more than the official price.

The diamond diggers should have benefited immediately from the floating of the leone six months ago. In fact, now that the leone is undervalued they should be very rich indeed, getting the world price converted at a favourable rate. Of course, it has been raining heavily for most of that period, so not a lot has been dug: perhaps they will get rich in the next six months or so?

The coffee and cocoa farmers have not benefited from today's undervalued exchange rate, because the prices paid to them this year were worked out at last year's overvalued exchange rate. The Agricultural Marketing Board always announces the farmer's price a full season in advance 'to give the farmers the confidence of a fixed price...'

If the diggers are not rich, and I do not see any sign that they are, it suggests that the diamond trade is run by a cartel of dealers. Not only is the export controlled, but also township buyers are being told to keep prices down. The next step would be for the cartel to lean on the people with digging licences to make sure that they sold to the cartel and did not smuggle on their own account. It does sound as though the industry is controlled by a ruthless criminal organization.

There is a lot of violence. The normal way of robbing a diamond digger is to kill him, remove his stomach and guts, and look for diamonds there, on the assumption that he will have swallowed the diamonds for safety.

Thank God I do not have to cover the diamond market in this job: it seems to be a very dirty business indeed.

★

Some of the projects seem to have been doomed from the start. For example, there is a very visible project digging wells in the countryside. This is Freetown-based, covering the whole country, rather than based in one area like the big projects I have been visiting. The big innovation here is making a bucket out of a bit of old car tyre, which is 'appropriate technology'. I cannot really see the logic behind this aid. The Sierra Leoneans have always known how to dig wells. The water table is near the surface, and they have plenty of people available to dig. This kind of aid pauperizes the people. It means that they will not dig their own well, on the off chance that some donor will come along and do it for them. Similarly, in other countries I have found villages refusing to build their own school or market on the grounds that other villages have been given them by aid projects – and this when nothing more was needed than a thatched shed.

Another project that failed to impress was a farm mechanization project. The foreign Project Adviser was bursting with enthusiasm, and saying that it was by far the best project in the country. As far as I can see, though, all it does is show that if you have enough dollars you can run farm machinery. You can buy tractors and machinery; you can buy spares; you can even buy fuel. This is no surprise to the people of Sierra Leone, and of no relevance to anyone who has not got an unlimited supply of dollars. What is surprising is that the Sierra Leoneans who do not have dollars still manage to keep fifty-year-old rice mills going in the villages, and can keep ten-year-old lorries on the road. A project that helped them do this by importing spares would be worthwhile. As it is, $2 million spent on the project is wasted.

Of course, you can't always blame the people who are implementing the project when it is a cock-up. Often the project has never had a hope of succeeding, right from the start. Little effort actually goes into identifying what is really needed and what can work.

For example, I have been sent out on a project identification mission in Pakistan, where I had a month to identify dozens of projects. I suppose that on average I was allowed two or three days to identify a project and draw up a proposal. Those two or three days include travel, courtesy visits, wasted visits, weekends, and so on. I came up with what I thought were possibilities, worth further investigation. What worries me is that the small projects, anyway, are financed on the basis of this quick visit, and the further investigation does not take place.

When they do send out a preparation mission to work up a project I have identified, there is strong pressure on the consultants to say that it is going to work. If they say that the project is not economically viable, or that it is misconceived from the start, then the international organization that employs them can get quite stroppy. It tells the consultants that they have failed to meet their terms of reference, and it can withhold their fee. It will certainly not employ them again.

It is worse with the large projects financed by a development bank. Project preparation for a large irrigation scheme, for example, can easily cost $5 million to $50 million, and this is before the project is accepted. The Asian Development Bank, for example, has been employing a UN organization to do some project preparation for them. Most unwisely, they have a clause in their contract that if the organization does not come up with a viable project, they do not get paid. This puts a lot of pressure on the organization to fake the facts. Two or three years ago they spent $5 million on the engineering surveys, the canal design, and so forth. As an afterthought, they brought me in to design a marketing system. I had to tell them that they had been doing all their economics on the assumption that they could sell the entire product at a high, scarcity, price. However, once the irrigation scheme was in place, output would increase a hundredfold, and its price would be less than half as much. My conclusion was that the project was uneconomic.

Consternation! The Asian Development Bank would certainly not accept the project with my price forecasts. The UN organization would be $5 million out of pocket. A lot of pressure was put on me, but I do not react well to pressure. They rejected my report and brought in someone else to fake my results without doing the field research I had done. This worked: the organization got paid; the Asian Development Bank got a project proposal they were happy with; and Pakistan will be paying off the debt for the next hundred years.

Nowadays I just refuse to take on project preparation work. I can do without the pressure.

Some people are more inventive than me in preparing projects. For example, in Pakistan the Director of Planning took me to the Murree Hills, near Islamabad, and we went on a chairlift to the top of a mountain. I was astonished to hear that it had been financed by aid, as it clearly did not add to the productive capacity of the nation, and there were no foreign tourists using it. It was purely for the entertainment of the richer Pakistanis. My host explained: 'When we first submitted the proposal it was thrown out, for exactly the reasons you give. Then we sent the same proposal in, with a different title. It is called "Project for the Uplifting of the Rural Masses". It was accepted immediately.'

Today I was in the richest town in the world. It is a small township, in the bend of a swampy river, with a few government offices, two or three Lebanese trading stores, and one or two hundred houses showing the normal rural poverty. There is no tarred road, except the main road that passes through it, and the railway crossing signs are still there from when there was a railway, twenty years ago. There is no electric light, or sewerage. I watched some kids playing happily at the side of the road, and saw their thin arms and legs, with bumpy joints, their stomachs distended, and I wondered what their life expectancy was, when they were already showing such signs of malnutrition.

Why do I say it is the richest town in the world? Because it is ex-President Siaka Stevens's birthplace, and he has a house there. Divide $1.5 billion by 1,000 inhabitants, and you have an average wealth of $1.5 million.

Every ten miles or so there is a police roadblock with a queue of cars and lorries before it. Mohammed just drove past without stopping.

'We do not have to stop, Sah,' he explained himself. 'It is not for government cars or projects, or us. It is how the police get their pay. They stop the lorries and the cars with passengers, the taxis, and the drivers have to pay them.'

'It is the same in Freetown. I used to drive a taxi there. There is a place near the Ministry where all the main roads come together. All the taxis have to stop there every time they drive past and pay the policemen.'

It seems to be universal in Africa. In Kenya and Tanzania, it started with government bans on transporting grain from one district to another during a period of scarcity. At first, the police just stopped the transport. Then they took a bribe to let grain pass, and then they just stopped all lorries and took a bribe. It became completely normal, and a percentage of the bribe was passed on to senior officers and so on, right up to the top.

The roadblock is strictly business. It has nothing to do with internal security or the secret police. In fact, 'security' does not impinge on me at all here. It is a real pleasure to drive through the bush and to stop and chat to a farmer working in the fields, or to someone working a rice mill, or to a government official. It is not just that they are friendly and open or that a lot of them talk English (I find that English is the second language in the tribal areas, not Creole); it is that they talk at all.

It is a complete change from socialist Tanzania, where I had to report first to the Resident Minister of the province, then to the Government District Officer and the District Secretary of the Revolutionary Party, both of whom who would accompany me to the village and introduce me to the Village Mayor, Village Party Secretary, and one of the Ten-House-Cell Leaders, responsible for keeping an eye on ten farmers. They would all accompany me to the fields, call out a safe farmer and stand there listening while I interviewed him. He was obviously terrified of saying the wrong thing in front of them, but this did not really matter, as they translated his words into partyspeak.

Zambia, Tanzania and Malawi were all strongly influenced by a group of Catholic priests who believed that National Socialism had not been given a fair trial, and that if its racism, extermination and other excesses could be removed, it was the answer to the world's problems. These countries all adapted its systems: the one-party state, the corporate state, the secret police, the concentration camps and the Hitler Youth. Zambia and Tanzania even adopted their version of

'Arbeit macht frei', 'Freedom and Labour', as their national motto. I have heard President Kaunda speaking to a mass rally, to thundering applause from the Youth Service, and using the words, the cadences of Hitler 'One Zambia! One Nation! One Leader! – Kaunda!' 'Ein Volk! Ein Reich! Ein Führer! – Hitler!' The other thing that Tanzania did was to force the peasants (i.e. subsistence farmers) into huge, uneconomic collectives, burning them out of their houses and villages, and breaking down the social structure, so that they would move into collective townships. The only consolation is that it cannot last: National Socialism is grossly inefficient for anything other than bringing resources together for a short war. The economies are collapsing.

Again, I wonder how the political control works in Sierra Leone. Perhaps there is a strong traditional society, and all that is necessary is to square the chiefs? There are no prison camps – nothing like the 8,000 political prisoners in Tanzania. In fact, so far as I can make out, Freetown still has only the same small prison as there was in the law-abiding colonial days. It must be a hell hole. It was built in the 1930s and must have three or four times as many people as it was designed for (but then so do British prisons). It is also at the bottom of Government's list for government rice and other food, so I imagine the survival rate is low. Still, this is part of the general malaise in the country, not any particular viciousness.

I do not ask these questions out of idle curiosity. Politics may mean that they cannot implement the food policy I recommend in my report. Politics may mean that my recommendations are not implemented or, on the other hand, that any opposition to them is ruthlessly crushed. Alternatively, the politicians may be making so much money out of the present system that no changes are possible.

I also have to recognize the possibility that the people I am talking to are telling me what they are being told to, or that they believe that Thomas is a secret policeman who will report back to Special Branch. I do not think so, but if it is the case, I cannot trust what I am hearing.

★

How can the people here always be so spotlessly clean? Few of them can have more than one change of clothes, and mine certainly get dirty and smelly in a single day. Washing the red mud out of clothes cannot be easy, especially when the water itself is stained red from bauxite mining. Drying them must be a nightmare during the rains when there is a constant downpour. Yet they manage to do it.

★

At today's project, I had a long talk with the Monitoring and Evaluation Officer, a Dutchman called van der Laan. He has just arrived in post and is depressed by what he sees.

The project was badly conceived and badly executed and is riddled with corruption. He saw it immediately (and so did I in my brief visit). However, if he writes a report saying this, he will be sacked: he will have grossly offended the local Project Director, and the person in Brussels who prepared the proposal, and the person in Brussels who was responsible for implementation and control.

The first Monitoring and Evaluation Officer, four years ago, took the easy way out. He shut his eyes to all this, and carried out a 'baseline survey' to find out what the position was before the project started, the theory being that if you do not know what the situation was at the beginning, you will never be able to prove that there has been a change. This survey occupied all his time for two years. His successor, two years later, said that the methodology of the survey was wrong, and repeated it, which took him two years. This criticism was correct: nobody has enough money to do the job properly. (Everybody knows the Awful Warning, the Nigerian project that did the baseline study perfectly, but spent $25 million on it, leaving no money for the project itself.)

Van der Laan cannot get away with doing another baseline survey and he does not know what to do. Meanwhile Brussels has realized that something must be done to remove the Project Director, who has stolen so much. They were actively campaigning to have him appointed head of the West African Rice Research Association, a major regional research organization, very important to the region. This is not funded by Brussels, so he would be off their hands.

Colonialism

Why am I enjoying Sierra Leone so much? The people are so open, cheerful and enthusiastic, in spite of the fact that the economy is on the rocks and they are broke. They have a self-confidence about them that may have something to do with the fact that the country never had European settlers. Britain did not want the place, but they were damned if they were going to let the French get it. British civil servants stopped tribal warfare, introduced a legal system, developed markets for local produce, and discovered diamonds and other minerals, all 'for the good of the native peoples'. They also educated the Sierra Leoneans to become the civil service for the whole of British West Africa. This may be the reason they have no chip on their shoulder. However, you might expect the same of Nigerians on this argument, and they are as aggressive as Glaswegians on a Saturday night.

In countries that were settled and fought for their independence, like Kenya and Zimbabwe, the people appear to be self-confident and polite. The real aggro comes from countries that were colonized and were then given their independence without a fight, like Tanzania and Zambia. They have built up a fictitious history of the Struggle.

For example, Britain decided to give Zambia its independence in the mid-1950s, before the Zambian independence movements had even started. The British colonial civil servants who had brought Ghana to independence in 1957 were then transferred to Zambia and told to do the same there. Six years later, they succeeded: Zambia was independent.

Soon after independence, I was working there, and had several expat friends staying with me. They were teachers in bush schools, and had been brought into the capital for a week to write the official History of Zambia for schools – previously they had been using books prepared by white Rhodesians. We had an alcoholic weekend, during which my wife, who was working in the government personnel division, told us the story of a District Commissioner who ordered his black clerk to carry him across the river. The clerk, of course, flatly refused. In fact, he spent the next ten years writing indignant letters to the Director of Personnel, demanding an apology. My teacher friends decided to incorporate this story, slightly amended, into the official History of Zambia. We were all anti-District Commissioner, mainly for political reasons, but partly because we were professionals and did not think that going to a minor public school or being Indian Army (retd.) was sufficient justification for their airs and graces. Anyway, this story was dressed up and put in the school history books.

When I returned to Zambia on a job last year, I found that this had become the defining myth to describe the colonial years. There are pictures everywhere of an African being forced to carry a sola-topied District Commissioner across a river. Whatever the Government does, however oppressive it is, however corrupt, people think 'At least I am not carrying the District Commissioner through a crocodile-infested river.' And I know the story is false: the clerk was able to refuse to do it and still keep his job.

Home Again

SATURDAY, 22 SEPTEMBER

Back from patrol, trek, safari, tour or whatever. It has been a week of working from morning to night, with both formal and informal interviews, and with up to four hours a day driving in a Land-Rover over bad roads, but even as I write this on Saturday night I am still buzzing with adrenaline. The introduction of project resthouses to Africa has meant that there is often somewhere comfortable to stay. Whistle-and-thuds, mosquitoes, lack of power, and lack of water are a minor inconvenience in a one week trip, though they could become an enormous and increasing burden in a two-year job.

Even the short time away has given me a new set of delights: living in a hotel with its own generator and water storage tanks, I have running water, electricity at the flick of a switch, lights bright enough to read by and an air conditioner.

★

I went out to dinner at the Armenian restaurant with Brendan. We were sitting watching the sun set over the sea, when a group of young girls walked up, carrying large baskets of fish on their heads. The restaurant owner went over to look at the fish, and started to negotiate in Creole.

'There used to be a lot of fish here,' said Brendan. 'A couple of years ago there was even a British trawler company operating out of Freetown, and sending frozen fish to Europe. Then didn't the Russians come and buy the fishing rights for $3 million a year, which is peanuts. The Russians vacuum up anything that moves on the continental shelf. Not only has the offshore fishing gone, but so has the inshore fishing, which was worth a hell of a lot more than $3 million to the local fishermen. They can't make a living any more.

'Yes, the Communists have a different way of doing business, I'd say,' he continued. 'They are quite open about it. 'What is your percentage Minister?' they ask. The aid agencies are too mealy-mouthed about it. It would be more to the point if we agreed that the Minister's cut was 10 per cent and raised all hell if the total taken by the Minister plus anyone else went above 10 per cent.

'I hear now, that your new Minister has raised his cut to 50 per cent. Mind you there is not much left here to steal, so his 50 per cent is the same as 10 per cent used to be.'

The lights failed soon after dark, and the waiter brought a candle to our table. After a bit, I went to pee, and a waiter accompanied me, holding a candle for me to aim by.

We stayed for a couple of hours, having a full mezze – dish after dish of Armenian and Lebanese delicacies, and we had rather a lot to drink. As we drove back to the hotel, we had a fevered discussion. We were agreed that the Sierra Leoneans drive on the wrong side of the road, but we could not agree on which was the wrong side. Brendan swerved from one side of the road to the other, depending on who was winning the argument at the time. Fortunately, we did not meet any cars between the restaurant and the hotel.

Financing the System

Thomas seems to be starting to trust me. He was explaining how the political system is financed. The money comes from rice, he says. The Government says that all rice that is imported must be distributed evenly throughout the whole country, so that no area goes short of subsidized rice. Every politician is allocated the same amount of rice, and it is their job to see that the rice is sold in their constituency.

'They are politicians, not rice traders, of course,' he said, 'so they do not collect the rice themselves. Instead, they give a chit to the rice trader, saying 'Please supply Sesay and Sons with ten tonnes of rice.' The trader takes this chit to the Agricultural Marketing Board depot, and they let him buy it. Then he is supposed to take it back to the constituency and sell it. There is nothing to make him sell it at the official subsidized price.

'The trader makes a lot of money out of this, so he has to pay the MP for the chit. That is how the politicians make their money.

'Also, once the trader has bought the rice, there is no reason why he should sell it in the MP's constituency: the country areas do not need much rice, but Freetown and the diamond areas do. The traders sell it where the price is high.'

It sounds to me like a beautiful system for giving money to politicians. They never have to do anything apart from sign the chits and collect the money. It is also a way of constantly asserting that the MPs have the power, not the traders.

'Three months ago,' continued Thomas, 'my father was in a bad situation. He is just an ordinary person, a worker in a shop in town. He had no food to feed my mother and his other children. I can help him, but only a little. So he went to his MP. The MP saw him, and gave him a bag of rice from the pile by the front door. It was a gift. For my father it means that he can live and feed his family for another three or four months. He is very grateful indeed.

'Now, you know, I know, and even my father knows, that this was not really a gift: the MP stole the rice in the first place, or else it was his profit from the chit system. Still, my father must be grateful, and he must support the MP in future, so must all the family. It is this gratitude that gives the MP his power.'

He spoke calmly, giving me information about what happened and how the system worked. He seemed to accept that this is the way it is. I could not detect any bitterness, or any suggestion that he might be able to change the system.

'Other people are also grateful to him. The more important people in the constituency sometimes want ten or twenty bags of rice, and they want it at the subsidized, wholesale price. He gives them a chit to collect it from the local Agricultural Marketing Board depot. Again, they are grateful, and they must support him in future.

'It is the same with sugar. When I came back from England after my M.Sc., I wanted to show what I had learnt, so I did a proper economic analysis of the sugar industry. I recommended closing it down, because it costs more, in foreign currency, to import the raw materials like fertilizer, than it would to import refined sugar.

'I wrote a Cabinet Paper on it, and my idea was rejected. My mistake was that I was trying to maximize the economic benefit to the country, like a good economist. The Cabinet came up with their alternative system, which had the objective of maximizing their own income. All local sugar is now allocated to MPs on the chit system. To keep prices high, no imports are permitted until all the local sugar has been sold. It is a brilliant system. For them.'

He shrugged his shoulders. He was explaining it as a matter of interest, as a new facet of the system that he had just learnt about. Possibly, most people here accept that all politicians are corrupt, and they take it that those who are most corrupt are more likely to be most competent, or possibly, as in Ireland, a politician gets a macho image from being seen to be blatantly corrupt.

'My report also mentioned that there was a distillation plant at the sugar refinery, which could turn sugar waste into industrial alcohol. The Minister saw this, and immediately arranged to buy all the alcohol produced.

'You know the small plastic bags of vodka you see in the shops and bars everywhere. You know: like the ice-lollies in England.'

I nodded.

'Well that is how his company sells the vodka. The alcohol was tested for safety once, when the still was installed ten years ago. It has not been tested since.'

I winced. I have lived in Ireland and I know that poteen can blind people – and kill them. One friend, Dan Twohig, promised to bring me some from the wilds of Kerry. He did not deliver for some months and I thought he had forgotten. When he did produce it, I shared it with some of my neighbours, and we all got filthy hangovers. Next day, Dan apologized for the delay in bringing it.

'The man who used to make it died. You see, the first stuff to come out of the still is full of meths and other impurities, so they throw it away and wait until the good stuff comes. They do not have lab equipment to measure the impurities, so they test it by taste: they keep taking sips to see if it is OK yet. This wasn't. The meths killed him.'

Another friend promised to bring me some from the Mountains of Mourne in the North. 'Grand stuff. It is made by a blind man and his son.'

What Happened to the Money

Why are the farmers so poor? Why has there been no corrugated iron roofing for twenty years? There is something strange going on. Their prices should have been sky-high seven to ten years ago, high enough to pay for roofs and a lot of luxuries. World prices rocketed to two and a half times their normal level.

Some of the money was taken in increased export tax, and some went to the Government in a hidden tax because of an overvalued leone, but what happened to the rest of the money? Well, the Agricultural Marketing Board made a fat trading profit, and the

Government told them to invest it in state farms and in the Agricultural Bank.*

One of the investments was the palm oil factory I had seen up-country. From what I have seen in other countries, any money put into state enterprises just vanishes. Usually, you can blame poor management, or corruption, or their trying to use technology that they do not understand. Usually, too, what should be a good investment becomes unprofitable when the currency is overvalued. In this case, there was the added complication of inflation accounting: the state farms were required to sell at cost, without allowing for inflation. As a result, when there was 30 per cent inflation, they earned 30 per cent too little to cover their costs next year. They had no money for maintenance, spare parts, fertilizers and insecticides and so production fell and they went bankrupt.

The Agricultural Bank went the way of the other credit schemes here. With a repayment rate of 10 per cent, the money soon vanished.

World prices have fallen since then, of course, but up to the end of last year, 1985, they were still above the 1975 levels, so farmers should have been comfortably off. However, once Government had got used to creaming off most of the farmers' income, they did not let go easily. The farmers' incomes are now well below what they were in the early 1970s in real terms.

---

* The cocoa price per tonne rose by $4,000 from 1976 to 1977. Coffee prices rose even more, by $5,000. Since you can get four tonnes of coffee from a hectare, that is an *extra* $20,000 per hectare – a vast fortune to someone who now gets perhaps $25 a year in cash. Even if they only grew a tenth of a hectare each, it was a lot of money.

But today I was looking at the figures. In fact the farmers did not get this extra money. Instead of $4,000 a tonne extra, they got $600. Nearly all the extra money was creamed off by Government and the Agricultural Marketing Board.

First, Government increased the export tax fourfold, from $600 per tonne to $2,400 per tonne or more. A third to a half of the total was taken as a hidden tax by the use of an overvalued currency and ended up in the Central Bank. This is another tax, of course, but it is invisible, and the farmers did not know what was happening.

How could this happen? How did the farmers let it happen? Why did the international organizations and the donor countries do nothing?

As far as I can see, the main reason the Government got away with it was that they called their taxation 'price stabilization'. Farmers are keen on price stabilization, as long as you let them believe that you are stabilizing prices at a high level. Government, and consumers, are also keen on stabilization, but they expect to stabilize prices at a low level. Western academics at the time were inspired by the high prices to write some dire economic justifications of price stabilization, and of the New World Order.

There is no economic justification for these stabilization schemes, in theory or in practice. All the banks in the world work on the principle that the last thing farmers and businesses want is a stable cash flow. The banks exist to turn a stable income flow into a lump-sum loan. Even private individuals do not want a stable income: they want a lump sum to buy a car or a house. They want the lump sums so much that they will pay interest to get them.

The first part of the stabilization process is easy, taking away farmers' money when prices are high. The second part, giving back the money when prices are low, never works. Government immediately spends the money it takes away, so there is nothing to pay back. It is not possible to tax industry to pay back the farmers, because there is no industry to tax. If Government gave all the money to a Stabilization Board to invest, the money would vanish – it would vanish even if everyone were honest. The fact is that the Stabilization Board could not find any investment opportunities as good as those that the farmers could find for themselves. Their unsuccessful investments in Sierra Leone are an example.

If Sierra Leone's farmers had got the full value of their coffee and cocoa, they would have spent some of it on necessities like corrugated iron roofs, which would have kept them healthier. They would have spent some on luxuries, no doubt, but they would have invested a lot on ploughs, fertilizers, improved seed, rice mills, and so on. They would also have invested in pruning their existing trees and planting new ones. The whole economy would have been better off.

I am here to look at food policy and food supply, so my first question is, 'What does this mean for rice supply?' I suppose Phillips, the fertilizer man, was clearest about what was happening on the ground. In the coffee and cocoa areas, farmers no longer buy fertilizer and sprays, and they concentrate on growing food. In the rice areas, farmers no longer buy fertilizer, and no longer produce a surplus. In both areas there is a food deficit. People use money earned from diamond digging to buy imported rice.

In both types of area, farmers are now no longer peasant farmers getting most of their living from cash crops. They are subsistence farmers who produce enough food for their families in a good year, and not enough in a bad year.

This retreat into subsistence agriculture is familiar enough in the rest of Africa. President Nyerere achieved it in Tanzania, President Kaunda in Zambia, for example. It is immensely depressing, as it will take a political and economic revolution to reverse the decline.

As far as my mission is concerned, I have to act on the assumption that rice production has indeed dropped to the extent that the country can no longer feed its rural population, let alone its urban population. Yes, the result of these policies is that today Sierra Leone must import rice or its people will starve.

Freetown

WEDNESDAY, 26 SEPTEMBER

I sat in as an observer at a meeting on the supply of credit to farmers as a way of increasing production. A Danish consultant was presenting his final report on a World Bank credit scheme to the Ministry of Agriculture.

Last year the World Bank lent Sierra Leone $1 million for a credit scheme, when the exchange rate was 7 leones to the dollar. This gave a credit fund of 7 million leones. Administration of the loan cost 7 leones for every leone lent out, so only 1 million leones were lent out. A World Bank staff member did the administration, so they cannot blame the incompetence of the local civil service.

Then when the time came to collect the money, only one-tenth of the money could be recovered – 100,000 leones. This recovery rate squares with what I saw up-country. It is what is to be expected when prices are so low that it is uneconomic to buy fertilizers and sprays. A certain amount of dishonesty by the credit officers also helps.

Today, the leone is worth a fifth of its old value, and it could be worth a tenth by the time the money has to be repaid. Even at today's exchange rate, the 100,000 leones produce $3,800 to pay back $1 million plus interest.

Larsen, the consultant, ended his presentation by saying that it would have been far cheaper not to lend the money to farmers at all. It would have been much cheaper and more effective to drive through the villages throwing the money through the window.

The World Bank man, Mukkerjee, was very angry indeed. He jumped up and down, dancing with fury. He shouted indignantly, 'Mr Larsen is quite wrong in his calculations. It would not be cheaper to throw the money out of the window. He has not costed in the petrol.'

I laughed, but I felt sorry for Larsen. I cannot see the World Bank, or anyone else, employing him again if he rocks the boat. If he uses criteria like this, whose job is safe?

A parade was marching down the main street. First was a jazz band, looking and sounding very much as I imagine the original New Orleans bands did, with worn and faded uniforms and army surplus instruments.

Leading the parade was a white-bearded man doing a wonderful cakewalk. He was wearing a straw boater, its straw dark brown with age, and its ribbon a faded maroon. His faded maroon blazer may have fitted him once, but now left a large white-shirted tummy on display. As he came close, I recognized him: it was the Chief Economist of the Central Bank.

Behind him was a block of a hundred men about the same age, also wearing straw hats and school blazers, also doing the cakewalk. Then there was a gap of 10 yards, and another block of a hundred men, this time somewhat younger, but still doing a credible cakewalk.

I turned to someone standing next to me watching, and asked what was going on.

'It is the old boy's parade from Freetown High School. It is the oldest school in the country, and every year the old boys march to the Cathedral for a thanksgiving service. The oldest people go first, then the next, and so on.'

I watched with pleasure, as old boys from more recent times came by, their blazers better fitting and less faded, their straw boaters whiter, their cakewalks less impressive. Every now and again, there was another jazz band to keep up the mood.

Finally came the present schoolboys, in bright scarlet blazers and new boaters gleaming white, totally embarrassed by the whole occasion, and making no attempt at all to cakewalk.

There is evidently a thriving local theatre here, because everywhere I see advertisements for plays. Most I cannot understand because they are in Creole, but some I can. Written on a sheet slung across the road was:

THE BIG SHOW UP
DISAPPOINTMENT
DEATH AT MARRIAGE
TRAGIC
DEATH LOVE AND PAIN
THE MOST TRAGIC LOVE STORY
DEAR MOTHER Parts 1 & 2
Shafumi Garber's Greatest Script

Another had:

> CHIVA CULT WORKSHOP
> UNGRATEFUL HUSBAND BLACK PHAROH

I would love to go, but I am certain I would not understand the Creole.

Getting Information

FRIDAY, 28 SEPTEMBER

I try and get information from as many sources as possible. This is the only way I can crosscheck, to see which source is correct: there is so much rumour, misunderstanding and misinformation to filter out. It is detective work. One of the sources is the local newspapers. I get one or two newspapers every day, and when I get back from work I have a shower and then sit on the terrace reading the paper before I write my diary.

Sierra Leone has the best newspapers in the world! I do not refer to the quality of printing, I am afraid. One sheet of paper is folded to give four tabloid pages. Typesetting is done with movable letters, so the typeface keeps changing as they run out of letters – *The Dawn* is short of 'e's and words appear as 'el€ctricity'. The paper they use is poor quality and the presses are old, so the text is often difficult to read.

Yet they tell the truth! Scandal after scandal is exposed here. Where I know about it from my work, the story is dead accurate. The story is not given in any great detail, as there is no space to spare, but they do give a couple of column inches to corruption, where the British papers give nothing.

A lot of what they write is incomprehensible to a foreigner. When they attack someone really important, they cannot be straightforward. They are allusive, using nicknames and hints, and they slip into Creole proverbs and phrases. I got Mohammed to translate, and to explain one of these stories – he is less constrained than Thomas, the civil servant. It proved to be a funny and entirely accurate attack on my Minister.

They must be the bravest journalists in the world. They are attacking powerful people, men who have no respect for human life. Every week there are reports of thugs breaking into the offices of one newspaper or another and beating up the reporter. Two weeks ago a reporter was killed.

Why do they take these risks? I can only guess. They can see their country collapsing around them. They can see all the wealth of the country being put into a Swiss bank. They can see their people starving. They can see their society disintegrating.

It is more difficult to understand why the authorities let them get away with it. Most of the papers seem to depend heavily on government advertising, and Government could easily bring them into line by moving the advertising to a pro-Government newspaper. However, it is a measure of their honesty that there are no pro-Government papers, just degrees of anti-Government papers.

Again, Sierra Leone is a one-party state, and in most one-party states they just nationalize the newspapers and use them to print government propaganda. Sierra Leone has a secret police force, which could easily arrest reporters on some trumped-up charge. The politicians who are exposed could sue them for libel. None of this happens.

I wonder, though, if all this was part of Siaka Stevens's way of keeping control. As long as the papers kept exposing corruption, he knew which politicians were building up a war chest sufficient to challenge him. As long as they kept exposing corruption, no other politician could sell himself as Mr Clean.

Maybe the Sierra Leoneans have more of a tradition of freedom than most of the countries with a controlled press. The people of the coast, the Creoles, are all descended from released slaves. The feeling of freedom when they were released from the plantations of the new-born United States during the War of Independence, or from the slave ships going there later, must have influenced generations. It must have had a more powerful psychological impact on a population than the Russian Revolution or any of the African nationalist struggles. The tribal people inland never felt that they had lost their freedom. They were a protectorate, not a colony, and British rule never meant much more than a District Commissioner persuading them not to fight each other.

I had a meeting with the Economics Department of the University this afternoon. It was at the top of the mountain which looks over Freetown and dominates the bay, where I had gone with Brendan on my first day here.

The economists were intelligent and helpful, though they know nothing about the food marketing system – they are macro-economists. There was a little embarrassment when they tried to get me to employ them as World Bank consultants. I had to explain that I do not have a budget for employing other consultants. This is one of the few countries where the World Bank encourages consultancy firms to employ local academics on their teams. The reason is that the academics here are paid so badly that the universities would collapse without the occasional extra income. In most countries we are told to avoid academics, on the grounds that they never deliver. It is not just that few of them have that rare ability to apply their theory to real life problems. It is because they have to work full time on a project, often travelling, if they are going to be of any value, and most of them are too conscientious to abandon their students completely for a couple of months in the middle of term. Some of them also think that the foreign consultant will be satisfied with a rehash of their lecture notes, rather than hard analysis of a new problem.

It is remarkable how fast ideas and rumours spread. Only a couple of weeks ago I heard Batangas, at the end of his visit from Rome, explaining his theory that nearly all the rice that came into the country was promptly smuggled out. Only ten days ago I was told in the strictest confidence, purely because I was working on food policy, that half the rice shipped here is not even unloaded. Yet in the week I got back from my trip up-country I have been told both these stories as gospel truth, by consultants in the Casablanca, by civil servants and now by the economists at the University.

It may be that everybody has known both these stories for years, and it is only because I am a newcomer that they seem strange. This may be so for the smuggling theory, but I do not think it can be true for the unloading theory. Why should the stories have spread so quickly? Why should everybody choose to believe them, even though they can have no evidence at all to support them? I think it is rather like the story of the District Commissioner making his assistant carry him through a crocodile-infested river: people believe the story because they want to; because it confirms all their prejudices. Here, people want to believe that there is total corruption at a high level: it is an easy explanation for the collapse of the economy, and it takes away any responsibility from the individual.

The problem is that when everybody believes a story like this, it is almost impossible to get them to consider alternative versions of the truth, let alone to change their minds. This is beginning to matter. I am certain to come up with a conclusion that contradicts the myths of half the population. It is becoming increasingly likely that my conclusion will also contradict the myths that most of the rest cling to as well.

The food situation is on a knife edge. There is no desperate shortage now, just a lot of people suffering from malnutrition, and a lot of children dying before the age of 5. There is no buffer, no safety margin, though. A slight switch in supply could trigger something serious. I have to get this message across, or they will never adopt a more rational food policy.

How Civil Servants Survive

MONDAY, 1 OCTOBER

I had a long talk with Thomas today. I wanted to know how civil servants got enough to eat. His salary is $100 a year. This is for a man of 29 who has a master's degree from a British university, a man who is married with four children.

A quick calculation shows that he would be spending all his income on rice at the new price.* Only half his family's calories come from rice: he also has to buy cassava, sweet potatoes, oil, and other foods. Then he has to pay rent, and buy clothes, fuel for cooking, and so forth.

A clear-cut solution. Almost no salary earners in Sierra Leone could stay alive on present salaries if they were paying current import prices for rice. I asked how he managed. In theory, it is not as bad as I thought: he told me that all civil servants should get a rice ration in addition to their salaries. Slowly, as he explained the system in more detail, it became clear that it might be quite as bad in practice, if not in theory.

'That is what is supposed to happen,' he said, 'But it does not happen. We used to have an Englishman running the department before Foday. When we got rice, he used to divide it out equally, half a bag for each person, even the typists and messengers. If there was any left over, he would raffle it. It was an honest raffle: I won it once, and even the messengers sometimes won. For the last few months since the Englishman left, though, the rice has not been coming. It just does not arrive, and we do not get our ration.'

'But what happens now, when you don't get any rice at all?' I asked.

'For me,' he said, 'it is difficult to buy enough food from my salary. I do not know how the typists and messengers live on their salaries. You have seen them sleeping at work. It is not that they are lazy. They have not been at parties all night. They have no food, so their bodies shut down. If they do no work and move very slowly, they can survive on the food they can afford to buy.'

He told me that the army are now getting most of the rice rations reserved for the civil service. They get much more than they can eat, so they double their salaries by selling the surplus. Army wives are

---

* This family eats at least as much rice as three adults, at 0.3 to 0.5 kg. per head per day. That gives 328 kg to 547 kg of rice per year. How much will it cost to buy this at today's exchange rate? The Agricultural Marketing Board pays $240 a tonne for rice (which strikes me as well over the world rice price), giving a price in the retail market of say $300 to $350. Even at the lower estimate of consumption, he will be spending his total income on rice.

now the main rice traders in the markets within two miles of the barracks.

He told me this without any apparent rancour, as though it was just how things are in Sierra Leone today. I do not know if it is just his manner or if he really feels so beaten down by what has happened to him, to his family, to his country, that he just takes it as another blow from the heavens.

Maybe it is just a rumour; maybe not. Still, it would explain why the other civil servants are no longer getting their rice ration. Again, I must ask why the rumour is believed. Thomas hinted that with the constant threat of a coup, the President had to keep the army happy.

It is easy for a foreigner to get completely the wrong idea about the exchange rate and inflation – and probably we economists are the worst of all. For example, I get paid in dollars. To me, the exchange rate is what determines the cost of living: as the leone falls, the leone price of everything goes up. This is because the sort of thing I buy is directly linked to the exchange rate: my hotel rate is set in dollars, for instance, and all the expat restaurants put up their charges in line with the dollar.

It is a different experience for the locals. The civil service salaries have not risen for a couple of years, and, as far as I can gather, most of the private salaries are stuck too. Farmers sold their coffee and cocoa in the middle of last year, then had no cash income until the middle of this year. The prices they were paid this year were based on last year's overvalued exchange rate. A lot of imported goods have not increased in price at all: they have just vanished from the market. This means that a lot of local prices are more or less unaffected by changes in the exchange rate.

This may explain why the expatriates are keenly aware of the changes in the daily exchange rates, but the local officials, even the economists, do not seem to be aware of what is going on. It may also explain the odd perceptions of expatriates, and especially macroeconomists, about inflation.

Trickle Down

I was in a stationery shop this morning, negotiating a price for a ream of paper, when a man who was waiting to be served struck up conversation with me. As people do, he asked me where I came from and what I did. He then said that he was an immigration officer. He was responsible for the work permits of foreigners. He could get people deported. He started to get heavy, obviously wanting me to bribe him. I walked away quickly.

When I recounted this at the Casablanca, Brendan told me not to worry. 'Whatever would they be wanting to deport you for? When a country is as dependent on aid as this, they are not going to let junior immigration officers deport people on a whim. If anyone is going to throw you out for a political reason, the decision will be made at a high level, and they will do it by severing your contract.'

I then asked for advice on another problem I had had in my shopping. I like to get my weekly Economist magazine, as that is where the international development jobs are advertised – though I have never seen any economist reading anything but the ads. I could not find any shop selling it. The people at the bar told me to buy it from the newspaper sellers outside the main post office. It seems that quite a few people and projects subscribe to the airmail edition. Someone in the Post Office then steals it, and his confederate sells it on the pavement outside.

'Damn it, I know I am paying for it twice, but I have to get a copy,' complained Brendan.

'Yes, this dishonesty is common here,' said Thor. 'The hubcap came off my car, so I went into the market and found the stall selling second-hand hubcaps and vehicle spares. I asked him for one for my VW Passat, but he did not have one. He asked me to wait a minute while he got some from his friend at another stall. I waited ten minutes, and he came back with three VW hubcaps and I bought one. Then I went back to my car, which was parked outside the market, and I found that all the hubcaps had been stolen.'

An Italian who was sitting next to us told us that he had been brought in to deal with the 'die men' in the Ministry of Health.

'What's a 'die man'? I asked.

'Well, if you are a foreman in charge of twenty people, you can pay out twenty wage packets every week,' he explained. 'Or else, you can invent one person, pay out nineteen wage packets, and keep the other one for yourself. That man is called a 'die man'.

'If you invent one, why not invent five or ten? One problem they have is that they must sign a receipt. Since most of them are illiterate, they do not sign, they press their right thumb on an inky stamp-pad, and then put their thumbprint on the wage sheet. So what does the supervisor do? He uses his left thumbprint for the die man. Then for the next die man, he uses his right big toe, then his left big toe.

'Last week I find a man using another part of his body for another die man.'

I laughed. 'But why do they call them "die men"?' I asked.

'When the auditors visit a project or department on payday, they insist to see everyone on the pay roll,' he explained. 'Every time they shout out a name and nobody comes forward, the foreman says in a mournful voice "He done die."'

He drank half his glass of beer, then stared at the table. He continued in a different voice, flat, depressed. 'Maybe two-thirds the workers are die men. The World Health Organization, and the donor governments and the World Bank forced the Ministry to employ me to find the die men, and to cut the staff by half. Of course, nobody in the Ministry helps me, because everybody in the Ministry gets a small part of each die man's salary. Most of the money goes to the Minister and the Permanent Secretary and nobody dares annoy them.

'When I leave next month, after one year's work, I will have cut the Ministry staff by one-tenth. I will tell everyone that it is a great success. The World Health Organization, the donors, the World Bank, even the Minister, will say it is a great success. I know, though, that the saving does not cover my salary. Anyway, everybody knows that they have already been replaced by new die men in new projects anyway.'

'A lot of them do exist, even if you never see them, they do of course,' said Brendan. 'They are the Permanent Secretary's nephews and cousins, the Minister's constituents, the Director's wife's relations. They all have to be employed, now.

'They exist, but there is nothing useful for them to do. The Ministry doesn't have paper, it doesn't have diesel, and it doesn't have cars. In fact, it has ceased to operate.

'When I arrived and set up my project, the Ministry wished 140 of these people on me. I had nothing for them to do, nothing at all, and the last thing I wanted was people sitting around my office doing nothing. Just to pass the time, wouldn't they be thinking of ways to steal from the project? So I picked out ten of the liveliest of them to work with me. Then I found a large empty building on the other side of the Ministry compound, filled it with chairs, and told the others to report for duty there. They are as happy as Larry being paid to sit and gossip all day. And the auditors are quite happy that they do exist and are being paid.'

And a deeply cynical me says that it is all the fault of foreign aid. In colonial days, the administrators wanted to pay themselves well. They were paid from local taxes, with nothing coming from Britain, and, of course, there was no international aid in those days. They could not just increase taxes to pay themselves more: there was an obvious limit to the amount of taxation the country could stand. If they wanted to pay themselves well, they had to keep the civil service as small as possible. If they had doubled the number of civil servants, they would have to halve their salaries. They only employed staff when it was necessary to do the job. Five hundred Brits ran India.

With independence this changed. The new governments guaranteed jobs for any graduate. They desperately needed them for the first five years, because the colonial powers had not trained enough people. After that, though, they had far more than they needed. However, it was politically impossible to stop this guarantee. Today for instance, Egypt is trying to get rid of 10,000 surplus graduate civil servants by giving them an acre of land each, and letting them be peasant farmers. At least as peasants they would be contributing something, however small, to the economy, instead of being a drain on it.

Aid made things worse. Every time a new project came, it employed new staff with aid money, or made Government provide staff as a condition of getting the money. At the end of the project, after two or three years, the aid money stopped. The Government still had to employ the people and pay their salaries, though.

Since the Government was getting the same income in taxes, and had to pay a lot more people, salaries dropped sharply. This is really when corruption started: the well-paid colonial civil servants had been honest, as they had too much to lose if they were caught stealing.

'There is another kind of "die man" boyo,' came the deep Welsh voice of Owen Veterinary. 'I was up in Makeni four months ago, before the rains, and the drivers outside the project headquarters asked me to take their photos, standing next to the cars they drove. Proud, they were, just as if they had bought the cars themselves. I did, of course, and I took the film back here to develop. Well I did not go there again until last week, and I took the photos with me. I gave out five pictures to the drivers who were there, and I asked where the other three drivers were. I got the reply: "They done die. Malaria."'

There was a silence as we took this in. I looked down at my plate and concentrated on my food. Three men out of eight in four months: that is a massacre.

★

Boss Seaga caught me at the bar on my way out. I do not know if I am a sympathetic listener, or if I just do not move out of his reach as fast as the others.

'Mr Peter,' he said, 'this country is getting too dangerous for Lebanese. The blacks all think that we are millionaires buying diamonds and stealing everything from this country. It is the new Lebanese who are doing it. I was born in this country, and my children were, but I am planning to get out. The problem is a passport for me. My wife is all right, she is Yugoslavian, and she has registered the children as Yugoslavian. My eldest son is just 18, and he is going to Yugoslavia next month to do his national service, then he will have a proper nationality and passport, and will be able to live in Europe. Of course, because he was raised here, he is a good swimmer and scuba diver, so he wants to be a diver in the navy for his national service. They will not have him in the navy, because his name does not end in —vitch, so he will be a private in the army.'

I wondered how a Sierra Leonean Lebanese would have met a Yugoslavian, let alone marry her, but it turns out that they are fellow Muslims — she comes from a Muslim area of Yugoslavia called Bosnia. Well, I wish him luck. Everyone in Sierra Leone wishes they had a similar safe haven in Europe, for when things blow up here.

I borrowed a book to read before I went to bed, If This is a Man by Primo Levi, an Italian Jew who survived Auschwitz. He is quite straight about it: the people who survived longest were the people who stole food from their companions, the people who stole goods and traded them for food, and the successful traders. Those who acted for the community, those who believed in fair shares, were the ones who weakened and were sent to the gas chambers first.

There comes a level of deprivation, of danger, when duty towards the large group is no longer a survival strategy. It may be replaced by a duty to the small group, to the extended family, to the nuclear family, or to oneself. This is only when the social structure breaks down completely — think of the social structure that got a million men to go over the top at the Battle of the Somme. Think of the Buffs taking 90 per cent casualties one day, and going over again next morning.

Many people in Sierra Leone today must have much the same belief in their life expectancy as people did when they entered Auschwitz. If they do not steal, they or their children will certainly die. Stealing from foreigners, aid organizations, Government or strangers is no sin.

And I was getting so twitchy about having to be constantly on the alert in case people cheat me!

How Much Food is There?

Well, I have been here for a month now, and what have I achieved? I have seen everybody I should have except the Agricultural Marketing Board people. I have travelled up-country. I have collected all the statistics and reports. In some countries, this would mean that I had done enough to sit down and start doing some serious analysis of the food market. Here, the more I learn, the more I realize that nobody knows anything.

For instance, the quantity of rice supplied is the key to my whole job here, but there are no hard facts at all on how much is produced. The meeting I attended on production surveys showed that two apparently identical scientific surveys disagreed by 80 per cent on the area under rice and by 60 per cent on the yield.

Similarly, on the demand side we have no idea at all of how much rice the average person eats. The high estimate is nearly three times the low estimate.* There are no hard facts to support any of the high estimates (which is not to say that they are wrong). The low estimate is based on the latest nutrition survey (Table 1) and it can be argued that consumption has fallen in the last few years. But I also have to allow for error: if you think of the practical difficulties of measuring what an illiterate population of rural farmers

---

* Some people say that Sierra Leone is a nation of rice eaters, of people who say that they have had nothing to eat if they eat cassava or bread instead of rice with their meal. They think that the average rice consumption is 0.75 kg (1.65 lb) per head per day, or 273 kg per year. However, they cannot produce any evidence at all for that estimate. Some people think that it is nearer 0.5 kg (1.1 lb) per day, much the same as in parts of India and Bangladesh, but this is a guess, based on international comparisons. One nutrition survey (Table 1) put it at under 0.3 kg (0.66 lb) per adult, not per head, but they emphasize that other starches and the oil in the food brings up total calories to 2,000 per day. I am inclined to believe this, not just because it is based on a serious study, but because the total calories and the high level of oil consumption seem to be realistic. With the medium guess at rice consumption, (0.5 kg) adult consumption would be over 3,000 calories a day and there would be a lot of fat people around: there are none. With the high estimate (0.75 kg per day) adult consumption would be nearly 4,000 calories per day and obesity would be the killer, not malnutrition.

TABLE 1 Mean annual consumption, all households, by commodity group, in selected rural regions, Sierra Leone, 1976

Item	kg/year	g/day	oz/day	calories/day	% of calories
Cereals	120	370	13.05	1223	56
Rice (milled)	115	315	11.11	1059	48
Other cereals	20	55	1.93	164	8
Roots and tubers	56	153	5.41	182	8
Cassava	50	137	4.83	150	7
Cassava products	5	14	0.48	30	1
Yam and other roots	1	3	0.10	2	0
Oils and fats	16	52	1.84	460	21
Palm oil	12	33	1.16	290	13
Other oils and fats	7	19	0.68	169	8
Fruits and vegetables	20	55	1.93	14	1
Fruit	5	14	0.48	4	0
Vegetables	15	41	1.45	9	0
Nuts, pulses and oil seeds	15	41	1.45	142	7
Sugars and honey	0	0	0.00	0	0
Meat and offal	2	5	0.19	8	0
Eggs	0	0	0.00	0	0
Fish and seafood	62	170	5.99	127	6
Milk	1	3	0.10	1	0
Spices	1	3	0.10	5	0
Alcoholic beverages	18	49	1.74	21	1
Grand total	329	901	31.79	2184	100

Source: Smith et al., 'Household Food Consumption in Rural Sierra Leone', Michigan State University Rural Development Series, Working Paper no. 7, 1979. Calculations of calories have been added.

eats, you recognize that even if the researchers had had unlimited time and money, they could not have been accurate. What if they had overstated consumption by, say, 15 per cent?

The FAO Balance Sheet (the guestimate that Batangas was working on) produces rather different figures, partly because it covers both rural and urban areas (Table 2). It is difficult to say what it is based on: probably figures invented by junior economists in the

TABLE 2 FAO Food Balance Sheet data, Sierra Leone, average 1979–81

Item	kg/year	g/day	oz/day	calories/day	% of calories
Cereals	118	323	11.40	1050	53
Rice (milled)	100	274	9.66	921	46
Wheat	7	20	0.71	45	2
Maize	4	10	0.35	43	2
Millet and sorghum	5	14	0.49	26	1
Other grains	2	5	0.19	15	1
Roots and tubers	36	98	3.45	130	7
Cassava	27	74	2.62	105	5
Sweet potato	3	9	0.33	14	1
Cocoyam	5	14	0.50	12	1
Oils and fats	16	43	1.51	405	20
Palm oil	13	36	1.27	339	17
Other vegetable oil	2	6	0.22	47	2
Animal oil and fats	0	1	0.02	20	1
Fruits and vegetables	75	205	7.24	67	3
Fruit	33	91	3.20	42	2
Vegetables	42	115	4.04	25	1
Nuts, pulses and oil seeds	12	33	1.16	133	7
Sugars and honey	7	20	0.70	75	4
Meat and offal	6	16	0.58	21	1
Eggs	1	2	0.08	4	0
Fish and seafood	19	51	1.79	41	2
Milk	14	39	1.37	14	1
Spices	1	2	0.07	8	0
Alcoholic beverages	43	118	4.16	47	2
Grand total	347	950	33.50	1997	100

Source: FAO, Standardized Food Balance Sheet, Sierra Leone, Average 1979–81, 6 May 1983.

Ministry of Agriculture. (As is often the case with essential information in Third World countries, the original documents of these studies cannot be found in the country – presumably they were stolen
by some visiting academic or consultant – and I have to rely on
tables quoted by someone else.) However, both studies come up
with an average consumption per head of about 2,000 calories, half

of them from rice. The FAO figures are also for the years of the coffee and cocoa boom, so today's figure would be lower.

This matters. If the low estimate is right, half of present consumption is imported, an unusually high proportion for any country. If the Government were suddenly unable to import, because of lack of foreign exchange or high world prices for instance, then a lot of people would die. If, however, the high estimate is right, then only 15 per cent is imported. In that case a reduction in the amount imported would not be nearly so serious.

But then, we do not know how much is imported and exported. The official statistics say that 160,000 tonnes was imported and none exported. There is also the myth that only half this amount is actually unloaded from the ship, while the other half is sold at the next port of call. There is the other myth, too, that while 160,000 tonnes is imported, up to the same amount is promptly smuggled to Liberia and Guinea.

The only possible check on these myths is to ask whether they describe people acting rationally. Do they? The myth of rice being left on the ship describes people acting rationally to maximize their income, so I have to take it as a strong probability. The myth of smuggling also appears at first sight to describe people acting rationally, if immorally, buying heavily subsidized rice and selling it in Guinea or Liberia at the world price. But can they sell it at the world price there? They cannot if the prices there are subsidized like ours. I do know, though, that these countries are pretty well self-sufficient, so they would not be able to use this amount of imported rice. It does not make sense to take it 200 miles on jungle roads to Monrovia, and then to load it on a ship and pay transport to somewhere you can sell it at the world market price. The costs would be prohibitive. Is it physically possible for that matter? To take 160,000 tonnes on 5- or 10-tonne lorries means 16,000 to 32,000 lorry loads (there are not many big lorries here). That is about 440 lorries a day on the main road. Somebody would have noticed. In fact, I would certainly have noticed when I went up-country. No, I am deeply suspicious of this myth.

To work out the economics of smuggling, I have to know transport costs. In fact, to work out why Japanese aid rice is on sale up-country, I have to know transport costs. I spent a frustrating morning trying to get transport costs for rice from the Ministry of Transport, the Ministry of Agriculture and the Ministry of Commerce. I complained to Mohammed as he drove me to the Casablanca for lunch. When he picked me up after lunch, he had all the prices.

'It is easy, Sah,' he explained proudly, 'I used to be a lorry driver, then a taxi driver before I join the World Bank. I went to the lorry market near Kissy. It is where the lorry drivers go and wait for business. If anybody want to send things up-country, to Sefadu perhaps, they go there and find a lorry that wants to go to that place. Then they bargain for the right price.

'So I went there, and spoke to three, four drivers going to each place, and I got the prices.

'These are the prices for today. The prices change all the time. When diesel is expensive, or when there is no diesel in the garages, then prices are high. When there is a lot of business, then prices are high.'

Thanks to Mohammed, I have some hard, reliable facts, on one topic anyway, even if they are only valid for today.

I do know something else though: that however much rice was grown in the past, there will be a lot less this year, because people are planting less, and they are not using fertilizer. I know, too, that there is little of the usual reserve food supply, cassava, because it was eaten in the last two years. This means that I know that the country is on a knife edge. While there is enough food for most of the population to survive on today, even a small reduction in supply would be serious.

Two other things I know. First, that politicians, and presumably other powerful people, get a lot of money and power from their control of the rice trade. Second, there is a new president, General Momoh, who does not seem to be as competent or as firmly in control as the old one, Siaka Stevens.

I have a nasty feeling that I have a lot more on my hands than a straightforward price policy study.

The World Bank Reform

An alarming development. When I went into the office this morning, I found a four-page, duplicated set of minutes on my desk with 'Is this of interest to you?' scribbled on the front by Foday, the Director of Planning. It was the minutes of a meeting on rice imports, between the Ministry of Commerce and a World Bank Economic Reform Team, headed by Murat. They have signed an agreement, which goes as follows:

- Government is to get $5 million from the World Bank, to be disbursed through the Ministry of Commerce.
- Government agrees 'that the rice price will be market determined and market prices will govern the sale of rice imported by the private sector as from 1st January.' [That is to say, all subsidies will stop in less than three months.]
- Government will only import rice for distribution to public servants and institutions. Government imports of rice will not exceed 20,000 tons a year. [They now import 160,000 tons, nearly half the rice consumption of the country as a whole.]
- All other rice imports will be done by the private sector.
- 'Government will finance the Agricultural Marketing Board to maintain any strategic stock, but this must not exceed 20,000 tonnes.' [This is about three weeks' supply for the country as a whole.]

These terse minutes set out a major change in national food policy. I rushed into Foday, and asked him what it was all about. He sat behind his desk, large and solid. He waved me to sit down, and finished what he was writing in a file. He closed the file and turned to me. I asked again what it was all about. He had no idea. He had not been invited to the meeting, and had only been sent the minutes as a courtesy by the Ministry of Commerce. He shrugged dismissively.

'I did not read it, because rice imports are not in this Ministry's remit. It would cause problems, also political problems, if I got involved. No, I just saw that it was about rice marketing and thought you might be interested.' He turned back to the file on his desk.

I went back to my office to work out the implications of the change. First, it meant that there will be no rice subsidy in future. All rice will be imported at the world price. This seems to be designed to reverse Government's policy of importing and selling below cost, which is a sort of 'bread and circuses' policy – keep the urban mob happy and damn the farmers.

The minutes do not say whether anyone had asked what effect this would have on consumer prices, but to me it is obvious. Prices will certainly be much higher than they are today. The rice on sale in the markets today was ordered when it was 7 leones = $1. Since Government floated the currency earlier this year, leaving it to the market to set its own level, it has fallen to 42 leones = $1 today (There has been another fall in the last few days.) This means that the free market price *ex ship* of any new rice imports will be at least six times the old price. In fact, if you allow for the fact that there will no longer be a subsidy, the new consumer price will be about ten times the old – and remember that incomes have not gone up in the meanwhile.

But the price will not be worked out in this way, on import costs, once the private sector is involved. It will be set by supply and demand. If they decide to import only a small amount, the price could go higher than this. They will certainly not import so much that the price drops below this price.

First question: who in Sierra Leone can afford to buy at these prices? Answer: hardly anyone. Even today, the typists in the office are so badly fed that they fall asleep over their typewriters. Amanda's slimness is not due to the latest faddy diet. Thomas is only just surviving at today's prices in spite of the fact that he sometimes gets his civil service rice ration. His father is not: he has to beg rice from his MP to stay alive. If the rice price goes up tenfold, some of these typists, economists and messengers, and their families, will die.

Second question: what on earth does the World Bank think it is going to achieve by this? Answer: God knows. It has not done any analysis and there are no stated objectives. It seems to be motivated by a dogmatic belief that the Free Market will solve all the world's problems.

Third question: why did Government agree to such an extraordinary proposal, one that seems to have been sprung on them out of the blue? Answer: this is an easy one. The World Bank had them over a barrel. Even today, Sierra Leone cannot pay the interest on its loans; it cannot pay its civil servants' wages; it cannot import the fuel or fertilizer it needs. If the International Monetary Fund and the World Bank put on any sort of pressure at all, things will suddenly get dramatically worse.

The threat is not an empty one. Everyone here is painfully aware of what happened in Ghana three years ago in 1983. The country had just had three years' drought, so the farmers were no longer producing enough food. The drought also cut production of their main export crop, cocoa. Then the forest dried out so much that it caught fire, destroying cocoa trees and timber, which reduced their possible exports still more.

The drought also meant that there was not much water in the Volta dam, so hydroelectric power production fell, and they had to cut their aluminium exports.

The fall in exports came at exactly the same time as the country needed more export revenue to import more oil and more food. Then came the final blow: Nigeria deported a million Ghanaian workers, and suddenly Ghana had to feed 10 per cent more people when it had perhaps 30 per cent less food than normal.

There were a few pockets of famine, well away from the world's television cameras. Mainly, though, the deaths were invisible. More children died from childhood diseases, fewer people survived their annual bout of malaria, and the old died early.

Schools and universities were closed and students were sent home so that their parents would feed them. The teachers and university staff were then able to spend all their time scavenging for food. The situation was desperate. The donors had Ghana by the balls. They squeezed. They halved their aid over the three years of drought.

The Government had no escape. They had to go to the International Monetary Fund in abject surrender, and accept the whole International Monetary Fund package – including all the provisions that every other country in the world had rejected as being far too onerous.

Everybody in Government and in the aid organizations is well aware that it could happen here. Everyone is aware that Sierra Leone has a much weaker economy than Ghana, one which could not survive any pressure. I, at least, am aware that food supply here is on a knife edge.

What really surprises me is that Murat and his World Bank team did not consult me, even though he knows that I am working on food policy. Nor did he give me any indication that this was in the air. Nor did he consult Foday. Nor did he consult the World Food Programme, in the shape of Brendan, or at least Brendan has not mentioned it if he did.

The Agreement is not based on any economic analysis that I have come across, and I have trawled the World Bank offices, the ministries, the projects and the aid organizations for any analysis, reports or statistics on food.

I went to Murat's office to discuss the Agreement. I knew it was going to be a difficult meeting, and I would have to handle it carefully. I could not barge in and ask him what the hell he thought he was doing. Instead, I went in as a seeker after enlightenment.

He was delighted with himself. He boasted that he had pulled off a major victory. He had got the country to adopt a Free Market system for rice, exactly what the World Bank policy demanded.

I tried to draw him out on this, but he made it quite clear that he was only interested in the workings of the economy at the broadest possible level. He knows nothing and cares nothing about agricultural policy and food policy, but believes that the Free Market would solve everything. He could not understand what I was asking or why.

He had got the idea clear in his head that an overvalued currency subsidizes imports, but he had not realized the corollary, that an undervalued currency taxes imports. Or perhaps he had, but he did not realize that the currency was undervalued: after all, the Free Market determines the exchange rate. I did not even try to explain to him that normally we are talking of the money market setting an exchange rate which balances imports and exports. Here the market is setting a rate that measures only how frightened businessmen are, and how desperate they are to get their money out of here and into a Swiss bank.

Murat was convinced that his victory would result in Sierra Leone achieving a perfect food policy. Rice prices would be high, so farmers would plant more rice and, as a result, the country would produce all it needed, and even export some.

As he explained his grand vision, I could see his namesake, sword in hand, exhorting Napoleon's cavalry to follow him in the charge at Waterloo.

Well, it would be wonderful if the policy achieved this, a safe food supply. The only question is how we get from the present disastrous situation to this fairyland scenario. This is the enormously difficult question that I have been engrossed in since I came here. I used all my interviewing skills in turn to try to get Murat to expand on this. I even asked him point blank. He could not understand the question: he had got the Government to sign the Agreement, so everything was under control.

I asked him what the import price would be under the Agreement, and what effect it would have on the cost of living. He had no idea: he had not given it any thought, and when I raised the question, he was clearly not interested. This when even the thickest skinned World Bank official must have noticed that there are always food riots when you double food prices overnight. No wonder there has been a trail of starvation following the World Bank and the International Monetary Fund reforms through Africa.

I tried to find out how he thought Sierra Leone was going to feed itself between the time the food prices rose and the time the increased output hit the market. He had not noticed that there might be a gap between the two. I asked specific questions:

- 'How many months of high prices would there be before farmers began to believe that high prices were here to stay, and decided that it was safe to increase plantings?'
- 'Why would farmers believe that Government would let prices stay high, and would not bring in subsidies again as soon as

there were riots? Government had done just this four years ago when rice prices had risen suddenly after a devaluation.'

- 'How would farmers get the capital to clear new land, buy high-yielding seeds and buy fertilizer?'
- 'How many months or years would it take farmers to clear new fields from the jungle, or build paddy fields in the swamps?'
- 'Once the farmers had finally decided to grow more, and then had made all their preparations, how many months would it be before the next planting season?'
- 'How long would it take the State Seed Corporation to increase production of improved, high-yielding seeds from the present low levels?' (There would be no chance at all of the increase required without improved seeds.)
- 'How long would it be before the crop was harvested and put on the market?'

He had given no thought to any of these questions, and I was about to suggest that it would be wildly optimistic to expect any increase at all in production for at least eighteen months, when he suddenly exploded.

'This is World Bank policy. You are employed by the World Bank. You follow World Bank policy, or you get out and work somewhere else!'

I tried to calm him down, to bring down the temperature before I left the room. I do not think I succeeded.

The shit has hit the fan.

★

I am furious. I am furious that they should have taken such an action without any thought. I am furious that Murat should have refused to consider my worries. I am furious that he should treat me like his personal employee and order me to toe the World Bank line. I am not his employee or the World Bank's. I am employed by Sierra Leone and owe my allegiance to its government and its people, especially its people. The World Bank may have given the Government the dollars to pay me, but I have no contract with them.

I am not in a position to tell him this, or even to argue any further with him. If I did, he would put me on the next plane out of the country, telling the Government that I was incompetent. He would also make sure that I did not work for the World Bank again. Somehow, I am going to have to work round him.

This Agreement cannot have been all Murat's own work. Surely, the Economic Reform Team which had come from Washington and which was in the meeting with him must have drawn it up? Surely there must have been some people on the team who would know that you cannot double rice production overnight, that it takes at least four months to grow a rice crop?

Surely, too, they would have acted cautiously, when they know that most of the world's economists disagree with them, and want the prices of staple foods decoupled from world prices. Even those like me, who would like prices to be broadly in line with world prices, have several provisos. For example, a *realistic* exchange rate must be used. The *average* prices over three or four years must be used, not a price that varies from day to day on the world markets – only a dozen years ago the world rice price jumped from $300 a tonne to $900 a tonne in a couple of months. In addition, of course, food security must be preserved, which usually means that the Government controls food security stocks, even if the normal trade is privatized.

Economists in rice-eating countries are particularly cautious about this, because rice prices on the world market are particularly unstable. In most countries where rice is the staple food, the countries produce solely for their own needs, and only a little is grown for export, so in most years only 3 per cent of world production is sold on the world market. This means that if China, Bangladesh or Indonesia has a poor crop and they try to buy rice on the world market, the demand in that market doubles, trebles or quadruples. In 1974, the price shot up to six and a half times today's price. If this were to happen today, the Sierra Leone Government could not afford to import – subsidy or no subsidy, realistic or unrealistic exchange rate. People would die.

I have just plotted the rice prices for the last thirty years or so on a graph, and have found that the situation is worse than I had thought. Today's world rice price is at a record low, about one-third of the post-war average in real terms, and half what it was a couple

World rice prices in constant 1980 dollars
(Thai 5% broken f.o.b. Bangkok)

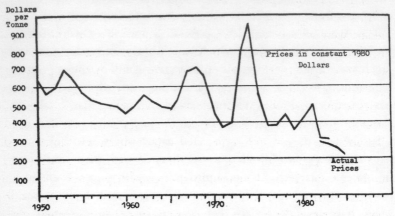

Sources: World Bank 'Commodity Trade and Price Trends'; FAO,
'Monthly Bulletin of Statistics'

of years ago. The World Bank Commodity Division in Washington is forecasting that the price will rise by a quarter in the next couple of years. Any price policy based on the fluctuations in the world market will destabilize the agricultural economy.

Worse, with a truly free market, traders would then go round the Sierra Leone farmers paying three times today's prices and buying up all rice that leaves the farm, which they would then export onto the world market, leaving nothing for the Sierra Leone urban sector. Several famines happened in this way in nineteenth-century India, because of the British Empire's free-trade dogma.

This does not mean that I am anti-free trade for cash crops like coffee and cocoa. I am all for their prices being closely linked with the world market. It is the only way that farmers will get what their crop is worth.

I went back to the hotel, then walked down the beach to Man o' War Bay, and sat under a palm tree at Alex's Beach Bar. I had a beer to try and calm myself down, then another, and another. All it did was work me up to a cold hard fury. My mind was racing as I analysed the consequences of the Agreement.

I tried to recognize the possibility that Murat and the World Bank people were well-meaning people who have made an error of judgement in this case. I know the pressures and temptations. I know that it is difficult to devise a way of getting from the present disastrous situation in much of Africa without killing a lot of people. There are times when an economist tells the Government, 'If you raise the price of grain to the farmers, certainly the immediate result will be that 200,000 more children per year will die in the city in the next two to five years. I am far less certain of the benefits, and they lie in the distant future. I believe that, after perhaps three years, the increased prices will mean a higher income in country areas so there will be, perhaps, 400,000 fewer deaths among farmers' children. I hope that in the medium to long term the increased prosperity in the countryside will spill over to the city, and child mortality will fall below today's level.

'I have very poor statistical data to back this. My economic analysis is not the sort that would be published in an academic journal. Nevertheless, I strongly recommend that you take this action.'

It is not pleasant to have to make such recommendations, but it goes with the job. I have had to make them before. I lose a lot of sleep when I do it.

Making the decision does give you a kick, though. It is a big decision, an important decision, a decision that will kill many people and save many people. It is a far more important decision than that made by almost anybody in Britain. The fact that you make the decision, on your own judgement rather than on hard fact and theory, makes you feel important, powerful. I recognize that the power is addictive.

I recognize, too, that the mind has to protect itself from insanity, and that it does so by telling me that, in spite of the chances and coincidences that put me in the job, I am the best person to do it: only my intellect, my judgement, my experience, are adequate.

Because I recognize the danger that I will become addicted to this decision, I watch out for it in myself and in others too. A lot of the World Bank economists are exposed to the same temptation, the same addiction. In fact, it may be that the organization as a whole is addicted. It does seem to go out of its way to make decisions that will cause millions of deaths or save millions of lives over the years, basing these decisions on judgements, rules of thumb, and political dogmas like the Free Market. It does seem to believe that harsh remedies are more likely to cure.

Cash Flow Problems

Several expats came into the Casablanca at lunchtime, announcing cheerfully that they had just been fired again.

They are all working on World Bank projects, and the Bank has given them notice that they are closing the projects. The Bank suspends all aid to any country that does not pay the interest on all its World Bank loans. They tell me that every three months Sierra Leone struggles to find the foreign exchange it needs to pay its interest. It never can pay in time, so the Bank suspends all its aid projects, and the staff are given three months' notice. They carry on working, knowing that the money will be found somehow. (I am OK, as my contract ends before then anyway.)

This time, so the rumour goes, not only has the Central Bank not got the $50,000 required, but also it has nothing at all in its vaults except the coloured glass marbles used in elections by people who cannot read.

$50,000 sounds small in terms of Third World debt. It turns out, though, that Sierra Leone is so poor that nobody lends to them on normal credit terms. They have a small debt acquired a dozen years ago, but since then all the money they have got from the World Bank and others is aid, not loans. The World Bank is primarily a bank, but it is a successful one, and it makes a profit. This profit is given as aid to the poorest countries. Very laudable, except that then they mess it up by holding up millions in gifts, because the country cannot raise $50,000 in readies.

'Yes, the Government is desperate for cash,' said Brendan. 'You know the stadium the Chinese built, next to the main government offices. It is just like all the other Chinese stadiums in Africa. When Chairman Mao built them, we all asked what could they be doing that for. We thought it was a monumental waste of money to put all that development money into pleasure, but it hasn't worked out that way at all.

'Every Saturday the Government has a struggle to find the money for civil service wages. How they manage is to pay people out of the gate money from the football match at the stadium. Last year, the run up to the Cup Final coincided with a time when things were very bad indeed, and they really needed the gate money. The Cup Final produced record takings, but the Government were not satisfied with that. They arranged for a riot to break out in the middle of it, and it was abandoned. The match had to be played again the next week, and they filled the stadium again at Cup Final prices.'

'It's all very well for the people in Freetown,' broke in Owen Veterinary, 'because the Government spends any money it gets right here: it never spends it up-country. I was visiting a project last week, and the staff were all on strike. The Government had not paid them for four whole months. I was well brought up, I was. Two things they taught us in the valleys. First, never spit in church, and, second, never cross a picket line. So I invited them down the road to the pub, and we did our business there.'

'It's hospitable they are,' he continued reflectively. 'That evening we were continuing our discussion in a bar where there was dancing. I was eyeing a young lady who was dancing most sensuously. Very sexy. The Agricultural Officer noticed and asked me, "Do you want to fuck her?"

'Well, I explained that I am a romantic, and I believe in true love.

'The Agricultural Officer listened attentively, then nodded. Then he lifted his head and called out "Hey girl! De whiteman wanna fuck you, but he no wanna pay you."

'She dropped her eyes demurely, then walked delicately over and sat down beside me.

'Of course, I did pay her,' he said virtuously.

The Agricultural Marketing Board

Any response to Murat must be based on hard facts, which means talking to people. Then I will have to start persuading them to act. This is dangerous. If Murat finds out that I am making waves, he will get me sacked, and sent out of the country. Also, I do not want everybody speculating on what is happening. If they do, there will be thirty different conclusions and recommendations floating around, only one of which will be mine. The politicians will accept the ones that agree with their preconceived notions. No, I must play it close to my chest, collecting all the information and analysing it secretly, so that when I come out with my conclusions and recommendations, they are the only ones around. I will do my visits without Thomas, and I will not tell Foday what I am up to. Most particularly, I will not say anything about it in the Casablanca.

Still no success at arranging an appointment with the Agricultural Marketing Board. I decided that the only thing to do now is to go there, knock on the door and ask to see the General Manager. This is the normal way of working in countries with dud telephone services. There is another advantage of not making appointments: if they do not know that you are coming, they will not arrange to be out of town when you arrive.

When I arrived at the Agricultural Marketing Board and asked to see the General Manager, the receptionist (a commissionaire actually) took my name and went up to enquire, leaving me in a small waiting room. He returned with the message, 'He cannot see you. You must write and ask for an appointment.'

This was not encouraging, as I had been doing this since I arrived. I thought that while I was there I would try and get some statistics out of them. The commissionaire made me write down what I wanted, then he took my note upstairs. I waited for an hour, then he came down with a few of the figures I asked for.

'That is all you can have.' he said abruptly. 'Now you must go. Goodbye.'

★

I cannot mess around any longer. I have to see the General Manager of the Agricultural Marketing Board and get some straight answers. He has been doing all the rice importing, and he is the only person who has the information I need.

There are all sorts of reasons why he may be avoiding me. There is the fact that I am working for the Ministry of Agriculture, rather than the Ministry of Commerce, which he is supposed to answer to. There is the hostility between these ministries. There is also the fact that most state marketing boards are terrified that a competent economist will start looking through their accounts. Or he may be afraid that he will talk too much and let me find out something I should not.

I went in to see Foday this morning and put it to him. I have asked him to arrange a meeting with the Vice President as soon as possible. He, or the President, has the job of telling ministries to cooperate.

Of Coups and Rumours of Coups

THURSDAY, 11 OCTOBER

I was woken up in the early hours of the morning by machine-gun fire. I kept my head down, below the window ledge to avoid any stray bullets. I carried out the standard procedures in the UN employees' handbook: I checked that my bedroom door was locked and chained, and I filled my bath with water, so that I would not die of thirst, whatever happened.

Nothing happened. There was no more firing. There was no roaring of engines as soldiers drove up. There was no sounding of fire alarms. I went to sleep.

Next morning nobody in the hotel had any explanation, nor did

Mohammed when he came, so I went into work as usual. Every-thing was as normal. Nobody had heard anything, but all the Sierra Leoneans lived in the north west of the city, while my hotel was in the south east.

In the Casablanca, Boss Seaga explained.

'It is just that two big diamond traders up the hill live next to each other. One is Muslim, one is Christian, but that does not matter here, because in Sierra Leone we are all Lebanese, and these two are friends. But these people get their security guards from the Lebanon, where it does matter. They started calling each other names, then they started shooting at each other. The traders are important and they have fixed it with the police. You will not hear anything more about it.'

An Italian told us that when there was a coup in Indonesia, one of his colleagues filled his bath with water, as instructed in the UN handbook, then had a bath.

Brendan looked up from his fried barracuda pikin, and assured us that if the machine-gun fire had been serious, he would have been the first to know about it.

'The UN are after making me evacuation coordinator, you see. It is a voluntary job for one of the senior expats. There is one in every country, but we try to keep it quiet. If there is a coup and it gets out of hand, I have to organize evacuation. I have a high-powered radio at home which links me to the US South Atlantic Fleet. They're the lads who will get us out, I'd say. In other countries, it may be the Brits or the Russians.

'We don't leave through the port. We leave from the beach out-side the tourist hotels, as it is far easier to reach from the areas where the Westerners live.'

The rumours of coups are passed on in the Casablanca in a low voice, but with an air of excitement. Everyone rather hopes that something will be done to topple this corrupt system and that the people responsible will get what is coming to them – assuming, of course, that any fighting will take place well away from the beach hotels, the clubs and the expat houses. Of course, nobody really expects any great improvement from a coup, but any new military government could hardly be more corrupt than the present one, and it is always possible that there will be a reformer.

I confess that I rather shared this thrill. Then, today it hit me. If there is a coup and there is a new government, it would certainly have to spend a couple of months consolidating its power before it could take any action on anything. It would be too busy even to look at food policy, and the civil servants would be too afraid of the new regime to bring the crisis to its attention. For the first few months, too, the junta would be on probation, with the World Bank and the Western governments deeply suspicious of them. They would not be able to confront the World Bank on the Agreement. Nor would foreign governments or donor agencies rush to give them food aid.

In other words, if things are as bad as I am beginning to believe, a coup means that a famine is inevitable.

How Much Rice is Imported?

Murat's argument is that removing subsidies from rice and privatizing imports will put up the price, so farmers will plant more and the country will be self-sufficient in the future. This theory contradicts the smuggling theory, but proponents of the smuggling theory will support the actions he proposes, on the grounds that they will reduce smuggling and leave consumption unchanged, saving the country a lot of money. This means I have to try and disprove both theories.

How can I possibly find out how much is consumed here? I think I can be pretty sure that not much is smuggled, because I saw a lot of imported rice in the up-country markets, because there is not a big market for the rice in Liberia or Guinea, because there is no sign of the 16,000 to 32,000 lorries carrying rice to the borders, and because, last year at least, smuggling did not seem to be particularly profitable. How on earth could I find out how much is left on the ship, though?

★

I started with Brendan, as he has been here eight years, working on rice marketing. I reasoned that he should know, if any expat does. It was difficult, though. I had to swear him to secrecy, and say that the information was vitally important, without giving him any indication of why it was important. I would not expect anybody else to respond to a request like this, but he is now a good friend.

He was still for a couple of minutes, then he spoke.

'I have never told this to anyone. I must have your promise that you will not tell anyone else, nobody at all, at all.'

I promised, taken aback that my demand for secrecy was met by his demand for secrecy.

'Obviously, it's part of my job at the World Food Programme to know how much food is coming into the country. Obviously, too, some is brought in by the Agricultural Marketing Board, some by the World Food Programme, some by countries who ask us to distribute it for them, and some by other countries like the USA, who distribute it themselves. Quite complicated, and plenty of room for error. Then, of course, I cannot rely on official statistics.' He smiled wryly.

'I worked out that there is only one way to find out how much is actually imported. I bribe the foreman of the dockers. He gives me figures of how much is actually unloaded from the ship.'

He smiled modestly, accepting my admiration for a brilliantly simple solution.

'It's very dangerous for him, it is. He'd be killed if anyone found out what he was doing. That's why you must keep it secret. Of course, I'd be shipped out of the country if they found that I had my own, accurate, import figures. I am certainly not wanting any passing consultants to know about this. I am only telling you because 'tis my belief that the food situation is pretty serious.'

His face was grave as he said this – more, I think, because he was worried about the food situation than because he had just put his informant's life at risk.

'My calculation is that, this year, one-tenth of the cargo was left in the ship on average. Two or three times, only half the cargo was unloaded, but for the last nine months it nearly all was.

'Of course, this is assuming that the foreman did not go straight to the GM and ask him what figures to give me. Sure, and you have to trust someone.'

What does this mean? My best guess now is that 144,000 tonnes were actually unloaded in the last twelve months, and a negligible amount was smuggled. Slightly less than half the rice consumed throughout the country was imported. Of course, they did not get enough to eat even with these imports: it would have been necessary to import much more than this in order to feed the population adequately.

This means that private importers will have to spend $15 million to $35 million on rice imports to keep imports at the same level as for the last twelve months. And a million pounds is an enormous sum of money in a country like this.*

I spent today trying to find out which private traders can raise this kind of money. It costs $2.4 million to import a single shipment of 10,000 tonnes of rice. There do not seem to be a lot of people who could raise that kind of money, and fewer still who could raise the money to buy seven to ten shiploads.

I started by going to Thomas's friends in the Ministry of Commerce. I was greeted warmly even though Thomas was not with me. They took me to the Chief Economist who had been so reserved when I came before. He was helpful now. Why, I could not work

---

* At the high level the private sector would be importing at least 140,000 tonnes at $250 landed, with a total cost of $35 million. At the low level, the imports would be, perhaps, 110,000 tonnes imported by private companies, with 20,000 imported by Government and 30,000 imported by donor countries as part of their aid programme (and we have no reason to be confident that they will do this next year). The private sector may also import much cheaper rice, at, say $140 per tonne. This would give a low estimate of $15.5 million. However, even if they could import at this price, they are likely to overstate the purchase price, as a way of getting the Government to let them change more leones into dollars.

out. Perhaps it was just that my questions were non-threatening now that the Agreement had taken rice importing away from them?

I started by asking them which traders had applied for import permits for rice, but they said that one of the clauses of the World Bank Agreement was that there should be no import permits. Presumably this was the free market principle, but maybe it was just so that nobody could extort a bribe for permits or refuse a permit out of sheer bloody-mindedness. The ministry economists pointed out to me, though, that even if people had applied for licences, this would be no guarantee that they would actually import the rice.

They gave me, off the record, a list of the businesspeople who might be able to produce $2 million for a shipload of rice. Then I went to Foday and got a similar list, and to Henry, thinking that as a businessman he would have a wider list of contacts. In fact, the lists overlapped, and I had only a dozen names.

Who Will Import?

FRIDAY, 12 OCTOBER

I spent today and yesterday calling on people who might be able to afford to import rice. I gave the first name to Mohammed, who, of course, knows everyone and everywhere. He drove me through anonymous streets of bazaar-like shops, open to the street. We stopped at one, and Mohammed spoke in Creole to the man behind the counter, asking if I could see the boss. I was led up a narrow flight of stairs at the back of the shop to a small, dark, cramped office, with basic furniture, which looked like the office of a small shop rather than the lair of a captain of commerce. I was amazed when it turned out to be the right place, but I found as we visited multi-millionaire after multi-millionaire that they all operated in this spartan, secluded way.

All of them were, of course, suspicious at a strange foreigner calling on them, but the moment I said that I wanted to talk about rice imports, they welcomed me warmly. Three of them actually cancelled what seemed to be important meetings in order to talk to me. They knew about the Agreement, whether because the Minister of Commerce had approached them, or because nothing can be kept secret in Freetown. All of them talked to me openly, and, I believe, honestly. Certainly, they said things that no civil servant would say. What they said was depressing, though.

About half of them were Lebanese. They said that they would not dare import rice. They said that consumer prices would certainly be much higher than today's prices under the Agreement. Everybody would blame the importers. There would certainly be food riots, and these would turn into race riots if the Lebanese were seen to be involved. It happened on a small scale during the First World War, and it was touch and go then whether they would all be lynched. They are under no illusions: the Lebanese are not popular here.

The black Sierra Leoneans also said that they were afraid of being lynched. They thought that the investment is far too risky for other reasons as well. If they were going to import rice, they would have to use a large amount of the foreign exchange that they had stashed away abroad, but then they would have to sell the rice for leones. They do not believe that the Government would let them convert the leones back into dollars – the Central Bank would reimpose exchange control – so they would be stuck with a declining currency.

Even if they were allowed to convert the money back to dollars, the exchange rate in six months' time would have moved against them, so they would not get all their money back.

Everybody said that Government could not, would not, stick to a promise to let rice sell at full market price. In the early 1980s the World Bank persuaded the Government to devalue and then let rice sell at the full market price. The result was a sharp rise in price from a heavily subsidized level. There were riots and the Government backed down. (This is yet another version of the story, but it complements the two versions given by the World Bank men and the one given by the Ministry of Commerce. Taken together, I think they give a good idea of what happened.)

In today's situation, Government will do the same, they believe. It will encourage private traders to import, according to the

Agreement, but the moment prices rise and rioting starts, they will clap a maximum price on rice, near today's subsidized prices. The traders will lose all their money.

The key worry that everyone had was that even if everything else worked, the cost of imported rice would be so high that nobody would be able to buy it. They would be left with unsaleable stocks on their hands.

I cannot fault their logic. The conclusion is terrifying. The private sector will not import. The Agricultural Marketing Board is only allowed to import enough for public employees, about 6 per cent of the country's needs. Result: the country will have half the rice it needs. The impact will not be evenly spread through the country, so that everyone suffers a bit. No, the farmers will hang on to any food they have, and Freetown, the towns and the diamond diggings will have no rice at all, and little other food. People will die.

I went into the office to see Thomas. He is working hard on the survey of retailers, which gives me a good excuse for not taking him on these interviews. I have also asked him to dig up some statistics for me, to keep him busy. I am playing my cards close to the chest on this one.

Foday saw me and called me into his office. He was delighted with himself. He had not known the procedure for asking the Vice President to knock heads together and get the General Manager of the Agricultural Marketing Board to see me, so last night he had called on his cousin who works in the Vice President's office to ask him. This morning his cousin sent a message to say that an appointment had been arranged for me to see the General Manager this afternoon. All it had taken was a simple phone call from the Vice President's office (and if the Vice President's telephone does not work, whose does?). Foday did not even know if the Vice President had been consulted. He was proud of his important cousin, and his ability to pull strings.

★

At the Agricultural Marketing Board offices in the docks, the General Manager was charm itself. He came down to reception, greeted me warmly, and took me up to his enormous office overlooking the harbour. I wondered how this could be happening, when he had fobbed me off again and again, and had only spoken to me under duress. Strange, but I would use his helpfulness while it lasted.

He said that the Agricultural Marketing Board wanted to hand over rice marketing to someone else. It would rather concentrate on its main job, marketing coffee and cocoa. The rice subsidy does not come from the Ministry of Finance – it should, but the Ministry never has the money to pay it – so the Board has to take the subsidy from the money it should be paying farmers. (This is another hidden export tax on the farmers, one which I had not known about.) The drop in the real price paid to farmers means that coffee and cocoa production is falling.

I probed a bit, and was told only slightly elliptically that the rice business is highly political, and that he could do without the constant political scrutiny. He did not come straight out and say that he was powerful and popular when he was importing rice that was heavily subsidized by the exchange rate, but that he would be extremely unpopular with everyone if he still had the rice monopoly next year, when the undervalued exchange rate pushed up prices to astronomical levels.

I asked him about the mechanics of rice importing. I took him step by step through the process, starting with placing the order, and ending with sale to the retailer. This is a powerful interviewing technique, but it does place demands on the person interviewed. I wondered again why he was so cooperative. But he was. He sat there, plump and prosperous, with a large gold ring on each finger (but no diamond) smiling at me, explaining the detail.

He said that since it was now mid-October, he would normally be in the process of buying rice for next year, but everything was halted because of the World Bank Agreement. His first task is always to arrange finance, which takes time, even though he already has the foreign exchange earnings from coffee and cocoa exports sitting in a London bank. Obviously, it will take the private-sector importers longer, as they have to assemble the money first, and they are not creditworthy abroad. Then he has to negotiate his purchase on the world markets, telexing London, Rotterdam, Bangkok, and so on. It takes him another two weeks to arrange a letter of credit. Say a month to the end of this stage.

He has to allow time for the Thais to bag the rice and load the bags onto the ship. It would be much quicker and easier for them to load it in bulk, but Freetown has no bulk unloading facilities, so dockers would have to go down into the hold, fill the bags using shovels, and then carry the bags ashore, which would take three weeks longer.

It then takes six weeks for the boat to come from Bangkok to Freetown. That makes at least thirteen weeks in all. If the private sector traders start ordering today – and they have said that they do not intend to do so – there will be no rice deliveries until the end of January.

I asked him what supplies were like from now until then. He said that the Agricultural Marketing Board still has a couple of shiploads due from last year's contract, enough to see the country through to the end of January. After that, nothing: he is not allowed to import.

I wondered if he was being excessively alarmist, in an attempt to persuade me (who he must have thought of as a World Bank employee) that the Agreement should be scrapped. The process he was describing seemed to be unnecessarily long. I challenged him on this, and he agreed that it was possible to cut the timings considerably if you have the cash available now, if you make all decisions immediately, and if you buy the first rice offered, regardless of price. In an emergency, you could also cut the time by getting rice shipped from Rotterdam or the USA instead of bringing it all the way from the Far East. This would cut the time to eight to twelve weeks, but it obviously puts up the price alarmingly.

I did not get the impression that he was making excuses for overstating the time before delivery. Instead, he gave the impression of being someone who knew everything there was to know about import, export and shipping, and who had considered all the options carefully. He was running through his conclusions rather than thinking aloud.

Sierra Leone is near the main shipping route from the Far East to Europe and I asked him why he could not get one of the rice ships to divert. He agreed that this was possible as an emergency measure. It is expensive, though. You have to find a ship that is carrying bagged rice rather than bulk, and rice that is cheap – not Basmati rice destined for European gourmets, for example. Then you must pay the shipping company a premium for upsetting their schedule. The commodity brokers know that you are desperate and they push up their prices accordingly. The result may be that the rice costs twice as much as usual.

I asked him about the 20,000 tonnes that the World Bank will let him import and store. He said that this is earmarked for government rations, and goes to the army, the police force, the civil service, the hospitals, the schools, the universities and the prisons (in that order, I gather). Government considers this to be a top priority, for obvious reasons, and he cannot imagine them letting him divert it to other uses – not even to feed the starving – unless he is actually unloading more rice from another ship.

Next, I asked for the figures on how much he had in stock, how much he was selling each month, and when he would run out of rice. He clammed up completely, and flatly refused to give me the information. Oh well, he gave me enough to be going on with.

But do I believe him? I think so: everything he told me seemed to hang together. Was he overstating the time it would take to bring in new rice? Maybe, maybe not. I have to work on the assumption that he was telling me the truth. What really worries me is the possibility that he was understating the time it takes to buy rice. If he was, there will certainly be a month or two with no rice on the market.

★

After the meeting, I got in the car and Mohammed drove off. We went through the Agricultural Marketing Board gates following a lorry loaded with sacks of imported rice. The sacks were piled ten high, with two workers sitting on top of the sacks. We travelled slowly, as the street was narrow and crowded. The lorry pulled out to pass an empty lorry at the side of the road and stopped at some obstruction. The workers on top jumped into life. Each grabbed one end of a sack of rice, and they swung it onto the empty lorry. Then another and another. There must have been ten sacks over the side in the thirty seconds the lorry was stopped.

★

I have just been trying to work out what the World Bank Agreement means in terms of storage. There will have to be a lot more grain stores built. These were not necessary in the past, because the Agricultural Marketing Board knew that there would be a ship arriving every three weeks, so it only needed to have enough in store to last three weeks, with a bit extra just in case. In the future, when imports are left to the private sector, there will not be the same regular, reliable supply. If nothing arrives – and the traders have said that they will not import – then, to be safe, Government should have enough strategic reserve to feed the country for the four months until a new shipload can be bought. How much will be needed? Say 45,000 to 60,000 tonnes (and this means that Government handles the import of the strategic reserve: they cannot gamble on the private traders deciding to import it). Even if the traders do decide to import normal supplies, there will not be a regular supply. There may be no ships arriving for several months, then four or five ships may arrive at the same time. For example, all the traders may delay their imports until August, because that is when retail prices are usually at their highest. Each importer will be delaying, hoping that the others do not, then suddenly four or five shiploads arrive without warning. If this happens, there could suddenly be a need for another 50,000 tonnes storage for trading stocks, in the months before August, in addition to the strategic stocks.

This means that the Government needs to hold a minimum of 45,000 tonnes in the strategic reserve, in case the traders delay imports or do not import at all. However, under the Agreement they cannot do this. The Agricultural Marketing Board is only allowed to keep 20,000 tonnes, maximum – 6 per cent of national consumption – and this is not a strategic reserve at all, just backup for civil service rations. God knows how Murat arrived at this figure. Just for the record, Kenya has one year's supply in its strategic reserve, as well as the normal trading stocks. This may be a bit excessive, but they can boast that they are the only country in Northeast Africa that has never lost a life through famine.

Also, Murat's arithmetic is wrong. The Agricultural Marketing Board will have nothing in stock at the end of January, I think. It is only allowed to import 20,000 tonnes a year, all for the public sector. How can they ever build up and maintain a strategic stock of 20,000 tonnes?

Where are they going to store it all? Apart from the Agricultural Marketing Board's own rice stores, the only weatherproof, ratproof stores in the country are the Agricultural Marketing Board's coffee and cocoa stores. The General Manager told me that he will not let anyone put rice in these, because the weevils would infest the stores and gorge themselves on the next coffee and cocoa crop.

Other than this, there are only the stores used by shopkeepers, merchants, and so forth. Often these are only tiny corrugated iron sheds, and anyway they are already fully utilized for normal trade.

The quality of the stores is also important. With good, purpose-built stores, there is almost nothing wasted – less than 2 per cent. With bad stores, the wastage will be phenomenal, because of leaky roofs, cracked or dirty floors, insect infestation and rats. There is high wastage in stores like this even when the rice is kept in its protective husk, but imports are all of milled rice, with no protection, so there could easily be losses of more than a quarter.

Rats pose a special problem in West Africa. They piss on the rice and spread a particularly nasty disease, Lassa fever, which is almost always fatal.

With any stores outside the Agricultural Marketing Board compound, there is going to be a major security problem, particularly when prices rise and there are food riots. If Government builds enormous new stores, they will be fully used for a few months of the year and empty the rest of the time. That is the optimistic view; the pessimistic view is that traders will not import and the stores will not be used at all. The cost per tonne stored per day will be enormous, probably enough to counter all the theoretical gains from privatizing.

At first sight, outdoor storage is a possibility. In Central Africa, they pile maize bags 40 feet high on concrete hard-standings, and cover them with enormous tarpaulins. They can and do store millions of bags in this way, quite satisfactorily. However, this method will not work here. First, the humidity here is 100 per cent, compared with perhaps 15 per cent in Central Africa, so moulds and rots will run through the grain. Second, in Central Africa, they store maize with its protective hull still on, and we would be storing milled rice, with nothing to protect it from insects or animals.

★

I went to Brendan's office, and asked him about the storage. Were the Agricultural Marketing Board's figures correct? Again, I was cagey, not saying why I needed the information.

He gave me a quick rundown of the stores and their location. He has to use Agricultural Marketing Board stores when his rice is unloaded in the docks, and he uses their stores up-country when he is distributing it. He has inspected them all. We spent half an hour going through the figures. Yes, the Agricultural Marketing Board figures were correct in one sense: they did have 30,000 tonnes capacity. However, most of the stores are up-country, where they were built by the now-defunct Rice Corporation in the producing area, to store rice bought from farms. They are in quite the wrong place to store imported rice destined for Freetown. There has been no maintenance for several years, and many of them are no longer fit to store rice in, so there is less storage available than there was in past years. In fact, there is barely enough adequate storage for 20,000 tonnes. Three to five times as much is needed.

How Do I Get Action?

I have now collected enough evidence to know that famine is inevitable unless the Agreement is scrapped. I have to get action somehow.

The first step is to assemble the evidence and analyse it, just to check that I am right. I then have to present it in such a way that politicians and civil servants will be convinced that something needs to be done, and that they will do it. This means that I cannot present a normal consultancy report, which would put everything in the context of food and agricultural policy and exchange-rate policy. Instead, I have to keep the message as stark and simple as possible: Government must import food and provide it at a price people can pay, or a lot of people will die.

I am furious that I have been bumped into recommending this policy. Because of the World Bank, it is now absolutely necessary to do this in the short run, but it is exactly the opposite of the medium- to long-term policy I was aiming for. I wanted the country to move towards having a prosperous agriculture, meeting all its food needs without imports. So did the World Bank, but their half-baked inter- ventions have meant that policy must now swing in the opposite direction.

I must put my message in a short report to Government, a Cabinet Paper that will be distributed to, and discussed by, the full Cabinet. The paper must be aimed at senior civil servants and politicians, not at professional economists. The logic must be so clear that it is self- evident even to a politician. The paper must be written in clear, plain English. It must be short, six or seven pages at most. At first I thought that an impending famine was so serious a possibility that I could not afford to pull any punches. In fact, the opposite is true. I have to pull all my punches except one. I do not want to offend powerful people or threaten their interests, and there is only one action I am asking for. This means that before I start writing, I have to work out all the possible motivations of the key people. Right now, I do not know what will convince them and what will make them act: I have met only a few of them, and that was for less than an hour each. But even if I thought I knew what they would do in this situation, I would mistrust my perceptions. I cannot afford to take risks just because someone seemed open and helpful.

I have to assume that people are acting for the worst of all motives. I have to work on how they would think and act in the worst of all worlds. I cannot afford to be optimistic.

First, Government accepted the World Bank Agreement because they had no choice. They have no money; if the World Bank puts the screws on, what is left of the economy vanishes. In the worst case, they – that is, the President, Vice President, Prime Minister and ministers – will take no action unless they think that a large number of people will die, or that they personally will be lynched by the mob, or that Government will be overthrown by a coup. I will have to make these dangers explicit.

The Ministry of Commerce made the Agreement, and, presumably, they will be the people to renegotiate it – unless the President takes over. Murat carefully gave $5 million to them as a sweetener. The senior officials may see this as a bribe, in which case they will be reluctant to let it go. Murat was also careful to negotiate with a ministry where there was nobody who knew about food policy or food marketing: it has a few industrial economists and a lot of administrators who handle import and export permits. I suspect, though, that the Ministry has no real authority over the Agricultural Marketing Board or over rice supply, and can be ignored.

The General Manager of the Agricultural Marketing Board told me that he is keen to get rid of responsibility for rice marketing to the private sector. I bet he is! If the Agricultural Marketing Board imports at today's exchange rates and sells without a subsidy, there will be food riots, people starving in the street, and a coup. And everybody will blame him. If there is a coup, the junta is likely to imprison or shoot him, as the most convenient scapegoat.

But what happens if the Government implements the Agreement to the letter? The private traders are not going to import, so the country will run out of rice in late January or early February – and there will be no rice on order, so it will be at least eight to twelve weeks before more arrives. The Government then goes to the World Bank, the United Nations and the donor countries and says, 'We did exactly as you told us, and the results were what we predicted. Give us lots of money to buy emergency food aid. Do not send us rice from your stockpiles, that takes far too long.'

In the worst case, the Agricultural Marketing Board can then buy emergency rice at a much higher price than today's imports, using cash provided by donors. They will arrange for a large proportion to go to a Swiss bank, up to a half, I would guess. This is not being unduly cynical: it is what usually happens in other countries, and I see no reason to believe that the Agricultural Marketing Board is more virtuous than anyone else. They will be allowed to sell the rice at a low price or give it away, because people will be starving. Then the Agreement will be scrapped and they will go back to their old role, selling subsidized rice. Yes, this could be very profitable indeed.

I think that the General Manager is not aiming at this, though. After all, he gave me the final information I needed to spell out the steps to famine. Evidently, he does not want to see corpses piled against the fence surrounding his rice stores.

However, he will still make a lot of money, though not as much, if the private sector does not import, and if I alert the World Bank and the donors in November or December. They will pump in money to stop a potentially embarrassing famine. The Agricultural Marketing Board will buy expensive rice as an emergency measure. The rice will arrive just in time to stop mass starvation and the Agricultural Marketing Board will be restored to its old role, selling subsidized rice. This could explain why he gave me the information I needed, just in time. But I must assume the worst, that the Board are willing to have a famine in order to get the maximum graft.

How will MPs react to the news? Their first reaction to the Agreement has presumably been that they have lost a lot of income and power because of it. They can no longer allocate subsidized rice to their cronies and constituents. They are presumably hostile to the Agreement and looking for any way to destroy it. But how will they react to the news of an impending famine? To be sure, some people will die, but the MPs will get their hands on a lot of subsidized and free rice supplied by the donor countries. They will sell some of this at a good price and they will use some to buy the undying [sic] gratitude of their constituents. The famine will be very profitable for them in the short run, and the short run is all that matters now — the country's economy and political structure are getting decidedly shaky, so few of them can expect to be in power for as long as two years. Of course, this requires that they take a cut of the money and watch people die as a result, but then, that is what the politicians have been doing for the last forty years.

They will act on what they believe will happen, not on what I believe will happen or on what really will happen. Personally, I doubt if there is a lot of scope for making money that way. Certainly prices will be sky-high for some weeks, as people desperately try to buy the small amount of rice available, but there are very few people in the country who can afford to buy at these prices. Within a couple of weeks, everyone who has any savings will have spent them on rice. After that prices will collapse, because all savings have been spent and so there is no effective demand. Rice imported after that will have to be sold cheaply or will have to be given away. This gives the MPs power, but not money (unless they lend the rice to the starving, and hope to be paid back in a couple of years when the economy recovers). Prices will also drop once the donors start sending in emergency food.

If enough important people believe, rightly or wrongly, that they will get money and power from controlling the rice supply during a famine, then they will make sure that a famine will happen. I must remind them that there is not a lot of money to be made from a famine. Most ordinary people live from hand to mouth as it is, and very few have any spare income that could be used to pay higher prices for food. Very few indeed have significant savings. Hardly anyone has any assets to sell to raise money for food: they cannot sell the roofs of their houses – the roofs are twenty years old and too rusty to move. Nor do they have cars, bicycles or television sets that they could sell, even if there was someone with enough money to buy them. The people in the city clearly cannot buy enough food at today's prices, and increasing the prices will just mean that they buy less. They will not stop buying luxuries and buy necessities instead, because they made that switch years ago.

Only a tiny number of traders, politicians, senior civil servants and expatriates would eat the same amount if prices doubled.

Diamonds! I had forgotten diamonds. Yes, when we were up-country, Thomas and the project engineer told me that diamonds were stolen from the diggings. Some were sold to the illicit diamond buyers, but some were taken home and buried under the floor of the house for a real emergency. Most families would have had at least one family member working on the diamond fields at any time in the last thirty years. Perhaps it would be too much to expect that each family had thirty small diamonds, each worth, say, $15 to $50. Suppose that each family has five diamonds worth $200 in all. In a famine, they would sell these, and with the present exchange rate they would get a lot of leones for their $200. I am talking of a big family group here, say twenty people. That means that there is $30 million worth of diamonds that could be cashed in to buy rice in a famine. Maybe two or three times as much. Most of this would go to the MPs and to the Agricultural Marketing Board. Yes, $30 million may not be a lot of money elsewhere, but here it is big money and a big temptation.

And, again, it is not the truth that matters, because people act on what they *believe* to be the truth. If politicians believe that there is an enormous wealth in diamonds buried under the floors of huts throughout the country, they may act on the belief.

What about people's houses? Could the MPs buy them for a few bags of rice, then charge rent on them for the next hundred years? Yes, they could. It happens in other countries in a famine.* Yes, there is plenty of money to be made.

It will be more effective to remind the politicians that there will be so much rioting and discontent that a coup is inevitable. No doubt they have thought of it already: there are constant rumours of coup attempts even today.

I can also warn them of something that they will not have thought of themselves, that at any time in the future, without any warning, traders may just not deliver any rice to the country. They may decide at the last minute that they can get a better price just down the coast – in Guinea, for instance. Or they may deliberately withhold supplies to create a famine. Or they may withhold supplies to bring down the Government.

---

* See Genesis for the particularly nasty example masterminded by Moses, who got all the Egyptians to sell themselves into slavery, by making it the only way they could get food during a famine.

I think I have developed a coherent strategy to persuade the Government to take action. What do I do about the World Bank, though? I am dealing with a wide range of people there, most of them well-meaning, nice guys like Welensky, some of them absolute shits. But the World Bank is an organization with a character of its own, and even if I could negotiate with one of the nice guys, the organization would act, not him.

Again, I must consider what their motives and intentions would be in the worst of all worlds. I must assume that Murat is an absolute shit. Sure, he could be just grossly incompetent but, if so, how did he get his job? He must be astute at the internal politics of the World Bank, or he would not have reached the dizzy height of Res Rep. It is an extraordinarily political organization. He knows what his superiors at the World Bank want to hear, and he has made sure that they hear it. Add to this the fact that, like all other World Bank staff, he has been fired, and told to apply for his own job, and you have a powerful motivation.

The Sierra Leone desk in the Washington offices of the World Bank consists of career staff who have to survive in a highly political environment. Again, they have been fired and told to re-apply to get their old jobs back. They are struggling desperately to notch up as many Brownie points as possible before the appointments are made.

Today, most Brownie points come from pushing the Bank's current political dogma, an extreme Reaganite Free Market policy which the USA is foisting on them (and which the USA would never dream of implementing at home – the corn belt would rebel if they tried).

Both Murat and the Sierra Leone desk in Washington will get a lot of credit for what they have done, instantly privatizing the sector. If the Agreement is cancelled because it is publicly and embarrassingly known that it is a total disaster, then they will all be out of a job. Even if it is just cancelled, and no reason given, they will have lost all the credit they got for the privatization, and more. Of course, if it is abandoned after they have been reappointed, it will be less serious for them, even if there has been a famine in the meantime. Possibly they will be dealing with another country by then, and Sierra Leone will be someone else's problem. The World

Bank is forgiving about past blunders. It must be, or it would have to fire most of its senior staff.

The thought arises that Murat and the Washington staff are absolutely sincere, nice guys, and absolutely incompetent. This is possible, but even more frightening, as I cannot guess how they will react to any information. Another likely and terrifying possibility is that the World Bank is composed entirely of competent, well-meaning, nice guys, but that when they come together in an organization, that organization works in a way that is both incompetent and malign.

I conclude that it is not enough that I keep my Cabinet Paper secret from Murat and the World Bank: I have to keep it from them that I am even working on it. This means that I have to keep it equally secret from any expats who might gossip about it. If the World Bank learns what I am doing, they will lean on the local officials to fire me as incompetent. I will immediately be shipped out of the country so that I cannot communicate with anyone in Government or anyone in the aid organizations. I have seen it done before.

This would be effective. Once I am out of the country, there is not a lot I can do. I cannot imagine the British newspapers taking any interest. Nor can I imagine the headquarters of the aid organizations and donors listening to a discredited consultant with a chip on his shoulder.

No, I have to stick to my idea of having a limited-circulation paper aimed at a few top officials and the Cabinet, and do my damnedest to see that nobody else, particularly no expat, sees it.

I am only hoping that I am not frightening myself into silence. Self-deception is so easy. Perhaps I am being silent because subconsciously I know that if I make a big noise I will certainly lose my job and may lose my career. Even if I am discreet, I will never work for the World Bank again, not in West Africa anyway. A big loss, since they are by far my best customers.

Everybody in the aid business is acutely aware that Steve Lombard, who was employed in Tanzania on food security, was fired after he prevented a profitable famine there. He was running the FAO Famine

Early Warning System, and he predicted a famine in an inland area. He reported it to the Ministry of Agriculture in plenty of time for action.

The Ministry made no effort to do anything about it, and time started to run out: it was touch and go whether food could be delivered to the area in time to avert the famine. It looked as though things would be left so late that they were not given food aid, but rather millions of dollars to buy rice from ships passing by – and some people would cream off some of the money. Steve started to take unofficial action. He told the World Food Programme in Rome, so that they could earmark international food aid for it. He used his contacts to get the story on the BBC World Service and in the British press. He also arranged for a friend in the World Food Programme to get the American ambassador to ask President Nyerere how much grain he wanted and when. It was the first time the President had heard about the famine, and he was furious with the civil servants. The Government eventually took action, under strong pressure from the donor countries and organizations he had alerted, but it was a close run thing.*

Then the Ministry of Agriculture asked the FAO to fire Steve, and they did. It was quite clear why this happened, yet the World Bank and the FAO, who employed him, did not protect him. He died of drink three years later.

To each one of us in aid, this is a potent threat: there are no circumstances in which it is safe to speak the truth. To me, in my present situation, the threat is particularly strong.

I lay awake most of the night, hearing the muezzin's first call to prayer, floating from the loudspeaker on the mosque a mile away, and being still awake for the second call.

I was thinking, thinking. I was turning over all the arguments trying to think of a better approach. There is no alternative: I am stuck with it.

---

* This was reported in *Africa Confidential*.

The Casablanca

Lunch at the Casablanca as usual. It was an odd experience: I was full of adrenaline and my brain was racing, but I could not talk of my concerns. Around me everything was normal, Boss Seaga behind the bar, his belly firmly on the cash drawer, Henry talking to him and sinking his second or third double gin. I went straight to a table where Brendan was sitting with a few people I did not know, and ordered something to eat.

Boss came round each of the tables, looking worried. He asked us all to give blood for one of the regulars, an Italian, who needed twelve pints because he had a perforated ulcer. I have O negative blood, but I refused to offer it because I have had hepatitis. However, nobody else seemed to think blood group or disease was important.

If I needed twelve pints of blood, I certainly would not come to the Casablanca. Most of the regulars here have worked in countries with AIDS, hepatitis and lots of venereal disease. To judge by their behaviour here, there is an even chance that any one of them is a carrier. With twelve pints of blood, you could expect six different diseases. If it were me, I would take my chances with local blood. Sure, you would certainly pick up malaria and a lot of other nasties, but they are treatable. AIDS has not really hit here yet, unlike Malawi, where one in six of the population has it. Here, there is far less chance of getting it from one of the locals than from one of the consultants.

Curiously enough, when I had my medical to come here, the English doctor refused to give me a hepatitis B vaccine, on the grounds that you could only get the disease from sex or blood, so consultants were safe.

The conversation switched to the problems of getting anything done in this country. A senior World Bank fixer, an American, started boasting of his success. He had been flown in specially because their big hydroelectric dam project was stuck. He was delighted that he had managed to unstick it by paying $50,000 to the right people. He had shown that he was someone who could get things done, so he would certainly get reappointed to his World Bank job.

This bribery is convenient for getting a single job done. In the long run, though, it wrecks things for everybody. Only the other day, a newspaper had the story about a hydroelectric dam project that would have produced all the electricity Sierra Leone needed. (This was not the one the World Bank man was paying his bribe for, but another dam on another river.) Fourteen years ago the Canadians had offered to pay for it in its entirety. However, they were putting in tight controls, so that all the money would be spent properly. This meant that there was nothing in it for the politicians or civil servants. They did not formally reject the offer, but they did nothing about it. Instead, they waited until someone with looser controls offered to finance another dam, which did not happen until three years ago. Eleven years were wasted.

I was wondering if there was any tactful way of telling him this. Then Brendan, who is not a World Bank employee, intervened.

'The trouble with this sort of bribe is that it gets out of hand entirely. A couple of years ago, I tried to get some information from one of the officials at the Agricultural Marketing Board. He said to me "I am now speaking as a consultant, not as an employee of the Agricultural Marketing Board. If you pay me a consultancy fee, I will certainly give you the information you require." Once you start doing that, of course, you will have to pay everybody for every-thing. So I told him to bugger off.'

The bitching about getting anything done here continued. Two telephone engineers were complaining bitterly about Sierra Leone. They have just finished putting in a new, state-of-the-art, telephone exchange which would have got the system working again. This was financed by British aid. Unfortunately, the Government told them to put it in a building whose corrugated iron roof was leaking. The engineers kept asking them to put on new corrugated iron, which would cost perhaps a thousand pounds. The Government kept saying that they did not have the money in the budget. Result: half a million pounds worth of equipment was destroyed before it was even used.

It never occurred to the engineers that they might have been at fault, that they could easily have squeezed the money out of their fee, or that the British Government was equally at fault in refusing to pay for the roof because it had not been budgeted for.

A glamorous Nordic woman of about 40 came and sat at our table. She turned out to be a doctor working on the World Health Organization polio immunization programme. I asked her what it was all about.

'You will see as you walk around town that there are a lot of cripples begging,' she explained. 'One group is aged about seven; another is in their mid-teens and another lot is in their early twenties. This year's polio epidemic will provide another group. Each time there is a polio epidemic, the World Health Organization or some donor country provides the money to set up an effective immunization programme, and one generation of children is OK. The donors do not provide enough money to keep up the programme in future, and the Government has no money. The vaccinations stop; seven years later when there is a new vulnerable group, there is another epidemic, and a new system is set up from scratch at vast cost.

'Immunization is not as cheap and easy as it would be in Europe. You cannot get to the children at clinics and at schools because there are no clinics and few schools.

'The vaccines also have to be kept refrigerated, but there is no electricity in most of the country, even in Freetown. This means that we have to have paraffin refrigerators. You have seen them up-country where there is no electricity. They work from a paraffin flame that powers a heat exchanger.

'I am a World Health Organization immunization and epidemics expert, highly trained and experienced. However, my value to this project is that I can repair and maintain a paraffin refrigerator. Nobody else can do this, and if the refrigerators break down the vaccines are spoilt and the whole programme collapses.

'I am also the conscience of the project. I go to all our depots through the country. I look in the refrigerators. I pull out the Coke bottles, the palm wine and the meat. Then I put back the vaccines. I can only hope that they are not yet spoilt, otherwise the programme is useless. Worse, we convince the population that vaccines do not work.'

Looking at this energetic woman, I wonder again that I have not met any woman in any position of power in Government. I have met women typists and a handful of women at junior professional level. Where is the famous power of West African women?

This discussion left me depressed. I did not want to be reminded how difficult it is to get action in this country. Particularly, I did not want to be reminded that the politicians and civil servants here will only act if there is money in it for them. I have to get action on the food supply and get it fast, and some people will certainly lose a lot of money as a result.

As we talked, I saw Owen Veterinary come in. He went straight to the bar, ordered two double whiskies, downed them quickly, then got another and came over to our table. He was obviously very upset.

'I have just got back from a trip up-country,' he said. 'In fact, I haven't been back home yet.' I could see he was sweaty and travel-stained.

'We were travelling near Bo in the central province. It was not the main trunk road, but a tarmacked feeder road. A group of people with machetes stood in the middle of the road and waved us to stop. We had to stop, as they were blocking the road. I admit I was frightened.

'In fact they were not threatening us. They wanted help. One of them had had his leg cut off. They had carried him as a headload, ten miles up bush paths to the road, and now were trying to get him to hospital. Well, we were trying to work out how to fit him into the Land-Rover when a truck, a poda poda, pulled up. They were able to lay him out comfortably and go with him to hospital.'

He paused, gulped down his drink and ordered another. He was sweating, in spite of the fan playing over our table.

'What gets me is how he lost his leg. A different political faction in his village chopped it off. It seems to be how they conduct political argument here. God knows what it was all about. It is a one-party state, and both factions belong to the same party.'

He wiped the sweat off his brow and looked down at his glass. Nobody said anything, as we took in his information.

Brendan broke the silence. 'It's quite safe for whites here, so it is. White women are dead safe: the rumour is that there was a rape in 1948, but the man was a lunatic.

'White men can go everywhere in perfect safety. When I first came here, didn't my assistants take me and some of the bar girls on an all-night pub crawl. We went to pub after pub in central Freetown, with no trouble at all, and ended up with breakfast on the beach.

'I wouldn't try it in Dublin, nor even in Cork, I wouldn't.

'True, each bar had a guard with a sub-machine gun, but that was only because they had had a spate of armed robberies; the customers were friendly as can be. The only time I got a bit worried was when my assistant, Sesay, who was rather drunk by then, went up to one of the guards and berated him for sitting at the back of the pub with his sub-machine gun, instead of sitting at the front, to protect his honoured visitor – me! I managed to defuse the situation.'

I listened to him and worried some more. Yes, it is an extremely violent society and this scares me. It is not walking in the street or going to a bar in the red-light district at three in the morning that worries me. It is what happens if my campaign annoys powerful people.

Two years ago in Jamaica, I was quizzing the manager of a nationalized industry about his accounts. He did not answer my question. He just looked me in the eye and said, 'Mr Griffiths. In this country, you can get a man killed for $150 – Jamaican.'

I did not think he was joking. It happens: only last year, in Uganda, three expats who were accountants for aid organizations were shot dead for asking awkward questions.

★

As we drove back from the Casablanca after lunch, we came to an intersection. The light turned red, and I expected Mohammed to

stop, but he went through the light and turned right. I asked him
what the hell he thought he was doing. He was quite offended. He
said it is legal to go through the red light if you are turning right
and there is nothing coming on the left. I am sure he is right, but
I asked him not to do it again, as I am a coward.

I suppose the reason I have not noticed him doing it before is
that this has been the first time there has been electricity for the red
light.

This evening I went to a cocktail party held by a Lebanese friend
from the Aqua Club, a builder. All my preconceptions were exposed.
I don't know what I had been expecting, whether some exotic house
from the *Arabian Nights*, which I have only imagined, or the ostentatious vulgarity of an Arab moneylender's house in the Sudan, which
I have seen. The house, its furnishings, its decorations, even the mix
of guests were those of any middle-class expat. The clothing was the
light casual European adopted by the expats. The food was Lebanese, but then most expat food is here – Sierra Leonean food is an
acquired taste. There was no separation of the women as I would
expect in Egypt, Sudan or Pakistan. Instead, they were having a
lively discussion about their aerobics lessons and their squash games
at the Aqua Club. No difference in status from the expat women,
except that they have a role in the family business.

The only culture shock was watching the Arab women playing
whist. They dealt, and played, anti-clockwise.

As I left, I wondered how it would have been in a Jewish house
in Berlin in the early 1930s. The same knowledge that you are hated
for your race and your wealth, the same knowledge that the economy
has collapsed, and everyone is blaming it on you, and the same
knowledge that major changes in the political system are inevitable.
And, I imagine, the same parties in middle-class households.

I worked to midnight putting the final touches to my Cabinet Paper.

Cabinet Paper

MONDAY, 15 OCTOBER

Scenario for a Famine
The Implications of the World Bank Policy
on Rice Prices

ABSTRACT

The World Bank is pressing for the Agricultural
Marketing Board to stop all imports of rice for the
public. This will be left to unrestricted private
enterprise. It is shown here that there is a very real
danger that the urban sector will be left completely
without rice in early 1987. Many people will die. The
proposed stockpile, of less than 20,000 tonnes, is
inadequate to prevent disaster. Keeping a stockpile
will mean that there is inadequate storage for normal
distribution.
Recommendations for urgent action are made.

INTRODUCTION

The Resident Representative of the World Bank reached
an Agreement with the Government of Sierra Leone:

'1. That the rice price will be market determined and
   market prices will govern the sale of rice
   imported by the private sector as from 1st January
   1987.
2. The government import of rice through the
   Agricultural Marketing Board should not exceed
   20,000 tonnes a year, and all of this should be
   used for issue to government servants, hospitals,
   schools, prisons, etc.
3. The Government will finance the Agricultural
   Marketing Board for maintaining any strategic
   stock out of the annual imports of 20,000 tonnes.'
   (World Bank wording)

It will be argued here that this programme puts the
Government, the economy and the lives of the people at
risk.

In this analysis, local production is ignored, as, in practice, it is nearly all used for subsistence consumption by the farmers themselves. In the period with which we are concerned, changes in the marketing system or production system will have no effect on the quantity sold to the towns.

QUANTITY IMPORTED

In the past, we have got used to the Agricultural Marketing Board importing rice regularly and distributing it regularly. In other words, there was a constant supply with no serious shortages or gaps in supply. Everyone was quite confident that there would be rice on the market next week and next month.

Under the new system, all this will change. We will not know in advance how much is to be imported and how much is to be distributed.

There is a strong possibility that the private sector will import little or nothing. Since the Agricultural Marketing Board will no longer be importing, except for the rice issued to government servants and institutions, there will be no food for the rest of the urban population.

Private traders will tend to avoid importing rice for the following reasons:

1. They cannot make enough profit.
2. The money needed is too great - $2.4 million to buy a single 10,000 tonne shipload and $38 million to buy the country's needs of 160,000 tonnes.
3. The foreign exchange is not available.
4. They think that they will not be able to sell at the free market price, because Government will change its policy and will order Agricultural Marketing Board to sell rice at a very low price.
5. The crop is too political. When the price rises, there will be riots against the importers. The Lebanese are particularly worried that if they import, the riots will turn into race riots.

We cannot check import licences to see how much the private sector intends to import, because there are no import licences. It was a condition of the Agreement that there should be no import licensing, apparently because it would have conflicted with the World Bank's ideal of a Free Market without any bureaucratic controls that could have been misused.

TIME SCALE

It takes 10 or 11 weeks to import from the Far East
after the money has been raised, for example;

2 weeks negotiating
2 weeks raising a letter of credit and confirming it
45 days' sailing

There may be a further loss of one week to load the
ship and three weeks to unload it.

In other words, if the traders had been going to
import rice in the new year, they would have started
making their arrangements in September, before the
Agreement was signed. It should be quite easy to check
with the banks whether people have been trying to
raise this sort of money for rice import.

If the private sector decides not to import, Sierra
Leone will run out of rice early in the New Year. The
cities will have no rice at all. Accordingly, it is
imperative that

1. Contingency plans are made for rice imports by the
   Agricultural Marketing Board.
2. The strongest possible efforts are made to see who
   proposes to import and when.

ERRATIC SUPPLIES

Sierra Leone would face starvation if the right
quantity of rice was imported but it came at the wrong
time. For example, all importers might postpone imports
until the hungry season, which is generally the higher
priced season. No rice would be imported between
January and August.

Importers might delay or postpone shipments in order
to push up prices. Alternatively, they might postpone
release of stocks.

RELIABILITY

Even if we did have the information on how much
importers proposed to import and when, we would not be
able to place much reliance on it.

The importer might divert a shipload to Guinea at
the last minute, if he was offered an extra $15 per
tonne for it there.

He might have no intention of importing at all, only
of getting his $2.4 million in foreign exchange. We
would only find this out when the ship did not arrive.

He might wish to cause political instability by a sharp rise in the price of rice.

OTHER FOODS

Normally, if there is a shortage of rice, people eat more cassava. However, the last two years were years of poor rice yields, and people ate a lot of cassava. As they ate 2- and 3-year-old tubers, there is very little mature cassava, or even 3-year-old cassava, available this year.

STOCKPILE

To some extent these risks can be lessened by the existence of a stockpile. To be effective, this stockpile must be sufficient to cover us for the whole time between when we discover that there is a danger of a shortage and the time that a new shipment can be delivered and unloaded.

It has been suggested by the Agricultural Marketing Board that we should be wise to reckon on 13-16 weeks if the shipment is coming from the Far East. If we buy hurriedly, and at a high price, from Europe or the USA, the delivery period could be reduced by up to 5 weeks, say 8-12 weeks. This assumes an instant decision, immediate availability of money, and acceptance of the first rice offered.

This implies a stockpile of 45,000 tonnes to 60,000 tonnes, assuming consumption of 10,000 to 15,000 tonnes per month.

However, the World Bank specifies a stockpile of less than 20,000 tonnes. Indeed, allowing for the fact that rice will be drawn out of the stockpile, and allowing for the fact that there is a minimum economic size for shipment, it seems that the stockpile will be below 10,000 tonnes for much of the time.

Even this assumes that the Agricultural Marketing Board starts 1987 with the full 20,000-tonne stockpile. If it does not, its stocks will fall frighteningly low, as it will use 10,000 tonnes every six months on government-issue rice. For example, if it starts with only 10,000 tonnes in stock, half of its total imports will go to building up stock levels. It will have the full 20,000 tonnes in stock for only a few days of the year. It has not proved possible to find out how much the Agricultural Marketing Board is proposing to have available at the end of the year.

Nothing is known about the private sector's willingness or ability to store. They are in any case storing for profit only, and are not providing a strategic reserve.

STORAGE

In the past the stockpile has been low, about 3,000 tonnes, because the regular shipments brought in by the Agricultural Marketing Board removed the risk. In the future, storage should be available for some 60,000 tonnes.

The Agricultural Marketing Board has 30,000 tonnes of rice storage space. Accordingly, it will be able to rent out 10,000 tonnes of space to private firms, and probably another 5,000 tonnes for short-term storage.

Obviously, it is intended that new rice is imported before old stocks are finished. This means that 10,000 tonnes of storage space is not enough to unload a 10,000-tonne shipload into. Still less is it enough to unload a 15,000 tonne shipload into. It is significant that the Agricultural Marketing Board felt that they needed 30,000 tonnes of storage space even with their carefully planned procurement.

Since different private traders would be importing at different times, there has to be enough space to accommodate several shiploads, if two or three traders want to unload at the same time.

Where is this storage space to come from? There is limited, but expensive, private storage. We have not been able to obtain any information on the quantity available or whether it is ratproof and weatherproof. We are told, though, that this storage is already fully utilized for normal distribution. There is a little Agricultural Marketing Board storage space up-country.

The Agricultural Marketing Board believes that it would take a year to construct new stores.

The Agricultural Marketing Board is strongly opposed to using coffee and cocoa stores for rice, because weevils would then destroy valuable export crops.

STORAGE COSTS

The costs of maintaining this stockpile have not yet been calculated by the Agricultural Marketing Board. They would include the following:

1. The cost of building an extra 20,000 to 40,000 tonnes of storage space (not necessarily incurred by the Agricultural Marketing Board).
2. The cost of purchasing the rice.
3. The financial costs at 40 per cent overdraft rate.
4. Administration, security, loading, etc.

In practice it will prove very difficult to extract this money from Government, and it seems probable that this will end up as another invisible tax on the coffee and cocoa grower.

RECOMMENDATIONS

The following steps are urgently required:

1. To make provision for emergency imports if the private traders do not import.
2. To determine which traders intend to import and when.
3. To determine how firm their intention is, and what steps have been taken. To determine what problems they are having, such as non-availability of foreign exchange.
4. To determine the safe size of a stockpile.
5. To determine availability of and stocks of rice up to 1st January 1987.
6. To determine the availability of and quality of rice storage space.
7. To cost the stockpile.
8. To ask the World Bank to consider whether the Agreement is in the best interests of Sierra Leone.

Getting it to the Decision-makers

TUESDAY, 16 OCTOBER

I took my Cabinet Paper in to Amanda to get it typed. She was delighted to have something to practise on, and we went in to town to buy some stencils, duplicating ink and duplicating paper. I have asked her to prepare fifty copies, enough to get to the right people. I left her, bashing away at the heavy manual typewriter, a smile on her face.

I should have the duplicated copies tomorrow, but what do I do with them? How do I make sure that they actually get to Cabinet? First, I will submit them through the proper channels, through Foday, who, as Director of Planning, is the man I report to. He should send it to the Permanent Secretary, who will give it to the Cabinet Secretary, who will put it before a Cabinet meeting. It is the same system as for other Commonwealth countries. There are a lot of people in the chain who could just sit on it.

Possibly there is another, political, chain: Permanent Secretary to Minister to Prime Minister to Vice President to President. Of course, as an outsider I do not know who has the Cabinet Paper at any moment, or who is sitting on it, or how the system really works. Just to be on the safe side I will also give a copy to the Permanent Secretary. I assume that he will have a different agenda, because he is an administrator rather than a professional, and he is a Creole freemason rather than a tribal member of a secret society. I will also give a copy to the Director of Agriculture. He is not strictly in the chain of command, but he is the most powerful professional in the Ministry, and I find him a lot easier to deal with than Foday. I do not know the other top professionals in the Ministry so well, the Director of Research and the Director of Veterinary Services, but they seem to be OK. I would like to arrange a meeting with the Minister, but this has to be done through the Permanent Secretary.

I told Amanda that this was highly confidential. I hope this means that she will keep it away from expats. I would not mind, though, if she slipped a copy to an influential cousin or uncle.

The trouble is that dictatorship is inherently inefficient. All the decisions are made by one person on the information available to him or her. Sometimes five or six people control all access to the dictator, sometimes as many as fifteen. When the dictator first takes power, the gatekeepers may represent different wings of his party, or different power blocs. Soon, though, they are replaced by yes-men, or they turn themselves into yes-men, knowing that they only keep their authority as long as the dictator is given the information he or she wants to hear.

When I was in Malawi last year, there was a food crisis. It was not a famine, which is to say the television cameras did not arrive. Just a lot of people very hungry indeed throughout the country, and a lot of people dying in some districts. The politicians and civil servants were terrified that the President would find out and blame them, then consign them to the prison camps. The gatekeepers put a complete block on the information, so no action was taken. Eventually, one of the FAO expats was able to feed the information to the President through the Malawi Women's Movement, the one organization in the country that could bypass the usual gatekeepers.

Is Sierra Leone a dictatorship? I do not think so, really; just an undemocratic way of balancing the interests of different power blocs. Maybe this means that the gatekeepers are not so important?

I have just done a little analysis of food riots here in the past. They happen when there is a sudden price-rise over two or three weeks. They do not happen when there is a slow rise over a long period, even though the eventual price is much higher. I suppose that by the time the price is that high, the people are half-starved and have not got the energy to riot. Or perhaps it is the story of a frog: if you put it into hot water it jumps out immediately, but if you put it into cold water and heat it up slowly, it stays until it boils.

It is obvious, I suppose, with hindsight. It does mean, though, that the World Bank Agreement will certainly cause riots. Indeed, it means that there will be constant riots throughout the year, because prices will go up and down depending on when and if ships arrive with more rice.

Handing it Over

I went in to the office first thing this morning. Amanda greeted me and showed me the reports, beautifully typed, then duplicated as well as the old Gestetner machine would permit. She was proud of what she had done. She did not comment on the contents of the paper, and she gave no indication that she had read what she was typing. Discreet? I hope so.

I kept a dozen copies for myself and picked up the rest to give Foday. I knocked and went in. He was sitting in his chair, looking grumpier than usual. I hoped that he was not as bad-tempered as he was the day I met him.

I sat myself down, gave him a copy and asked him to read it. He picked it up casually, obviously ready to glance at it briefly before switching to polite conversation and shooing me out. He held it up, glanced at the first few lines, then put it on his desk and started to read it, carefully, slowly. He came to the end, then he read it again.

'What do you want me to do?' he asked.

'I would like you to get it to Cabinet,' I replied. 'You often put up Cabinet Papers. You know the drill.'

He was silent for a minute. Then he read it again. Then he was silent for three or four minutes.

'OK,' he said. 'I will do it. You realize, of course, that it will make you enemies?'

He looked at me for confirmation, and I nodded.

'Well, it will also make me enemies. That means that I must make a distance between you and this department. I will make it clear that this is the work of a consultant, not the department.'

He paused, and considered again.

'Also, it is better that you do not use the office here, or work with Thomas. I will find something else for Thomas to do.

'Now you must leave me please. I have to think.' He looked again at the paper before him.

★

The meeting had gone a lot better than I had expected. It looked as though 'official channels' might work. However, his nervousness suggests that I am right with my political analysis.

I busied myself preparing for another trip up-country. I could go mad sitting here and waiting for a response to the Cabinet Paper. I am far too tense to do any serious work, or to play or lie on the beach. I will certainly not hear anything for ten days. It will take a couple of days for the paper to reach anyone important. Then everyone will buzz around like blue-arsed flies for a couple of days, checking my facts with the Ministry of Commerce, the Agricultural Marketing Board and the private traders. Then they will worry about what options they have. If I am lucky, the paper will go before Cabinet on Friday next week.

It is too bad that Thomas cannot come with me up-country, but I can manage quite well with Mohammed. I do not need an interpreter when I am visiting officials, as they all speak perfect English, and Mohammed will be an excellent interpreter if I talk to people in the fields and markets. He is also great fun.

On Trek Again

MONDAY, 22 OCTOBER

Mohammed fetched me at dawn, and we started out for the diamond fields in the eastern part of the country, which I had missed on my previous trip.

After we had been travelling a couple of hours, we stopped and had our breakfast at the roadside. I had bought a smoked chicken, imported, from Choitrams, the Indian supermarket that supplies expats. This, with bread and butter, made a good meal.

By 9 a.m. we were passing Bo, in the centre of the country. As we drove past on the bypass, Mohammed told me that the university students were rioting there. The usual causes, he thought – high fees and bad food.

Half an hour later, we were driving towards the diamond fields on a surprisingly good road. It was 7-metre-wide tarmac, with good drainage, and raised high above the swamps it was passing through. The tar is still in good condition, as it was built only five years ago, by French aid, according to Mohammed.

It was a beautiful day, bright and sunny with a cloudless sky for a change. It was just starting to get hot so I opened the window as wide as it goes, for a breeze: we were only doing 50 mph, so it was not too windy. Perhaps it was a reaction from the strain of writing the paper, but I was looking at the fields and enjoying the sun on the different greens of the trees, of the rice and of the roadside grass, rather than taking an intelligent interest in what was growing. I noticed that the Land-Rover was yawing across the road. I looked around, but Mohammed had corrected, and it was on the right side of the road again. I returned to the scenery. Half a minute later it yawed across the road again. I looked at Mohammed. His eyes were closed. He was asleep.

'Mohammed! Wake up!' I said sharply.

He started, opened his eyes, and pulled sharply at the wheel to get to our side of the road. He pulled too sharply, a 45-degree turn at 50 mph. The top-heavy body of the Land-Rover lurched to the side, then started to tip over.

'This looks like the end,' I thought, and I remembered that four boys in my class at school had been killed in a car crash. 'I had not meant to die in a car crash in the middle of Africa.'

I clasped my arms around my head, and bent it down below the level of the dashboard. The Land-Rover crashed down hard on its side, paused, and turned upside down, thudding flat on its roof. My body was thrown against the seatbelt. Then we rolled upright again.

'That's OK then. I'm alive.' I looked up. 'Oh no! It's going over again!' I covered my head again, felt the Land-Rover going over with a crash. It crashed onto its side, then upside down, then over again.

Again and again it rolled over – two, three, four times. Each time it came upright, it seemed as if it would settle, and I would be safe, then it went over again. The rolling seemed inevitable, and I stopped wondering whether it would go over again. Then it rolled towards the edge of the road, where there was a 10-foot drop into some bush. I covered my head again as I felt the weight of the Land-Rover rise and tumble over.

It stopped and there was silence. I opened my eyes. I was hanging upside down, and I could see the car key still swinging in front of my eyes. My head was resting on the dry, dusty, grey earth. I released my seat belt, slumped to the ground and rolled clear – I was not sure how, then I saw the door had come off.

The Land-Rover was upside down, its body crumpled, in dusty open bush. I looked round dazed. 'Where's Mohammed?' I wondered. I looked inside, but he was not there.

I looked on the ground around the wreck, but still I could not see him. Half a dozen peasants emerged from the bush, looked at the wreck, looked at me and asked me if I was OK, in English. I inspected myself; they inspected me. No broken bones. No cuts. No bruises even. Amazing. Then they all started asking questions, and I stopped understanding them, and looked around wondering.

The diesel drum was ten feet in front of the Land-Rover. It had gone out through the roof over my head, missing me by an inch or two. A close call: it must weigh the best part of 500 lbs.

Just behind the Land-Rover was a flat bit of grey sheet metal, 10 feet by 8. I did not recognize it, then I realized it was the roof of the Land-Rover.

The crowd had now grown to twenty or more. They were going through the bush finding things that had been thrown out. My suitcase, the spare wheel, the big scale for weighing grain bags. Then there was a shout from the scrub behind the crash.

They had found Mohammed, a good 20 feet behind the crash. He was on his knees, his bum in the air, his head on the ground, looking rather comical. I ran to him. He was unconscious, but alive. I could not see any injuries, but he must have been hurt. He would not wear his seat belt, so he had been bounced round the cab as we rolled, then he had been thrown clear when the roof came off.

'Who was driving?' a man asked, and the crowd stiffened, ready to lynch the person responsible for harming this man.

'He was: he is my driver,' I said, and they relaxed, on my side again.

A passing car stopped, a red BMW going from Bo to the diamond fields. The driver took one look, and said 'Put him on the back seat. I will drive you to Bo hospital.'

They carried him gently to the car, and laid him on the seat. I took my suitcase, and asked the villagers to look after the wreck and its contents. Then I knelt on the floor beside Mohammed, and held him, to stop him falling off.

As we drove, the driver, a Mr Kamara, told me that the student riots in Bo had started to turn nasty, and had spread into the city, but he would try to get us through to the hospital. I tried to understand what this meant, but gave up.

When we hit Bo, Kamara drove through the backstreets, avoiding the university area and the city centre, and pulled up by the hospital. It was a 1930s building, black with mould, looking even more decrepit than most government buildings. We carried Mohammed inside. When I looked around, I realized that it offered no guarantee of treatment. There were no sheets on the beds, just mattresses broken open. Everything was old, worn out. It was filthy by most standards, but I suppose it was as clean as is possible when you have no money for soap or cleaning materials.

The doctors and nurses were all British-trained and very professional. They examined Mohammed carefully and decided that he was quite undamaged apart from his head. There was a possibility that he had damaged his medulla oblongata – something in his head. He should have an X-ray and a shot of penicillin, but there were no medical supplies in the hospital.

I took the senior doctor aside. He admitted that the local German aid project had brought in medical supplies, but they were for the use of project staff only. A couple of dollars removed this problem, and Mohammed was wheeled in for the X-ray. I gave the doctor some more money in case Mohammed needed any other treatment.

He gave me a check-over, but all we could find was faint bruising at my waist and shoulder from the seat belt. Very lucky. He insisted on giving me a shot of penicillin, though I do not know why, as I had no cuts. I, in turn, insisted on seeing the needles removed from their sterile pack, and checking that the penicillin bottle was new and unused. The last time I let someone inject me in an African hospital, I got hepatitis.

★

Mr Kamara was anxious to go. His Good Samaritan act had cost him four hours, and he could lose his car, and perhaps his life, in the rioting. However, generous to the last, he gave me a lift to the Ministry of Agriculture headquarters. Fortunately, the Chief Regional Officer, Charles Nyama, was there, and he took me in hand. I thanked Kamara effusively, as he drove off into the burning town.

Charles Nyama had never met me before, but he treated me as a member of the Ministry, as one of his own. He put me in the ministry resthouse, a basic two-room-and-a-parlour house, built of unplastered brick, which was in the suburbs well away from the rioting. There was a servant in charge of the resthouse, a thin, dried-up man in his fifties. I gave him some money to get food, then sat down and tried to take it all in.

An hour later Charles was back with a Ministry truck and two ministry mechanics. We were going to look at the wreck. We drove out and looked at it. Nobody could believe that anyone had survived. All the flotsam had vanished: camera, scales, tools, spare wheel, oil drum etc., but I was not up to making a fuss. I thought of the Cornish wreckers, and was grateful only that they had not beaten my head in.

Charles decided to tow the wreck back – in fact, I now realized that this was the purpose of the trip. I noticed everybody trying to find out how seat belts worked, then fastening themselves in securely. They no longer thought of them as effeminate.

Charles made his excuses and went off to see if he could get a message to Freetown, by the Ministry of Internal Affairs radio – telephones stopped operating years ago. He said that he would get a message to the Ministry and the World Bank that we were both alive and the Land-Rover is scrap.

Mohammed is dead. The doctor said he never regained consciousness. They will do a *post mortem*, but they think it was a brain injury, a ruptured medulla oblongata.

I am shattered. This morning they had said he was completely uninjured, and I was expecting severe concussion at worst.

We had only worked together a few weeks, but I had got to like him, and rely on him. He was a friend. I am devastated. I keep asking myself what I could have done to prevent it. Logically, I know I could not have made him sleep longer the night before we left. I think that we were sufficiently friendly that he would have told me if he was nodding off, so he could have a nap at the side of the road, or I could drive. I keep telling myself that I also tend to fall asleep while driving, and it was only after a couple of close shaves that I made a rule that I would always pull in for a nap if I felt myself getting tired.

It is the guilt of the survivor for having survived. I know it logically, but I still feel guilty.

★

TUESDAY, 23 OCTOBER

This morning I woke up still in a state of shock, and mourning Mohammed. Physically, I felt fine. In the mirror, I could see the bruises on my shoulder and hip starting to come out. Actually, I could not be sure how much it was the bruises, and how much it was the fact that I had sprayed them with iodine last night. I gave them another squirt, and they looked even more dramatic.

Charles collected me at 8 a.m. He was bustling, trying to do his own job and to look after me at the same time. First stop was the Ministry of Agriculture offices. I had not taken it in yesterday, but it used to be a railway station; with its grey-painted wooden buildings, it looks like any English country station.

Charles proudly showed me two hundred bicycles stacked on the platform, a gift from the Germans. They are for the agricultural advisers, so that they can get out in the bush and visit the farmers they are supposed to be advising. This is a major breakthrough, as for the last dozen years they have only visited the farmers within easy walking distance of their offices, so they have been ineffective. He has also been given some small motorbikes for the supervisors, but he is less enthusiastic about these. The Government only allocates the supervisors half a gallon of petrol a month, which is just about enough to get them from their outstation to district headquarters and back, so that they could collect their next month's half-gallon.

I let myself be led around. I had no thoughts. I had no idea what I wanted to do. I supposed I wanted to get back to Freetown, but I had no idea how.

Charles was in an expansive mood. He is obviously an efficient civil servant, but he is also someone who knows his way round – a bit like poor Mohammed. He explained his plan for today, 'The Vice President has flown in by helicopter to see what is being done about the riots. We will go along with his group, and I will try to talk to him and get you a lift back in his helicopter.

'The rioting is mild. It is just the university students running about in a mob and throwing stones, though they have burnt a couple of cars. The police have tried to keep them in the university grounds, but they have taken over the city centre.' He did not seem to be disapproving. I did not know if he thought that this is what students do, or if he thought that a bit of rioting was quite justified.

'Still, Government is taking the riots seriously,' he continued, 'even if it is only a student demo that has got out of hand. The country is at flash point, and anything could set it off.'

We drove around until we saw a cavalcade of twenty cars outside a burning building. It was not dramatic, as it was a 1960s concrete-and-glass building with nothing to burn, except the files. It was the Ministry of the Interior, according to the sign outside. Everyone was looking at it and saying 'Disgraceful!' Charles joined in, of course, but I think with no great conviction – inter-ministerial jealousy or something more?

We could not get through the crowd to the Vice President, in spite of the fact that Charles, as head of the Ministry of Agriculture, is an important man here. Instead, we followed the cavalcade to the next stop, the Ministry of Commerce. This was not looted or burning, so we drove on to the Ministry of Transport, which was also untouched. As the Vice President was congratulating the police, someone exclaimed that the Ministry of Commerce was now burning too. It had been set on fire as soon as we left. We jumped in our cars and rushed over to watch the fire. No one was trying to put it out, which surprised me, until I realized that even if there was a fire brigade, there probably was no water. The Vice President barked out a lot of questions, to show he was in charge.

Then somebody pointed out that the building we had just left, the Ministry of Transport, was now burning, so we rushed back and looked at it.

'Who is guarding the helicopter?' I asked. Panic everywhere. Someone senior forced his way through to the Vice-President and whispered in his ear. He barked out orders and a Land-Rover full of policemen armed with sub-machine guns tore off to guard the helicopter.

Charles used the disruption to get close to him and ask if I could have a spare seat in the helicopter. There were no spare seats, so we will have to think of something else.

'Agriculture!' came another cry. We turned around and saw smoke coming from Charles's office. The cavalcade rushed there, but there was nothing left. The wooden buildings were burning like straw. The bicycles are beyond repair. Charles was near tears.

Back to the hospital to sort everything out. I had not realized what had to be done. They wanted to do an autopsy, which was straightforward: they have scalpels and needles, and they got some thread from the tailor down the road. Then they asked me to pay the local photographer to take a photograph of me with poor Mohammed, as 'evidence' – of what I do not know.

They wanted to embalm him, however they do it here. I suppose that otherwise the body would have to be buried today in this climate. I thought that this was the Muslim rule anyway, but presumably it is modified by the local custom of burying people in the village where they were born. Since there is probably no electricity for refrigeration, embalming is the only option. We were told that embalming was not the mortuary attendant's job, but that he does it privately as a way to add to his salary. He quoted me 75 leones, and I was pulling the money out of my wallet when Charles went bananas.

'75 leones! That is a whiteman price. You are cheating him. Mohammed is one of us: he is Agriculture. I will give you 40 leones. I will collect the body this afternoon.' He slapped my money on the table and stormed out.

It is good of him to think of Mohammed as one of his own, even though he worked for the World Bank.

We moved on to the police station to report the accident and make a statement. The compound was crawling with police in their blue riot gear, some with batons and shields, some with rifles and sub-machine guns. As I walked across the compound something caught my eye, and I bent and picked it up: an empty .45 cartridge case. 'Drop it!' hissed Charles, 'You see nothing. You hear nothing.' I did, and we walked on, discussing the weather.

In spite of the rioting, they could spare one policeman to spend half an hour taking my statement, and two others to drive out to the scene of the accident and make their report. They pulled out their tape measures, and told me it was 272 metres from the first skid to where the Land-Rover had ended up. The marks on the tar confirmed that it had gone over five times. I am surprised that any vehicle travelling at 50 mph would have that momentum.

When we returned, I spent the evening at the resthouse. Charles came to check I had food and drink. I certainly got the impression that this was Agriculture protecting its own.

WEDNESDAY, 24 OCTOBER

After breakfast, I was sitting on the verandah bare-chested to catch the breeze, when a car pulled up. Out stepped Thomas with one of the other Ministry economists and a Ministry driver. Foday had sent them to rescue me – evidently, I am no longer a pariah.

They were appalled by my iodine-enhanced bruises. I suppose that if you are black any bruises that are visible must be very painful indeed.

'Where is Mohammed?' they asked. They were shocked when they heard that he was dead. They had not heard anything since our first radio message. I realized that the Ministry of the Interior radio must have gone up in the fire before Charles's second message had gone. If Charles had thought of asking the police or army to send the second message, it had probably been lost among the messages about the rioting.

While we were talking, Charles drove up, furious. The mortuary attendant had refused to do the job for 40 leones, and the body had deteriorated to the extent that they had buried it quickly. He had made the hospital dismiss the attendant, which I thought was hard on him, but I said nothing.

We made a detour as we left, to see the wreck. It left everyone silent. I noticed that everyone wore their seatbelts as we drove back.

When we hit Freetown, it was already dark. We stopped in a side street, and they told me to wait while they went in to tell Mohammed's family. Two minutes later, I heard children's voices in a despairing wail.

God knows how they will survive. I do not know if the World Bank has any pension or life insurance. Of course, I will see that something goes their way. I do not know what else I can do.

Charles had asked me to call on his wife, whom I had never met. She lives in Freetown, and was very worried, since everybody knew that there was rioting in Bo, but there was no news on the radio or television. I was able to tell her that he was in no danger. I was interested to see that in spite of his tiny salary, a senior civil servant here had a standard of living not that different to an academic in Britain.

And then I had to check in to the hotel again, find my room, and collapse in bed.

Mother Theresa

SATURDAY, 25 OCTOBER

The English newspapers have been doing their annual exposé of how the aid workers spend their weekends and evenings lying on the beach enjoying themselves. The implication is that 'We [Sun, Mail, Express, Guardian] readers give our money to help the Third World. We are helping the poor, the starving and people living in squalor.

We pay aid workers to go out and live on very little food, in total discomfort next to the poor. We do not want to see them enjoying themselves.'

They really want a Mother Theresa figure. They get a wonderful warm glow of virtue from the fact that she lives in poverty next to the very poor. They may not do it themselves, but they share in the saintliness. A few of them may even go so far as to contribute to her order, so that they may share even more deeply in this sanctity.

And that is precisely what she is providing – a glow of virtue to the rich. If I had been given so much money to spend and I had achieved so little with it, I would cut my throat. The poor starve in India because of its strange macroeconomic policy, its extraordinary agricultural policy and its wildly eccentric food policy. A tiny fraction of the money spent by Mother Theresa on making the rich feel virtuous could have been used to persuade the Government of India to adopt economic policies that would not leave the poor starving to death on the streets of Calcutta. Instead, she gave the entirely false message that sanctity can ameliorate the suffering caused by bad economics.

No, I do not feel wicked for taking a swim after an extraordinarily stressful week in the extraordinarily stressful climate of Sierra Leone. No, I do not feel wicked sitting on the beach for a few hours after a week on trek. I have to make tough decisions and I have to be right, or tens of thousands of people die. I have to be relaxed, efficient and on the ball. I will not be, if I am living in squalor to make [Mirror, Times, News of the World, Observer] readers feel virtuous.

Waiting for Action

TUESDAY, 29 OCTOBER

Thomas came out to the hotel this morning, with George, the new World Bank driver, who has taken over from poor Mohammed. They both asked me worriedly how I was. I gather I did not look good when they picked me up from Bo. I must have been in clinical shock. Today, I think I looked calm and fit, though I am still tense, and I get a bit shaky from time to time.

Thomas's visit must mean that I am no longer totally unwelcome at the department, though he did not suggest that Foday wanted to see me, or that I would be welcome at the office. Is it just their human response to my accident? Or is it that there has been some feedback from the Cabinet that it may be safe to be seen with me after all? I do not know: certainly Thomas did not give any indication that he had read the Cabinet Paper, or that he had heard about it.

He did tell me another bit of gossip about last week's Cabinet meeting. One minister had demanded that the police should be told to shoot the rioting students. There was the usual 'hear, hear' from the yes-men, then someone said, 'That's our children you are talking about.' Indeed, everyone in the room had sons, daughters or at least cousins at the university; their friends and supporters likewise.

This is a major advantage of a system where higher education is confined to the rich and powerful. The police do not shoot the sons of the rich and powerful.

He then told me, as something of passing interest, that the police staged a coup attempt yesterday, but it fell through because two police officers each wanted to be president. It was easily put down by the army, even though the police are better armed.

This is the same police force that was violently putting down the riots in Bo last week. If they had supported, or even tolerated, the riots, they would have spread, and the coup would have been a walkover. The new junta would have had too much on their hands to look at food supply for at least another couple of months.

Still, it means that the politicians must be very worried indeed, and they will not risk food riots if they can help it. A good sign.

I have made a surprising and significant discovery: local retail prices of rice have stayed stable over the last year. I had expected that they would have changed with inflation and the fall in the value of the leone. Certainly, the leone price would have shot up if people were

Prices in Freetown Markets, 1986 (cents per 10 oz)

smuggling, because the smugglers would be getting many more leones for their francs in Guinea or for their US dollars in Liberia. The fact that the leone price has stayed steady means that there cannot have been any smuggling. That means that Sierra Leone is importing half the rice it consumes. Which means that the threat of famine is very real indeed.

Before I started interviewing prospective importers, I had given Thomas a job to keep him out of the way. I had asked him to go to the Central Statistics Office and get all the food prices they had recorded for the last ten years. They use these for calculating the consumer price index, but they never publish the raw data. Thomas gave them to me yesterday morning, and I spent most of yesterday and all of today analysing them and plotting them on a graph.

What seems to have happened is that the Agricultural Marketing Board made contracts for this year's rice deliveries in September last year. They paid in advance, at the old fixed exchange rate of 7 leones = $1. They are now selling at cost, still based on this exchange rate. This means that their selling price has stayed static throughout the year. It also means that the Agricultural Marketing Board is not getting nearly enough leones to pay for importing next year's rice crop. No wonder they do not mind the private traders taking over.

The only price fluctuation was a brief fall after the February rice crop was harvested, which is to be expected.

The graph shows a different price progression for bread, but this only confirms my analysis. Bread is made from wheat imported by the Agricultural Marketing Board. They sold the wheat at the same price for the first six months of this year, as it was all bought under a contract made at 7 leones = $1. When supplies bought under that contract ran out in June, they started selling supplies bought under the next contract, from July. This was done at another exchange rate, so the price was higher. The price rise in July was not as big as I expected, but then I realized that the contract would have been made in April or May, before the really big fall in the value of the leone.

Cassava is produced here, not imported, so its price is not directly affected by the exchange rate. Its price goes up and down, depending on how much cassava is on the market and how much of alternatives like rice is available. The price is usually highest in the hungry season, before the main rice crop is harvested in October.

With the leone rice price steady and the leone collapsing in relation to the dollar, there is an enormous incentive to smuggle rice out. Before the leone floated, smugglers would have pocketed a maximum of 25 per cent of the value of anything smuggled, and that is ignoring transport costs and bribes payable. Today they would get seven times as many leones for one bag of rice, so they would pocket at least 90 per cent of the value of the rice they sold. But if they had smuggled, the supply in Freetown would have dropped sharply, and the price would have risen to nearly as much as the smugglers got for it in Guinea or Liberia. (And no, the Agricultural Marketing Board did not import enormous quantities of rice to keep the price down.)

No, there cannot have been any smuggling. The politicians must have exercised ferocious control to prevent it.

★

How many people will die? If the World Bank holds Sierra Leone to the Agreement, the death toll as a percentage of population will be higher than for any other famine this century.

There are about 3 million people living on farms in the country, and about three-quarters of a million others living in the city, in towns, on diamond diggings and on the large diamond, bauxite and titanium mines. Most people get half their calories from rice. The urban people eat only imported rice, so they will have half as many calories as usual. The rural population will also have less rice to eat.

The urban adult population used to eat nearly 2,000 calories a day in the good times, but probably eat 1,800 calories or less today, to judge by the obvious malnutrition. They get over 1,000 calories from imported rice. If there is no imported rice, they will eat only 800 calories a day. It is difficult to say what the starvation level is: healthy adults can get by for some time on 1,250 calories if they do not do any work. However, the people of Sierra Leone have no reserves of fat: they are malnourished and riddled with disease today. Also, adolescents need considerably more than adults, and adults doing hard physical work need 3,000 to 3,500 calories a day. I would guess that 1,200 calories per head, not per adult, is starvation level, and 800 calories certainly is.

The unemployed people without friends or family will die almost immediately. Then families will ask their unemployed relations to leave, to fend for themselves, and to die. People like carpenters, shoemakers and hairdressers will not earn anything – their customers will spend every penny they have on food – so they will die. Workers who are laid off will be next. Families will restrict the food intake of the young and the old, and they will die. Then, within weeks, normal families with a steady income will die.

Who is safe? The expats, of course, and some rich traders. The large mining companies will try and buy food for their workers, but there will be none on the market. The civil servants may survive if they get their rice rations, but the chances are that these will be diverted onto the black market. Even if they do get their rice rations, they will not be able to afford the other half of their food – the prices of cassava, yams, palm oil and vegetables will also be sky-high.

At first sight, the farm population seems safe, because only 10 to 15 per cent of their calories come from imported rice: they will suffer from serious malnutrition, but that is all. This 10 to 15 per cent is an average, though, and it hides big discrepancies. The farmers in the main rice-producing areas will have enough to eat and will do very well indeed if they have any surplus to sell. They will not be keen on selling, though, unless they are quite sure that their families will be fed for the foreseeable future. This will not be the normal famine, which ends with the next good crop. No, this will only end when rice is imported, and farmers have no way of knowing when this will be. The farmers will store any food that can be stored.

Other farmers, those who normally buy rice using the proceeds from coffee and cocoa sales or their earnings from diamond digging, live on bought rice, perhaps buying all their rice. They will not be able to buy any. They will starve.

What about the diamonds and the money that people have buried under their floor? Can't they use these to buy rice? Can't the big mining companies use their money to buy rice for their workers? No. There will be no food to buy. When people dig up their valuables to buy food, when they stop spending money on anything but food, it just means far more money chasing the same amount of food. Prices will rocket. Diamonds will be sold for a few cups of rice. High prices do not change the amount of food available. Nor do the high prices change the number of people who will die. They just ensure that at the end of the famine, all the wealth of Sierra Leone will be in the hands of a few powerful people.

Those city people and townspeople who were born in villages will go back there and claim food, as their right. I do not know what reception they will get. Even if they are accepted back, it will not change the total amount of food available. The village will have to divide the food among more mouths, so it will run out of food perhaps a month earlier than usual, and people will starve in that month. This could actually increase the death rate – the whole village would starve, instead of just the people from the city.

The food shortage will hit immediately and it will hit all the urban population and half the rural population at the same time. This is quite unlike the normal famine caused by crop failure, where the starvation creeps up slowly, hitting one group then moving on to another and another, giving the aid agencies time to prepare before everyone is hit. Sierra Leone has no strategic reserve, and it does not have any of the other reserves. Unlike Britain, say, the farming sector does not produce a food surplus, so there is no commercial food reserve. Unlike India, it does not have rapacious landlords who take food from the peasants and offer it to the highest bidder, which may leave the peasants to starve, but which feeds the urban population for a few months. Also, there is no reserve of cassava. Here the peasants will stick to what they have, leaving everyone else to starve.

We cannot hope for a slow progression, with 10,000 or 20,000 people dying in front of the television cameras, so that there is a build-up of publicity, food aid arrives and the World Bank backs down before things get too bad. No, everyone will be hit at the same time.

Virtually all the miners and the urban population will be hit immediately. Those farmers who buy most of their food will be hit a month or two later. Three-quarters of a million people will be hit immediately, and another million within two months.

Then disease will hit a weakened population. How many will die? A quarter of a million? Half a million? More?

I did not sleep much last night. I woke up thinking how soon the country would run out of rice. I worried that I was not doing enough about it. I kept thinking of new angles on the rice problem, of new arguments I could use to convince different people. I was trying to think of a strategy I could use to get the information to the aid organizations who would provide emergency food. For hours and hours I lay awake under my net, listening to the whine of mosquitoes. I was wide awake, thinking hard.

I have not slept much the last few weeks. Always it is the same worry. What can I do? Am I helpless? Is anyone listening to me?

Then sometimes I start thinking of poor Mohammed, how cheerful he was, what a pleasure to be with, of his girlfriends around the country, of how he died and I lived.

The Marketing Board

Still no response to my Cabinet Paper three weeks later. Has someone sat on it? Has anyone important read it? Are they going to take any action? What more do they want to know?

I went into the office to see Foday, armed with my analysis of rice prices, smuggling and the number of people who would die. I knocked on his door and walked in. He looked up from the file he was writing in, and his face went blank.

'I am sorry,' he said flatly. 'I have no news for you. I have not been told anything myself. Goodbye.'

He went back to the file on his desk.

I could not leave it there. I went out to the Agricultural Marketing Board offices at the docks and gave my name to the commissionaire who had been so unhelpful on my first visit. He went upstairs and a couple of minutes later the General Manager came down, smiling and greeting me like an old friend. He led me up to his office, sat me down and ordered me a cup of coffee. Perhaps he is just a nice, honest, concerned person. Perhaps, but I cannot afford to rely on it.

He was cooperative, more cooperative than before. This time he gave me the figures on the rice he had in stock. I had mentioned in the Cabinet Paper 'It has not proved possible to find out how much the Agricultural Marketing Board is proposing to have available at the end of the year.' I hoped that this new openness meant that someone at the top had read what I said and told him to stop buggering about.

He has 14,000 tonnes in stock, and another 10,000 tonnes arrives at the end of this month. Government has instructed him to sell 11,000 tonnes a month, so he will sell another 8,000 tonnes before the end of November, and 11,000 tonnes in December, leaving him with 5,000 tonnes on New Year's Day. This 5,000 tonnes will not be available to the public: it will be strictly reserved for priority users – the army, the police, senior civil servants and politicians. He thinks that he will only be allowed to dish out this 5,000 tonnes to the starving if a new shipload is actually being unloaded in the docks.

That means that in less than two months there will be no imported rice in the country, and starvation will begin. The normal procurement takes about four months, so that is no longer an option. The rapid and expensive procurement from Rotterdam or the USA takes two months, so rice can be brought in before things get too desperate, but only if Government acts today – and he does not see any sign of this happening. If there is any more delay, the expensive emergency procurement will be necessary, diverting ships passing West Africa.

I was encouraged to hear that the decision on how much rice to release on the market is made by Cabinet, not by a junior civil servant.

He made a suggestion. He would like to stop all sales of Agricultural Marketing Board rice from now until the end of the year. This would mean that he started the New Year with 24,000 tonnes, enough to keep the country going until the end of March at a pinch. The country would not run out in the meanwhile, as the USA is selling 20,000 of imported aid rice right now. He had asked Cabinet to give him permission to do this, but they had refused. He asked me if I could put some pressure on from my end. So I am being taken seriously! Was he asking for another Cabinet Paper?

He is clearly worried, and much more subdued than he was last time.

A Sundowner

I was sitting at a table on the beach, watching the sun set, brilliant red. I sipped my beer and thought that some things about Sierra Leone are perfect.

One of the English businessmen who lives here permanently came and joined me. Jim something or other – I have met him at the

Aqua Club. He had obviously had quite a bit to drink, and he was bubbling over with good humour.

'You know Mary, the bar girl who sometimes goes to the Casablanca. Well, I took her home last Friday. We had a great time. Then I paid her and she got dressed. Then I happened to look in my wallet: she had pinched all my money.

'She denied it of course. I grabbed her and searched her. Guess where she had hidden it?'

He giggled.

'Well, one thing led to another and we were at it hammer and tongs for another couple of hours.' He grinned reminiscently.

'But she pinched my money again. She denied it and she flatly refused to give it back.'

He giggled.

'What she didn't know was that I pay the police station at the end of the road every month. I gave them a ring, and they came and fetched her.

'They kept her for their amusement for four days, and then let her out, completely exhausted.'

He giggled.

Revisiting the Importers

THURSDAY, 8 NOVEMBER

After yesterday's meeting with the General Manager of the Agricultural Marketing Board, I decided that I must work on an update of my Cabinet Paper, something that will show that the situation is much worse than it was when I wrote the first one. I spent most of yesterday and all of today checking whether the private traders have changed their mind.

The first stop was the Chief Economist at the Ministry of Commerce. He greeted me from behind his desk and asked me to sit down. I thought that this time I was being treated as a civil service colleague, one of us, rather than with the cold reserve I had felt at the first meeting. He told me that the Ministry was now issuing import licences and keeping notes of anyone who had enquired about importing. (Good: another top-level response to my Cabinet Paper.) Unfortunately, though, nobody had applied for an import permit, and only one person had enquired. He gave me the name. This was all formal, but I got the impression that he was tense about the situation rather than anti-me.

I then went round all the private traders I had seen before. They repeated even more firmly that they would not import. Their reasons were much the same. The first thing they said was that the recent rioting and threats of coups had made it even more clear that it was too dangerous: they would be lynched. Equally important, it was commercial suicide: they could bring in the rice all right, but they could not sell it. At the beginning of this year the Agricultural Marketing Board had been able to import rice and sell it, subsidized, at retail for 2 leones a kilo. The collapse of the leone meant that if the Agricultural Marketing Board or the traders imported at today's price and sold it unsubsidized, the retail price would be 20 leones. Incomes had not gone up in the meantime. People who are hard-pressed to buy rice at today's price certainly will not be able to buy it at the new price.

I have to keep reminding myself that this is not Western inflation caused by printing banknotes. That means that incomes rise at the same time as prices. Here incomes are constant or falling. Wages stay the same in leones. Farmers' prices today are much the same as last year's because they were calculated on the old, fixed exchange rates, but they are producing less for sale, so their incomes have fallen. How do I know that this situation has not been caused by printing more banknotes? My contact in the Central Bank assures me that the Government would like to print more but cannot. They still have not paid the printer for the last lot, four years ago, so nobody will print any others for them.

With these two objections to any import, any others may seem superfluous, but they are not. The traders said that even if they did import, the high prices would cause such an outcry that Government would set a maximum price, one that people could afford. Or they would just seize the rice and sell it off cheaply. Either way, the traders would lose everything.

They were even more worried than before that they would be left with leones that they could not convert back into dollars. They know that the Central Bank desperately wants to impose exchange control to stop the haemorrhaging of the country's wealth, and only pressure from the International Monetary Fund and the World Bank stops them. If they do, then the traders will be stuck with leones. They are well aware of the 'pipeline' system of exchange control in some West African countries, where it takes four years to get your foreign exchange, by which time the exchange rate will have turned against you.

One thing comes out of this clearly. Risk is an economic cost, and private-sector imports are far more risky than public-sector imports. This means that it is far more expensive for the private sector to import than the public sector.

I went to see someone else, the man that the Chief Economist had told me was interested in importing. His name had also been on Henry's list of those Sierra Leoneans who have enough money to buy a shipload or two of rice. I had tried to see him in my first round of visits, but they said that he had gone to the Canary Islands, where he had a string of hotels.

Like the other multi-millionaires, he had one of these small offices over a shop in a bazaar. He recognized my name immediately, and took me into his office. He introduced me to the man he had been talking to, his chief accountant, then shooed him out, so we could talk alone.

He said that he had seen my Cabinet Paper and he had been asked to import rice by the Government. He sees all the problems that the others see, but he is trying to do something to overcome them. He is negotiating with Cabinet to get guarantees that he will not lose money from the deal. He also wants guarantees that he will be able to change his leones back into dollars, and to change them at a realistic rate. He was open with me, probably because he thought that anything I would report to Cabinet must help his case.

I suppose this is a ray of hope, but it is no more than that. There is an outside chance that one person, who is not a rice trader, will import an unknown quantity of rice at an unknown date and sell it at a price nobody can pay.

Time is ticking by. Already it is too late to get rice in the usual way. Emergency imports will be needed.

The buck stops here. I cannot stop the famine myself: a lot of people in Government will have to make unpopular decisions and take unpopular actions. But if I do not do my bit, there will be a famine. There is nobody else to do it for me: in this country, unlike in most African countries, there is no food security unit, no early warning system, no agricultural policy unit, nobody who examines food supply, either in Government or in the many projects.

The civil servants are clearly terrified of knowing anything, saying anything or doing anything. Even if one of them, or the Government itself, approached the aid organizations, whether officially or unofficially, they would not be believed. The fact is that if a local raises the alarm, the aid organizations will ask themselves what the scam is this time. The ubiquitous corruption means that everyone is suspect.

Even if the aid organizations did take the story seriously, they would send in an independent observer to do just what I am doing now. That would mean a delay of two months. We do not have two months to spare.

I have to write another Cabinet Paper.

Who would have raised the alarm if I had been killed in that accident?

The consequences of making a mistake in this job are too big. Even in my normal food policy work, I know that the wrong advice will kill tens or hundreds of thousands of people. The deaths will not be dramatic and no foreigners will notice what is happening. There will be a higher infant mortality rate, fewer toddlers surviving to age 5, undernourished adults not surviving the next malaria attack, or not having the stamina to resist TB. In the present crisis, any error, any failure to get action, will kill many more.

I could go mad thinking about it. Instead, I try to think of it as a purely economic problem, a numbers game, and to forget that the numbers may mean children starving.

And when I write my report, I have to present it as a simple economic exercise, and keep any passion, any emotion, out of what I write. I also have to censor it for other reasons. I would like to write the truth, the whole truth and nothing but the truth, but this would mean that everything I do would be wasted: I would annoy a lot of people, my report would be rejected, and nothing would be done. Also, I would be fired.

Anyway, everyone knows that the whole system is corrupt, so why mention it? The international aid organizations tell you to turn a blind eye to it. Sometimes, though, the corruption is not just redistribution of wealth: it is causing the whole system to collapse, as it is here. Can I hush it up and still sleep at night?

Some consultants do. They make a good living telling clients what they want to hear, and making any criticisms so bland that the client does not notice them, and certainly does not act on them. No doubt they tell themselves, as I tell myself, that they are only making the minimum number of cosmetic changes needed to get their reports accepted and acted on.

The only way to avoid deceiving yourself like this is to work to the limits. If your reports never get an outraged reaction, you are lying. If they are never rejected, you are lying. If you are never fired from a contract, you are lying. You are lying to your clients and you are lying to yourself. You are killing people.

I was sitting in the hotel lounge, having a cold beer, when a Sierra Leonean came and sat next to me. He told me that he was an ex-army officer who had been dismissed because he had been suspected of planning a coup. He wanted to tell me all about it, and get my sympathy. He was a little drunk, wild-eyed and very indignant.

It was possible, of course. On the other hand, how could a dismissed officer afford to get drunk in a beach hotel? Probably he was an *agent provocateur* for the Special Branch. Either way, I wanted no part of it. Even if I was a CIA or KGB agent, even if I had known everything about the local political situation, I would not have talked to someone approaching me in a hotel like this.

Not that I would have been unsympathetic if I had believed him. Most expats here, even the most right-wing, think that the system is so rotten that a Maoist revolution is the only answer. They say so loudly in the Casablanca, even though it is probably bugged. I doubt if the Special Branch minds what expats say to each other, so long as they do not say it to a local.

It was too dangerous to listen to him, or even to continue to sit near him, so I took my drink outside, and sat by myself on the terrace and watched the moon on the sea.

I started thinking of Mohammed, of how he had died and how easily it could have been me, and I felt guilty for having survived. Then I wondered if his wife and children could survive a famine. I got very drunk indeed.

A Second Cabinet Paper

FRIDAY, 9 NOVEMBER

This morning I submitted my new Cabinet Paper to Foday, and I discreetly slipped copies to the Permanent Secretary and the Director of Agriculture. I spent yesterday writing and polishing it. This morning Amanda calmly and efficiently typed it and ran off fifty copies on the duplicator. She is the best typist I have ever had and is quite wasted here: she could get an excellent job anywhere in Britain.

I took it to Foday. He looked up warily as I went into his office, saw that I was carrying papers and guessed what they were.

'Is that another Cabinet Paper?' he asked, 'An update?' I nodded.

'Well,' he said cautiously, 'I will pass it on, but you must know that I can do no more. It is something for the top people. They tell me nothing. I have heard nothing about your previous paper. They have not even sent me the Cabinet minutes.'

He was not saying that he normally gets the full minutes of Cabinet meetings, only that if they discuss something which concerns him the Cabinet office sends him the relevant decisions, a paragraph or two of green duplicated paper cut out of the minutes and stuck on a sheet of white paper.

Well, I left the papers with him, and I am keeping my fingers crossed.

★

This Cabinet Paper set out the crisis even more starkly. I have repeated the main argument, of course, but I have emphasized that the time for action has run out. I also mentioned the Agricultural Marketing Board's proposal to stop selling rice now, so that there will be some left on New Year's Day. I hope it works.

However, I must assume that it will not work, and come up with some alternative actions.

First, I can have some discreet talks with the more competent heads of the various aid organizations. The Americans and the Russians are out, because they are here to push a political dogma and have no credibility. The British show no interest in policy and are quite happy as long as they are allowed to dig wells in the jungle. Danish aid in Africa seems to be confined to giving Danish-made dairy and abattoir equipment to state organizations that do not need it, so I can ignore them. The Swedes are obsessed with cooperatives. The Canadian, the German and the Frenchman seem to have their heads screwed on. So does the FAO Res Rep, Abensberg. The others I am not sure of.

There is no food security unit I can go to, like the ones the FAO set up in East Africa and the Sahel. The equatorial rainfall here is variable, but even if there is 70 inches less than usual, there is enough to keep everything green, so foreigners do not realize that there is a drought. Anyway, there has always been enough money to import food in the past. It is a pity there is no food security unit, because their reports go direct to the intergovernmental committee of the World Food Programme in Rome, the people who actually get food aid moving.

Brendan, of course, works for the World Food Programme, though in a different capacity — dishing out food aid — so he should have contacts within the organization. He is my best bet. I have carefully not told him what is going on, but he must have some idea, from my questions and from his other contacts.

I could let the story loose in the Casablanca, and within a week all the expats in Sierra Leone would know. My worry about this is that nearly all of them believe the smuggling myth — that everything that is imported is promptly smuggled out, so cutting imports would have no effect on supply. If so, they would rubbish my story, and knock all chances of intervention on the head. It is a big risk, as it could so clearly backfire on me. This is the very last resort, as the World Bank will certainly whisk me out of the country if they hear of it. But I am within seven days of the last resort.

Again, if there is no action within seven days, I could bypass Murat, and get copies of my Cabinet Paper to acquaintances in Washington. Time is the problem: the post takes weeks, and Murat will not let me use the diplomatic bag to send criticisms of him to Washington.

How will Government react if I leak it? It could turn nasty. I am hoping, though, that someone — Foday or the Permanent Secretary, perhaps — will take me aside in the next two or three days and tell me whether or not they want me to leak it. They could use my leaks to put pressure on the World Bank. This solution does not save face for the World Bank, but the Government has a scapegoat — me.

The Government probably wants to save the face of Murat and the staff of the Sierra Leone desk in Washington. The Government could act tactfully, and just import the rice without any announcement at all, possibly not even telling the Bank officials privately. By the time the World Bank officials noticed (or by the time it was so blatantly obvious that they could no longer pretend that they had not noticed), they might have been reappointed to their old jobs.

Dishonest Expatriates

For once, the talk in the Casablanca was about dishonest expatriates, not dishonest locals. Generally, you can trust any expat with anything up to ten thousand dollars, because it is not worth losing your job for chicken-feed.

Andrew from Belfast was complaining that his expatriate Project Adviser had siphoned $100,000 out of the project over two years. What was worse, the Project Review Mission from headquarters had decided not to mention it in their report, even though they had been told about it and it was quite clear from the accounts that the money had vanished. Nobody was surprised. It happens.

Most of us at the bar were more annoyed at the officials in the Res Rep's offices here and at the officials in Washington, Rome and Brussels. They handle vastly more money than any Project Adviser, and a lot is stolen. If someone is lending a corrupt official $100 million with no adequate controls, the official could be making $10 million himself, and he would be happy to pay a million or two to the man in the international aid organization.

A lot of them, particularly in Brussels, also demand a bribe from any consultancy firm wanting to work in the Third World. The money comes out of the pockets of the people in the Third World, and, of course, out of the pockets of consultants like me. There is not a lot the consultancy firms can do about this: they pay up or go bust.

The consultancy firms are not spotless, either. Some of them cheat the client.

'Yes, I have even had them faking my CV,' came an English voice from the corner. 'My first job was as an economist in a well-known English consultancy firm. They sent me out to India with a fake CV saying that I was an expert in mango growing. I ask you! I had never even seen a mango then, and I knew nothing about agriculture or horticulture. The boss gave me two pieces of advice which have stood me in good stead ever since. "First," he said, "mangoes grow on trees, not in paddy fields. Second, keep your mouth shut and your eyes and ears open. Save your opinions for your final

244 / PETER GRIFFITHS

report." I did just that, and my report was well received by my client.'

A depressing conversation. I am going to have to rely on people like that to take action if the Government docs not.

Alerting the World Food Programme

THURSDAY, 15 NOVEMBER

No news, so I went to Brendan, whom I had been keeping in the dark, even though I trusted him more than anyone else here – which shows how carefully I have been playing my hand. I swore him to secrecy, and showed him my two Cabinet Papers. He reacted with alarm, but no great surprise.

'Well, sure, I could see that something was going on, but I couldn't quite put my finger on it,' he said. 'Indeed, what you say makes sense. It also makes sense of some things I knew, but you could not possibly know.'

'Let's look at the evidence now.'

And we spent three hours going through my statistics and analysis, checking and double-checking. He kept getting up, going to the filing cabinet and pulling out his own figures to see if they were roughly the same. They were.

Then he spent the afternoon writing a report to go to five people he knew in the World Food Programme in Rome.

We decided we could not trust his typist. She is a nice girl and competent, but we must assume that she reports everything to the Special Branch, or worse, the UN Res Rep, and that could upset everything.

Instead, I borrowed her typewriter, some paper, carbon paper and flimsies, and I typed his report out twice, each time with three copies, the bottom one barely legible. It was hard work: I had not used a manual typewriter for years. I had got used to the much lighter touch of an electric typewriter, and then, for the last two years, the heaven of my own computer.

After all that rush, Brendan revealed that the letters could not leave Freetown until next Tuesday. He is sending them in the FAO diplomatic bag to Rome, and the next bag leaves on Tuesday's flight.

★

The latest rumour is that the President has nipped another coup attempt in the bud, and fifty officers were thrown out of the army before they managed to do anything. I have no doubt at all that every junior army officer is constantly considering whether there will be a coup and, if so, which side he should be on. I am equally sure that every senior officer is wondering when the time will be ripe to make his own attempt.

It is the numbers that make me suspicious. If fifty officers were thrown out last week, thirty-five two months ago, and forty-two six months ago, how many are left? I have made a point of not asking about the army's strength, to avoid attracting the attention of Special Branch, but my impression is that there are two battalions. I would guess at twenty officers per battalion, plus some headquarters staff. Surely they cannot recruit fifty new officer cadets a year to fill the vacancies?

Still, even rumours of coups will get the politicians rattled, and increase the pressure on them to do something about food.

Breaking the Rules

FRIDAY, 16 NOVEMBER

I have decided that if I do not hear anything by this evening, I will have to try everything else I can think of to get action. I will write all weekend, letters to everyone I can think of. I will ask Brendan to send them off, either in the diplomatic bag to Rome, or using the UN's internal mail service, which takes them in the diplomatic bag to New York where someone will post them in the normal US mail. Either way they will get there a lot faster and more reliably than by Sierra Leone's postal service.

I have been waiting all week for some response to my second and more alarming Cabinet Paper. If they are taking it at all seriously, it will have gone to the Cabinet Secretary and the President last Friday afternoon, and it will have gone before a full Cabinet this week. If they are not taking it seriously, the country is in big trouble. Perhaps it is too much to expect any bureaucracy to act that quickly?

I am desperate: I have not had any feedback and I do not know what is happening, if anything. It was a couple of weeks before I got any feedback at all from my last Cabinet Paper, and even then at first it was isolated hints and comments that made it clear that someone had read it and acted on it, before someone completely outside the civil service told me that he had read it and was negotiating with the Cabinet to get foreign exchange to import rice.

I am far too anxious to work. I wake in the middle of the night and lie in the dark, checking the figures in my head, checking delivery dates, and trying to think of a strategy. The answer always comes out the same: it is now mid-November, and the Agricultural Marketing Board will have no commercial stocks on New Year's Day, in six weeks' time. It takes two months to get expensive rice from Rotterdam or America, and if it is a bulk shipment it could take three weeks to bag it in the hold and unload it.

Still, if my Cabinet Paper is accepted, the Agricultural Marketing Board will stop sales immediately, so it has enough rice to get us through January and part of February. This will give them time to bring in emergency supplies.

★

As I write, I can see out of my office window the fence surrounding the Friendship Building. There is a crowd of two or three hundred people waiting outside the fence. They are waiting to buy aid rice distributed through Brendan's World Food Programme. Judging by the length of the queue, the price is well below the going retail price in the markets.

I asked Thomas if he could find out what the price was. He said that he could not go and ask, because the women in the queue would tear him limb from limb if he walked straight to the front of the queue, and anyway the market women would quote the price they were supposed to charge, not the price they were really charging. Instead, I gave Amanda a dollar's worth of leones, and told her to buy as much rice as she could, and bring it back for us to weigh. Just to encourage her to get the best bargain, I said that she could keep all the rice and keep the change for herself.

It took her four hours of queueing in the hot sun to get served. The market woman only let her buy three cupfuls, enough for a family of four for two days. We weighed the rice and calculated the price. It was about a third less than today's price in the main market, so some of the benefit of the subsidy is being passed on, which I had not expected.

People must be desperate if they are willing to queue for three hours to save a few cents on a few cupfuls of rice (and I am talking of Sierra Leone cents, which are one-fiftieth of a US cent.)

I saw Abensberg, the FAO Res Rep, at the Aqua Club this evening, and went over to see if I could fix a meeting with him on Monday. He agreed, then told me that he has managed to get donor finance to establish a policy and marketing unit in the Ministry of Agriculture. It will have three expats to set up all the systems and train local staff. I was delighted. If they had had a unit like this in place for the last five years, they would not be in this mess.

He then asked me if I would be willing to be head of the unit on a two- or three-year contract. I was taken by surprise: I didn't know that he knew anything about me, except for our brief meeting when I arrived. Then he let it slip that he had seen my Cabinet Paper. Evidently government has started approaching the sharpest people in the aid agencies to get allies against the World Bank. Something is happening!

I am not keen on the job even though it means two or three years on the salary of a top international civil servant, pensionable and tax free, with perks like a duty-free car and diplomatic passport. No, these long-term jobs have a completely different dynamic to short-term consultancies. Instead of being an outsider looking with a fresh eye, you are an insider, working as a civil servant within a ministry. You rapidly become institutionalized, and you end up defending the institution and its systems instead of changing them. You also get embroiled in office politics.

I suddenly felt feverish as I got back to the hotel last night. Being hot and sweaty is normal here, but I came out in a muck sweat and started shivering. Malaria! I went straight to my case and got out the medicine bag. Half a dozen chloroquine before going to bed, then four more when I woke up this morning. I seem to be OK today, but I have taken it easy all day.

The Showdown

MONDAY, 19 NOVEMBER

I went to town, ready for the final showdown. As a last, feeble, hope, I went to Foday first, just in case he had heard anything since Friday evening. I knocked and went in through the open door.

'The Minister wants to see you urgently,' he said, his face expressionless, his voice flat. 'He said that you should go to his office as soon as you arrive.' He looked away from me, then got up and busied himself pretending to look for something in the bookshelf at the back of the room.

I went upstairs, wondering what it was all about. It did sound very much as though they did not believe me, and were terminating my contract. I knocked on the door of the Minister's secretary. She recognized me: I had waited for an hour in her office on my first day here. She lifted her phone and told the Minister I was there.

'He says you are to go straight in,' she said, pointing at the door.

He stood up and walked up to me as I entered, then shook my hand. A good sign. He offered me one of the armchairs, and sat in another opposite me. Another good sign. He looked alert: he is slight, immaculately dressed and has a carefully tended imperial beard.

'You will be pleased to know that Government has ordered the Agricultural Marketing Board to import rice as a matter of urgency,' he announced formally. 'They will sell it at a price that people can afford to pay. It is decided, too, that the Agricultural Marketing Board is not to sell any more rice this year. Meanwhile the question of the future role of the Agricultural Marketing Board in rice marketing is under consideration.' He spoke flatly, unemotionally, as though he was reading out a press release.

Then he relaxed a little and said, 'Of course it is not a simple action to take: it will not be easy for Government to find the leones, or for the Central Bank to find the dollars. It will mean, among other things, cutting other imports.'

'However, the Government does not wish to publicize the fact that we will amend the Agreement with the World Bank,' he continued (I liked the use of 'amend'). We are pleased that you have kept the matter secret in the past and we would like you to continue to keep it secret. It is better that the World Bank does not know officially until the rice arrives.' He said it firmly and forcefully.

'Oops!' I thought to myself, 'Better get Brendan to destroy the letters before the diplomatic bag leaves.'

'Meanwhile, you will of course continue your work here as though nothing has happened.'

I breathed a sigh of relief: at least the mortgage will be paid.

'I thank you for your work here.' He shook my hand gravely and showed me out.

It worked! I did it! The food will come! Nothing has been done about the long-term problems, but at least there will be no famine.

And I can get out of this muggy heat and enjoy the pleasures of England in November.

And Then What?

I stayed in Freetown until my contract ended, in mid-January.

From Christmas rice prices rose, as the USAID rice ran out. The Agricultural Marketing Board released only small quantities onto the market, determined to ensure that there was enough to feed the people until the first rice ship arrived at the end of January and its contents were unloaded.

As prices rose, people ate less, and they obviously had no energy to do anything at work. More and more of them fell asleep at their desks. More and more could be seen asleep or half-asleep in the streets.

They were tired, too, because they had to walk to work. The country had run out of petrol and diesel. Presumably, the refinery had made the same calculations as the rice importers. Who would buy fuel when it cost ten times as much in leones as it did a year ago? (The value of the leone had fallen again.) How would the refinery get the dollars to buy the oil? Would the Government let them turn the leones they earned into dollars at a fair rate?

First, there were long queues at every filling station. Then it became clear that the only people who would get fuel would be those willing to pay black market prices, and this meant the taxis, some of the lorries, and some of the rich. Then even this fuel ran out, and fewer and fewer taxis were running.

When George drove me to the airport, using some of the emergency diesel stored in the World Bank compound, it seemed as if we were the last car in the city.

We drove through a dead city, people silent, traffic silent, and I wondered if the ship would arrive in time.

Dear Jane,

Yes, it ended as suddenly and as undramatically as this.

Needless to say, I never got another job in Sierra Leone, which is just as well, as the corruption I saw led to the nastiest civil war in Africa's history.

Nor has the West African branch of the World Bank employed me again. It was a risk I took. Fortunately, the Bank is a large monolithic organization, and the news did not get to other divisions, so they have employed me in Eastern Europe and Asia.

Love,

Peter

Glossary

CFA francs	The currency used by ex-French colonies in West Africa.
EEC	European Economic Community, sometimes called the Common Market or the European Community. It developed into what is now called the EU.
EC	Sometimes this is the European Community (now the EU), sometimes it is the European Commission, the governing body of the EC and now the EU.
ECU	European Currency Unit. Now called the Euro.
FAO	The Food and Agriculture Organization of the United Nations, which has its headquarters in Rome. The other UN agencies work together under the UNDP, but FAO operates separately, with its own Resident Representative.
IMF	International Monetary Fund, based in Washington. At this time the exchange rate was approximately $1.5 = £1.
Res Rep	The Resident Representative of an organization like the World Bank, the EC, FAO, the UNDP. Some of these have ambassador status.
UN	United Nations, especially the UNDP.
UNDP	United Nations Development Programme. The organization that manages the UN's Third World aid.
USAID	The United States Agency for International Development: the US government aid organization.
WFP	World Food Programme, based in Rome, and closely linked with FAO.